TERMS FOR ENDEARMENT

BUSINESS, NGOs AND SUSTAINABLE DEVELOPMENT

Contributing Editor: Jem Bendell

D1114428

❝ *Terms for Endearment* breaks the mould. It brings new voices to the debate on the future of business. The writers explain why business needs to put the important things in life first and how to translate such principles into practice. We're all challenged to do the same. ❞

Anita Roddick, Founder and Co-Chair, The Body Shop International; Founder, New Academy of Business

❝ At a time of rising concern over where the world is heading, the experiments and innovations detailed in this book provide new insights into the possibilities of humanising capitalism. Rich in case studies and challenging in its conclusions, *Terms for Endearment* lays out an exciting agenda for NGO–business collaboration in the 21st century. ❞

Michael Edwards, Director, Governance and Civil Society, The Ford Foundation and author of Future Positive

❝ This is a must-read for the champions of corporate responsibility, for those that want to go beyond the PR stuff and really engage with stakeholders. Its combination of case studies and commentary goes beyond exhortation to provide insights into the potential benefits as well as the pitfalls. ❞

Barry Coates, Director, World Development Movement

❝ This well-structured book draws on many practical examples to show how business and society can collaborate to achieve a more socially just and ecologically sustainable world. Moreover, its analysis provides innovative ideas and concepts which will both speed up and increase the possibility of attaining development that is sustainable for the many, rather than for the few. If you are concerned about improving the quality of the world you will live in tomorrow, whether as a corporate manager, social activist or citizen, this publication is for you. ❞

Alan Fowler, Co-Founder, INTRAC

❝ We are all stakeholders in sustainability, and *Terms for Endearment* moves the practicalities of collaboration between all stakeholders in society well and truly onto the agenda of the 21st century. This is a timely, necessary and significant contribution to the expanding worldwide debates on effective partnerships between business and civil society organisations. The book is essential reading for all involved in securing sustainable change in the future. ❞

Professor David Birch, Corporate Citizenship Research Unit, Deakin University, Australia

❝ This book is a true treasure chest. It gives a unique insight into the dynamics and motives of the actors involved and it describes dilemmas and possible responses that are at the forefront of social change. Communicating this insight will hopefully only be the beginning of a much-needed debate on the role of business in society in an era of globalising markets. ❞

Georg Kell, Senior Officer, Executive Office of the United Nations Secretary-General

❝ *Terms for Endearment* effectively explores some of the fascinating and important highways and byways along which NGOs pass in seeking to influence business practice, and thereby being deeply influenced themselves. ❞

Simon Zadek, Chair, Institute of Social and Ethical Accountability

❝ This book is a timely contribution to the burgeoning debate on civil society and business engagement. ❞

Kumi Naidoo, Secretary-General and CEO, CIVICUS

❝ Global business and civil society are the superpowers of the 21st century. This book shows that, in both battle and détente, they are shaping our futures. Anyone interested in novel ways of achieving the sustainable governance of markets should read it. ❞

Professor Richard Welford, University of Huddersfield, UK

❝ Managing relations with stakeholders is an essential aspect of modern business. More than suggesting a strategy, *Terms for Endearment* presents a philosophy for success. ❞

Maria Sillanpää, Director, KPMG Sustainability Advisory Services

❝ A sustainable future can only be guaranteed by responsible business practice. This book provides many practical examples of how companies can work with stakeholders to develop more effective solutions for a sustainable future. ❞

Teresa Fabian, PricewaterhouseCoopers

❝ This book is helpful to anyone involved in sustainability management, accounting, auditing and reporting, because, without ongoing dialogue with local and international stakeholders, no organisation can develop and implement locally acceptable solutions to global issues. ❞

Dominique Gangneux, Bureau Veritas Quality International

Terms for Endearment

BUSINESS, NGOs AND SUSTAINABLE DEVELOPMENT

CONTRIBUTING EDITOR JEM BENDELL

Published in association with
NEW ACADEMY
OF BUSINESS

Greenleaf
PUBLISHING
2000

© 2000 Greenleaf Publishing Limited unless otherwise stated

Published by Greenleaf Publishing Limited
Aizlewood's Mill
Nursery Street
Sheffield S3 8GG
UK

In association with
The New Academy of Business
17–19 Clare Street
Bristol BS1 1XA
UK
www.new-academy.ac.uk

Typeset by Greenleaf Publishing.
Printed and bound, using acid-free paper from managed forests, by
Creative Print & Design (Wales), Ebbw Vale.

British Library Cataloguing in Publication Data:

   Terms for endearment : business, NGOs and sustainable
     development
     1. Public relations – Environmental aspects
     2. Non-governmental bodies – Environmental aspects – Public
     opinion
     I. Bendell, Jem
     658.4'08

     ISBN 1874719284 (hbk)
     ISBN 1874719292 (pbk)

CONTENTS

ACKNOWLEDGEMENTS

Thanks are due to: David Murphy, for helping me start in this line of work; John Stuart, for his enthusiasm about *In the Company of Partners* and running with the idea for a special issue of *Greener Management International* and now this book; Dean Bargh for working on the text; Tom Davies, for encouraging me to express myself openly—even emotionally—in my academic and professional work; all the contributors, for their work and for being very accepting of all the chops and changes to their contributions; the appropriate persons on the Aspen Institute Non-Profit Sector Research Fund and University of Bristol grants committees, for supporting my plans over the past months; Olman Segura, for making my stay at Universidad Nacional possible; Jonathan Cohen, for keeping me up to date with informative e-mails about recent developments in this field; Elena for reminding me of the important things in life; Leigh, for teaching me to surf—a great escape from labouring on the laptop; Manu Chao for creating the right kind of music to lighten the solitude of writing; and to those good friends of mine who don't rely solely on e-mail circulars to keep in touch; Mum and Dad for supporting me at crucial stages throughout my life; and Mark for always reminding me to finish my PhD (so I'll finish these acknowledgements and get on with my thesis!).

Jem Bendell
Playa Jaco, February 2000

FOREWORD

Anita Roddick

Founder and Co-Chair, The Body Shop International;
Founder, New Academy of Business, UK

There is an old-fashioned concept of business and there is a new one. Old business places profits before principles and shareholder interests above those of society as a whole. New business recognises the link between profit and principles and demonstrates accountability to all stakeholders. Although this new concept of business has yet to be generally accepted, it is becoming more prominent and influential. One of the main reasons why the new business agenda is on the rise is the growing role of non-governmental organisations (NGOs) in influencing corporate policies and practices on social, ethical and environmental matters.

NGOs are both the agents of change and the answer to many of the tough issues facing business in the 21st century—not just those found in the financial pages of newspapers, but many more that make up the mismatch between business and modern life. The mismatch was always there, but, at the height of global capitalism, it has never been as sharp as it is now.

You can remember the old-fashioned view of business from the way popular culture usually depicts big business as the bad guys. The old-fashioned view of businessmen—it usually was men—portrayed them with their gimlet eyes fixed on the year-end results, pushing aside anyone who gets in the way. That's why I could never think of myself as being 'in business' when I started The Body Shop.

My idea of business when I started was provided by my mother's café. Working there taught me that business wasn't about financial science. First and foremost, it was all about trading—about buying and selling—and about a different kind of bottom line, which meant that you could bring your heart to work.

Today business is the dominant sociopolitical force on the planet, so we can no longer pretend that the economic bottom line is the only thing that matters. If we did, then the organisations most able to make a difference to life would be shirking their responsibilities. Like Nero, corporations would be doing the modern equivalent of fiddling while Rome burns—and to some extent they are doing just that. We can't afford for business to so limit its ambition when it is faster, wealthier and more creative than governments. There is a new responsibility that we in business must face up to.

NGOs help us face up to our responsibilities. This book describes the role of NGOs as the watchdog of globalisation. Their vigilance around the world makes the great abuses which humanity once brushed aside visible for all to see. Together, they now represent billions of people—often the least powerful and the people whose voices are heard the least—determined that trade should be more equitable, just and sustainable. *Terms for Endearment* describes how NGOs are creating a 'civil framework' for new business, by making socially and environmentally responsible decision-making a prerequisite for future commercial success.

Not everyone is converted. The NGOs and the world's biggest corporations clashed in Seattle at the end of 1999, and I came away choking from the CS gas and feeling a deep sense of shame at the way that multinationals and politicians can behave. New millennia are traditionally periods of great fear and great hope. The week's events certainly engendered fear for the future, but there is also a corresponding hope.

For one thing, NGOs provided the only bridge between the different sides in Seattle. They were the only ones who could talk to everyone, to political and corporate leaders as well as activists. It was a small example of how NGOs have been able to get people to communicate, and a reminder of some of the most creative partnerships that NGOs are now creating. All over the world we can see these emerging: unusual alliances between human rights groups and education institutions, alternative trade associations, progressive consumer groups, and often they are in partnership with business.

That is the context in which business has to interact with NGOs. Often the former's first contact with the latter is to come under effective public attack from them. And one of the most powerful things a business board can do is to respond to this attack by risking working alongside them.

Increasing numbers of businesses are doing just that: some of them in a genuine spirit of partnership, some of them quite the reverse. And they are likely to do so all the more in the future. This is partly because consumers demand it. 'We don't care about the legislation,' one corporation told me in Seattle, 'but we do care about consumer revolt.'

Partnership is a new business model that gives NGOs a central role, and it turns business into a lever that can change perceptions and change the world. The point is that, although it is fashionable to talk about the relationship between the two as one of charity or *noblesse oblige*, it is actually precisely the reverse. As the stories in *Terms for Endearment* show, businesses now need NGOs.

What's really important is the reflexive learning that can occur when businesses engage with NGOs. This kind of business education and learning breaks the MBA mould and its narrow focus on accounting, financial management, economics, marketing and public relations. Breaking this mould is at the heart of the work of the New Academy of Business, an alternative business school which I founded in 1995. The New Academy brings together both company and NGO managers to develop new business strategies for the common good.

Terms for Endearment breaks the mould. It brings new voices to the debate on the future of business. The writers explain why business needs to put the important things in life first and how to translate such principles into practice. We're all challenged to do the same.

FOREWORD

Georg Kell

Senior Officer, Executive Office
of the UN Secretary-General

The emerging relationship between business and civil society, especially NGOs, epito-mises fundamental ongoing changes. Its potential significance in reshaping the roles and responsibilities of the private and public sector is increasingly recognised by decision-makers and engaged citizens.

If pursued in a constructive and informed manner, this relationship may help to find new common ground between commercial interests and broad societal goals and thereby contribute to solving some of the most pressing questions of our time: how to couple rapidly expanding markets with a social response and purpose.

The need to do so is most obvious at the global level where contrasts between eco-nomic rights and wealth-creating capacities on the one side and the neglect of other concerns are most striking and consequential. Finding new ways to use market power to address issues such as providing economic opportunities for the poor, giving practical meaning to universal values such as human rights and labour rights and addressing envi-ronmental problems may fill some of the void that a weakening collective commitment of governments has left behind. At the same time, this may help to secure a more stable underpinning for global markets to function.

The debate around trade has shown how this relationship has evolved at the global rule-making level and how important it is to find common ground. Sustaining a commit-ment for openness—a precondition for spreading benefits—is no longer an exclusive case of liberalisation versus protectionism but increasingly a question of whether we can find a response to expanding markets by dealing more effectively with other concerns such as poverty, human rights, labour issues and the environment.

It is no coincidence that the very same concerns are also at the heart of the relationship between business and NGOs at the micro level. Motives, issues and actors are the same. But it is at the local level where the potential for finding innovative solutions is greatest. After all, it is individual people, leaders who are willing to take risks and committed actors whose motivation is strong enough to cross traditional dividing lines that can identify, formulate and communicate new approaches.

This book is a true treasure chest. It gives a unique insight into the dynamics and motives of the actors involved and it describes dilemmas and possible responses that are at the forefront of social change. Communicating this insight will hopefully only be the beginning of a much-needed debate on the role of business in society in an era of globalising markets.

FOREWORD

Kumi Naidoo

Secretary-General and CEO, CIVICUS

This book is a timely contribution to the burgeoning debate on civil society and business engagement. Considering the dramatic increase in business activity, the growing influence of business organisations and the declining power of governments, it is an opportune time to discuss what responsibilities coincide with the growing power and influence the business sector wields. There are several sceptics within civil society that question whether business engagement in the social sector can yield true progress or whether it simply co-opts and silences civil society organisations. Given that the relationship between civil society organisations and businesses either have been adversarial or have been at the level of chequebook contributions by business to those non-profit organisations whose goals they supported, these reservations are no doubt understandable. However, a categorical dismissal of all business engagement, especially in light of the breadth and scope of business activity and its influence in development and globalisation, potentially overlooks an important opportunity. Many civil society organisations have come to recognise that the power of business has to be engaged in a range of different ways. Sometimes this will take the form of regulation and monitoring, and sometimes it will take the form of advocacy. But sometimes it will take the form of long-term strategic relationships aimed at fostering social progress. In short, there is some value if the inherent power and resources of business can be harnessed to advance the progressive agendas of civil society groups.

It is worth recognising that there remain businesses that still behave with impunity in terms of how they deal with issues such as the environment and human rights, even though this approach is becoming increasingly untenable. For civil society organisations, engaging with business is similar to engaging with government in several ways. Perhaps most important is the fact that the autonomy of civil society organisations must be protected so that, if vigorous advocacy against business organisations are called for, then this should be possible. In the coming years, one of the biggest issues that civil society organisations face is how to deal with a world in which inequality, both between nations and between the rich and the poor countries, is growing. Another distinction that needs to be consciously made is the fact that business is a very stratified concept today. Far too often when we talk about business, we think solely of big business. However, it is imperative that any discussion on business must look at the small and medium-sized enterprises as well. Civil society activists have come to realise that several businesses are striving for more socially and environmentally responsible ways to conduct business. This has become a business imperative that big businesses in particular simply cannot ignore.

There are now some cases in which social improvements have resulted from businesses working in partnership with civil society organisations and with government. The potential return from this engagement benefits from the comparative advantages that different sectors are able to contribute. Whereas the business sector enjoys vast resources and is known for its managerial skills, civil society organisations have the proven ability to highlight issues, mobilise resources and organise quickly and effectively. Clearly, engagement does not necessarily need to mean co-option, nor does it mean that there will not be levels of disagreement between the two parties on both substantive and tactical matters. However, given the unprecedented size and influence of the private and the non-profit sector, it would be irresponsible for civil society organisations at the local, national and international levels in this day and age not to consider developing a strategic approach on how to engage business. And, if business engagement means that the position of the poor and the socially marginalised can be advanced, or that the development challenges facing a community, a country or the world can be addressed, then civil society organisations are duty-bound to accept the challenge.

In approaching this challenge successfully, both civil society organisations and business must be cognisant of the possibilities and pitfalls that surround new ways of working together. Clearly, engaging two seemingly polar sectors yields the challenge of addressing the interests of both parties who can bring different values to the table. However, provided that the interests of the communities we seek to serve are being advanced and that no dishonourable deals are being done behind the scenes, such relationships should undoubtedly prove to be both mutually beneficial as well as publicly defendable, and will ultimately help to promote a healthy society. How this relates to the macro-economic questions humanity faces today is of course complex, and even more challenging. Engaging on a programmatic basis where appropriate, and keeping our eyes on the bigger issues of global social and economic justice, is the challenge of the times we live in.

INTRODUCTION

Working with stakeholder pressure for sustainable development

Jem Bendell

New Academy of Business, UK

> Monsanto's [cotton] field trials . . . will be reduced to ashes in a few days. These actions will start a movement of direct action by farmers against biotechnology, which will not stop until all the corporate killers like Monsanto, Novartis, Pioneer etc. leave the country . . . [T]hese actions can also pose a major challenge to the survival of these corporations in the stock markets. Who wants to invest in a mountain of ashes, in offices that are constantly being squatted (and if necessary even destroyed) by activists? (Professor Nanjundaswamy, quoted in Cummins 1998: 1).

In 1998, Indian farmers in the Karnataka region, chanting 'Cremate Monsanto' and 'Stop genetic engineering', uprooted and burned genetically engineered cotton fields in front of a bank of television cameras and news reporters. Non-governmental organisations (NGOs), including the Karnataka State Farmers' Association, were calling on the biotechnology company Monsanto[1] to 'Get out of India', and for the government to ban field tests and imports of genetically modified (GM) seeds and crops.

This sort of antagonism between business and NGOs is not a new phenomenon. Back in 1962, Rachel Carson's *Silent Spring* sparked the contemporary environmental movement with an exposé on the dangers posed by pesticides for people and the natural environment. The chemical industry responded with a scathing attack on environmentalists, branding them 'a motley lot ranging from superstitious illiterates and cultists to educated scientists' (quoted in Hoffman 1996b: 53). From *Silent Spring* to the present day, relations between representatives of business and their NGO stakeholders have often been antagonistic.

---

1   On 3 April 2000, Monsanto Company merged with Pharmacia & Upjohn to form Pharmacia Corporation.

The mid-1995 confrontation between Shell and Greenpeace over the disposal of the Brent Spar offshore oil platform confirmed the long-standing image of two tribes engaged in perpetual war over values, words and ideas. Yet this was not the end of the story. Eventually the protests led Shell UK to engage the Environment Council, a British NGO, to facilitate a series of European-wide 'Dialogue Forums' between the company and a wide range of NGOs and other stakeholders on alternative disposal options for the Brent Spar (see Chapter 2). Subsequently, Shell UK's chief executive officer said that his company 'had no option but to pursue the goal of sustainable development' (quoted in Cowe 1996: 17). Similarly, since the outcry over Shell's operations in Ogoniland, both before and after the Nigerian government executed environmental activist Ken Saro-Wiwa, the company has consulted with Amnesty International on its business principles and new corporate human rights policy.

At daybreak on the 21st century, relations between businesses and NGOs range from the strongly antagonistic to the 'strangely' collaborative. In the following pages there are examples of international NGOs, such as the World Wide Fund for Nature, as well as local groups in both industrialised and less industrialised countries, all pursuing sophisticated market-oriented strategies to pursue their objectives. Examples of stakeholder pressure on timber companies (Chapter 4), biotechnology companies (Chapters 6 and 13), mining companies (Chapter 5), and companies investing in countries with repressive regimes (Chapter 3) are provided, as well as the case of an NGO action against a proposed intergovernmental agreement on investment (Chapter 3). However, the main focus of this book is on how and why companies are working *with* stakeholder pressure for sustainable development, by collaborating with NGOs on various initiatives.

In recent years there have been a number of books published that seek to help corporations defend themselves when 'under siege' from stakeholders (Neal and Davies 1998: 1), and advise them on 'Managing Outside Pressure' (Winter and Steger 1998) by providing a 'practical roadmap to protecting [a] company's reputation' (Peters 1999: 1). Indeed, models of effective stakeholder relations management can be proposed, which focus on: (1) defending the organisation's position against stakeholders who represent a high threat and a low potential for co-operation; (2) collaborating with stakeholders who represent a high threat and a high potential for co-operation; (3) involving stakeholders who represent a low threat and a high potential for co-operation; and (4) monitoring stakeholders who represent a low threat and a low potential for co-operation (Savage *et al.* 1991).

If this is the type of advice you are interested in, then you might consider closing this book now. In these pages you will not find advice on how to manage stakeholder pressure to corporate advantage. This is because much stakeholder pressure is motivated by belief in the principles of social justice and environmental sustainability. To try to analyse this pressure from a utilitarian approach both misunderstands these principles and denies the humanity of both managers and students of business. Therefore this book examines cases where business can work *with* stakeholder pressure for sustainable development; if you are interested in how businesses can become part of a better society, and cases when unfortunately they cannot, please read on.

◢ The rise and rise of civil society

In this book we make interchangeable use of the terms 'stakeholders', 'non-governmental organisations' (NGOs), 'non-profit organisations' and 'civil society groups'; the term 'third sector' is also used. Before proceeding, we need to clarify some terms and concepts.

First, there are 'stakeholders'. The idea that companies have stakeholders has now become commonplace, in both the academic literature and business practice, and relations with stakeholders are considered key to the strategic planning process (Starik *et al.* 1996). Freeman (1984: 52) suggests that stakeholders include 'any group or individual who can affect or is affected by the achievement of an organisation's purpose'. This definition is too broad for some as it includes interested parties as well as affected parties, and therefore an argument has been made for restricting the term to those 'who have a "stake", or vested interest, in the firm' (Carroll 1993: 22). In much management practice, however—for instance, in stakeholder reporting and social auditing—Freeman's approach holds, and stakeholders are defined as primary or secondary, depending on an assessment of whether they are immediately affected by, or can immediately affect, a firm's operations.

NGOs are often stakeholders in a company, whether they are formed by groups of people who are affected by a firm's operations (either immediately or in a broader context), or groups articulating on behalf of other people (or wildlife) that are affected by a firm. NGOs have been defined in a number of different ways, and in this book they are defined as 'groups whose stated purpose is the promotion of environmental and/or social goals rather than the achievement or protection of economic power in the marketplace or political power through the electoral process'. This definition includes groups that are non-profit as well as non-governmental, but excludes non-profit groups that work for economic interests, such as the International Chamber of Commerce (ICC), and those non-profit groups without an explicit social or environmental purpose, such as a school choir. Even so, NGO is a broad term, covering major international organisations such as Amnesty International, on the one hand, and a local development group such as FUNDE in El Salvador, on the other.

The total number of NGOs worldwide is unknown. The Union of International Associations estimated in the early 1990s that there were more than 20,000 international or transnational NGOs. This total included some 1,000 NGOs that have consultative status with the UN Economic and Social Council (Willets 1998). Within many nation-states, NGO numbers are much higher. At the end of 1998, there were 186,248 registered 'non-governmental' charities in England and Wales. Ten years ago, Rajesh Tandon (1989) estimated that there were several thousand voluntary agencies in India, including relief and rehabilitation agencies, philanthropic, charity-owned NGOs, social action groups and intermediary organisations. Researchers at The Johns Hopkins University reported that NGOs trade at least $1.1 trillion worldwide, provide more aid than the World Bank, and employ more than 19 million people. The Netherlands leads the way—12.4% of its citizens work in NGOs, with other European nations following closely behind (Salamon *et al.* 1999).

NGOs are now widely regarded as nodes of civil society. The term 'civil society' has a long history and there are currently many competing definitions in use. State-centred definitions of civil society have strong historical routes—even Marx wrote about civil society and the state—and were given new vibrancy by political activists in Eastern Europe who spoke of it as the networks and markets that existed outside the totalitarian state (Walzer 1995). However, I agree with those who contend that 'the two part model . . . whereby civil society includes everything outside the state sector, is [not] useful today' (Cohen 1995: 35). A three-part model that draws on the work of Antonio Gramsci (1992) to differentiate between civil society, the state and the economy is more helpful. In this way organisations can be classified as either belonging to the state (government), market (business) or civil society (NGO) sectors—or a hybrid of them. What are the key differences between organisations in these sectors that make a book about relations between them of importance? Each organisational type has a different overriding imperative. Governments' primary concern is with a political system focusing on the creation of rules that can be enforced through coercive means such as the police and courts. Businesses' primary concern is with economic systems where owners are in control and people are induced to do what the organisation desires through monetary rewards. In contrast, NGOs focus on social systems and networks based on values and beliefs; they derive their power from their ability to speak to tradition, community benefit and values.

Why is civil society on the rise today? One argument is that it is because of people's alienation from the institutions established to serve them. The evolution of the modern nation-state has caused the public sector to take the form of large institutional structures that can create a sense of alienation among citizens. The same seems to have happened with the private sector as well, where individual enterprise has given rise to large institutional structures that rival nation-states. Indeed, the contemporary multinational corporation has the size and scope of many public entities. Alienation with state and private institutions may have necessitated the growth of organisations in the 'third sector', or civil society. In this book we concern ourselves with the relations between businesses and those NGOs that are working on aspects of sustainable development. These NGOs come from two main 'camps'—environment NGOs and development NGOs.

◢ NGOs and sustainable development

Many NGOs focus on issues related to the goal of sustainable development. Although there are intriguing relations between businesses and NGOs on issues such as black, gay or women's rights, the focus of this book is on those interactions relating to sustainable development. As a result of global environmental degradation and widespread poverty, the World Commission on Environment and Development (WCED), better known as the Brundtland Commission, presented the concept of sustainable development as a solution in 1987. The Brundtland Commission diagnosed the source of environmental and social problems as the conflict between an open economic system pushing against a closed ecological system. Therefore they defined sustainable development as 'development that meets the needs of the present without compromising the ability of future generations to meet their own needs' and stated that it embodied 'two key concepts . . . the essential needs of the world's poor . . . [which] should be given overriding priority; and the idea of limitations . . . on the environment's ability to meet present and future needs' (WCED 1987: 43).

Because of the broad nature of the term 'sustainable development', it has been adopted by many, from local activists to multinational corporations (Adams 1993). The term has been somewhat co-opted, so that it has become synonymous with strategies for sustained economic growth that include economically viable environmental protection measures. Despite its basis on an existing industrial economy, the growth of the new digital economy is seen by some as evidence of the possibility of environmentally benign economic growth. This approach sets aside the original attention of sustainable development with the need to reconsider the environmental limits to production and consumption and the nature of human progress. Originally, sustainable development was about creating happy, just, secure and environmentally sensitive communities. Despite neo-liberal convictions about the efficacy of international trade and economic growth in creating such communities, the amount of money that changes hands per annum has never been a good indicator for sustainable development.

The concept is widely used by NGOs involved in environment and development. In the North, environmental NGOs have evolved towards a sustainable development orientation through three waves of environmentalism (Murphy and Bendell 1997a). The first wave of environmentalism began in the 1900s as a residue of the Romantic Movement, which championed a return to nature in the wake of the Industrial Revolution. This led to the establishment of the first national parks. The second wave in most Northern, industrialised countries began in the 1960s, fuelled by socioeconomic changes at that time and the emerging science of ecology. The first major environmental campaigning groups were established and they focused primarily on increasing regulation to protect people from industrial pollution. The third wave of environmentalism began in the mid to late 1980s as environmental NGOs began to seek practical ways of implementing solutions. The global environmental problematique began to be broken down into everyday issues with practical remedies. Third-wave environmentalism places increasing emphasis on market-oriented campaigns and on seeking workable solutions to environmental problems.

Many development NGOs based in the North have also begun to embrace the sustainability agenda and the advocacy route. Korten (1990) describes three generations of development NGO strategies. First-generation development NGOs focus on the provision of disaster relief and welfare—the original role of Northern NGOs such as Oxfam; second-generation strategies focus on promoting small-scale, self-reliant community development; and third-generation strategies involve increasingly large and sophisticated NGOs 'working in a catalytic, foundation-like role rather than an operational service-delivery role . . . facilitating . . . other organisations [to develop] the capacities, linkages and commitments required to address designated needs on a sustained basis' (Korten 1987: 149).

Korten goes on to describe the need for fourth-generation NGOs which aim to build 'a critical mass of independent, decentralised initiative in support of a social vision'

(1990: 127). Part of this strategy is building links between different NGOs and addressing the more structural issues at the heart of social and environmental problems. Whereas third-generation NGOs 'seek changes in specific policies and institutions', Korten suggests that fourth-generation NGOs will facilitate the coming together of loosely defined networks of people and organisations, across national borders in the North and South, to transform the institutions of global society (1990: 123).

For many Southern NGOs, community and activist groups, however, the division between environment and development is not so clear. When local Southern groups protest against their lands being acquired, or their rivers being poisoned, they are fighting for their mutual, material interests (Collinson 1996). Therefore many Southern groups have a natural orientation toward the goal of sustainable development.

Although NGOs around the world remain extremely heterogeneous, there is evidence of an emergent, shared discourse based around a critique of economic globalisation (Lynch 1998) and the promotion of sustainable development. Despite valid concerns over the way the term has been abused by vested interests, David F. Murphy and I recognised how sustainable development has become

> a new organising principle, perhaps an emerging, positive myth, which has the potential to bring together diverse and often competing causes. The mythic quality of sustainable development lies in its capacity to clarify the Earth's complexity and facilitate commitment to new collaborative models (Murphy and Bendell 1997a).

◢ Driving factors for business–NGO engagement

The power of the sustainable development concept to convene different people and organisations and provide an apparently common vernacular on which to base a dialogue has been key to the growth in relations between corporations and NGOs. However, a number of other macro-level changes in economics and politics have been driving factors behind increased engagement between the sectors, and these are summarised here.

The first dynamic, explored by Peter Newell in Chapter 1, is the emergence of the global economy, the perceived decline in the role of the nation-state and the problem this is causing for regulating economies. In the less industrialised world, many governments have always had limited capacity to provide services or regulate business activities, yet today they are under pressure from financial organisations to adopt economic restructuring programmes and slim down even further. Meanwhile, in industrialised countries the range of functions that governments are expected to perform is contracting. This marks a decisive shift from the past when national markets were subject to state regulation by governments in order to deal with key market failures and externalities, and were taxed in order to provide public investment and welfare services to address issues of poverty, equity, security and justice. Today's markets have broken free from the state as 'alliances of various kinds have given rise to the stateless corporation in which people, assets and transactions move freely across international borders' (Snow *et al.* 1992: 8). This new situation is largely unregulated and not effectively taxed. It has imposed a discursive discipline on governments because all their domestic policies must be based on an overriding imperative to export cheaply and attract inward investment. In this way the international economy is determining state monetary and fiscal policy and drawing governments into a process of competitive deregulation. This situation makes it more likely that market externalities, such as social and environmental 'goods', will be ignored and market power will be monopolised.

We see, then, that the problem is not globalisation itself but rather our lopsided globalisation: while the globalisation of trade and finance is proceeding at a hare's pace, the globalisation of governance is dragging behind like a tortoise. Intergovernmental organisations have been notoriously slow in delivering meaningful regulatory systems, as Peter Newell argues in Chapter 1:

> Often, international agreements are vaguely worded, slow to negotiate and difficult to enforce. The greatest indictment of all is that, despite the proliferation of inter-state accords relating to the environment, the rate of environmental degradation in most areas proceeds unabated (p. 33).

The resulting governance gap at the global level creates a need for those with new-found power to act responsibly, as indeed the United Nations hopes:

> [E]stablishing new international legal agreements and building or reforming international organisations can be difficult. This makes the call for corporations to adopt responsible practices in return for the rights they have gained even more significant.[2]

Similar calls for corporations to adopt responsible practices are coming from a variety of stakeholders in a variety of contexts. In Chapter 4 the failure of state and intergovernmental processes to reverse the role of the timber trade in tropical deforestation is described as an antecedent of direct action against companies and subsequent efforts to set up an independent system for regulating responsible forestry. In Chapter 10, Simon Heap and Penny Fowler describe a similar process whereby a political stalemate over fishing restrictions led the World Wide Fund for Nature to work with a company that had a major frozen fish business, Unilever, to set up a system for regulating responsible fishing. Meanwhile, frustration over the inadequacy of regulation for genetically modified crops produced a wave of protest against the biotechnology companies, with no easy solution in sight (Chapter 6).

A second dynamic behind the rise in business–NGO engagements is the disintegration of some traditional views on the difference between political and economic institutions. Previously, business has often been regarded as an apolitical endeavour. With the growing recognition of corporate power in shaping political realities, this fallacy has been exposed, thereby creating a challenge to corporate legitimacy. Corporate legitimacy is a general perception that the actions of a company are desirable or acceptable within some

---

2 www.unglobalcompact.com, p. 1.

assumed value system. Traditionally, corporate legitimacy was conferred by the nation-state and legality was within a system of state law, yet this can be questioned today. Companies find themselves having to work harder at legitimating themselves: statements defending a corporation's legitimacy and reputation such as 'we obey the law' or 'that is the government's responsibility not ours' are not sufficient in the 21st century.

In Chapter 2, Cheryl Rodgers illustrates this dynamic with examples from the oil industry. Shell once argued that 'politics is the business of governments' and that it should not interfere with national government policies, while critics countered that companies such as Shell held significant political influence and therefore considered this position dishonest (NGO Taskforce on Business and Industry 1997: 19). Rodgers shows that, since conflict with NGOs over the Brent Spar oil platform and the company's operations in Nigeria, the senior managers of Shell and their competitors have begun to change their approach, and corporate codes on human rights are now commonplace.

In parallel to these changes, the previous apolitical, or asocial, approach to the development of corporate policy is changing. The technique of employing only the advice of experts within narrow technical fields is being replaced by processes that include dialogue with stakeholders. More companies now realise that environmental issues are 'social and political dilemmas' with 'a range of possible answers' (Herkströter 1996: 9).

The implications of these changes are heightened as a result of the growing profile of major corporations and their brands around the world. A brand image is an aggregate of the thoughts that customers or investors associate with a particular company symbol, from a product logo to a stock market listing. Brand image has become so important that changes to it can have significant effects on company profitability or value (Griffith and Ryans 1997). Environmental and social issues hold both positive and negative potentials for companies with global brand images. Meanwhile, many NGOs carry public opinion with them on environmental and social issues, which means they have the ability to affect corporate brand image in these areas.

A third dynamic is the development in telecommunications and information technology. Global access to computers, fax machines, modems, satellite communications, solar-powered battery packs and hand-held video cameras has provided many NGOs with greater knowledge, voice and power. Although the vast majority of the world's poor and powerless do not have direct access to information technology, growing numbers of NGOs do. The flow of information around the world during political uprisings and following the disappearances or murders of notable campaigners lends added political weight to these events. 'Thanks to cyberspace, absolute control over information access is no longer possible' and atrocities can no longer be covered up easily (Johnston 1997: 336). In Chapter 3, John Bray presents examples of how NGOs have used the Internet to co-ordinate campaigns or send out information about problems such as human rights abuses, abysmal working conditions and environmental degradation, even at the very end of a company's complex supply chain. Once this information reaches the global media it can flash around the world by satellite, appearing in headlines and on television and radio within minutes. In this 'CNN world' no company can hide from the media searchlight. Therefore companies such as Unilever are well advised to proactively take responsibility for what happens in their supply chains and to begin working on problems with local and international NGOs (Chapter 8).

◢ Why business is endeared

The preceding section sketched out the 'big picture', explaining the growing importance of civil society to business in a globalising economy. Now the practical reasons why individual companies should seek constructive relations with NGOs are covered. In Chapter 14 Steve Waddell argues that NGOs are able to *do* things that business corporations cannot, and this is why they make attractive partners for business. By joining forces the partnering organisations combine their resources and strengths, and offset their weaknesses:

> NGOs are providing a means for linking the economic and production-oriented world of business with the social and value-generating one of civil society. At one level this translates into providing linkages to low-income people and interest groups that the comparatively wealthy, expensive, and elite world of business has difficulty connecting with and understanding. At another level this means making business aware of issues not immediately involved in production, such as the environment, poverty, inequality and social justice (Chapter 14, p. 205).

The reasons for working with NGOs can also be understood in terms of a management's building of intellectual, social and reputational capital, as well as efforts to reduce risks posed to this value creation.

First, there are benefits to the intellectual capital of a corporation. The skills, expertise and ideas of staff are key to the success of companies, especially those involved in knowledge-based industries. It would be a mistake to think that the intellectual capital of a company is confined within the four walls of the office. Companies can access new forms of expertise and ideas externally by working with NGOs that have a wealth of knowledge in their respective areas of interest. For example, the DIY retailers in the WWF 1995 Group had complex supply chains and often strained buyer–supplier relations, so they benefited from their partner NGO's free advice in implementing their forest product sourcing and certification programmes (see Chapter 4). NGOs are also a source of new ideas and critical thinking. If companies are to be able to meet growing social and environmental demands, they will need to undergo profound organisational change. In future, business leaders need to consider fundamental questions such as 'Who really needs this product?' and 'Will the community be healthy and prosperous enough to produce and to buy our products in the future?' In order to address such challenges, managers can work with other sectors of society and share ideas. Networks are also important elements of intellectual capital. Northern companies can tap into NGO networks in order to address sustainable development issues on the ground in countries where their suppliers are operating. Anne Weir of Unilever believes this to be important in helping to 'ensure that the standards and values applied in our business are appropriate for the societies in which we operate' (Chapter 8, p. 124). International NGO networks also offer opportunities for Southern suppliers to access socially and environmentally progressive markets in the North.

Keeping the best staff so that a company does not lose its intellectual capital is increasingly recognised as fundamental to the success of companies in knowledge-based industries. Staff may be more inclined to continue working for a company if it is a good working environment—something that is partly shaped by a company's relationship with society. Therefore trust, or 'social capital', is a valuable asset for a company. The need to develop and maintain this social capital is another reason for being endeared to work with NGOs. The concept of social capital is based on the idea that companies can achieve greater productivity and higher quality because of trust generated by good labour relations, and closer relations with suppliers and other stakeholders. Working with NGOs on causes popular with the workforce can only stimulate a better working environment and thereby enhance the social capital of the company, while working with NGOs can help in sustainability-related supplier programmes (Chapter 8).

The social capital of a company is not locked up at night when the staff go home, as the level of trust shown for the company by communities and wider society has a bearing on the success of that company. Credibility is a cornerstone of trust, and it is an area that many have problems with today, due in part to society's questioning of traditional values, as outlined above. For example, a study by the Investor Responsibility Research Centre outlined how environmental reports and claims by companies suffer from a lack of credibility with customers and stakeholders (Coates 1998). Northern retailers of products from Southern countries are particularly in need of credible information to reassure consumers, while Southern producers require credibility for their social and environmental claims in order to access ethically or environmentally sensitive markets in the North. Rightly or wrongly, NGOs are warehouses of ethical and environmental credibility. Eurobarometer's poll found the same thing that BP's market research did a few years ago: people believe NGO campaigners more than spokespeople in industry or government (Coates 1998).

Perhaps a new term is required to capture this: what I am talking about here is a company's need to build 'reputational capital'. Recent research undertaken by Columbia University in the USA suggests that around one-third of shareholder value in many industry segments is accounted for by corporate reputation. Another study by Ernst & Young estimated that the intangible assets of skills, knowledge, relationships and reputation averages two-thirds of the total market value for companies focused on knowledge creation and/or market position (Coates 1998). This might be why, in the US, the Domini Social Index developed by investment research firm Kinder Lydenberg Domini, tracking companies with high social and environmental standards, has consistently outperformed the Standard & Poor's 500 Index. Corporate reputation is valuable, in real terms, and corporate reputation is affected by civil society, in real terms.

Intellectual, social and reputational capital can be built up over years but lost in a day. Mitigating this risk is another reason for working with NGOs. A selection of boycotts, protests, resignations, awkward shareholders, terrible media coverage, or negative knee-jerk reactions from corporate customers and legislators can constitute the fallout from a media 'bomb'. The lessons from the oil industry (Chapter 2), timber industry (Chapter 4), biotechnology industry (Chapter 6) and fish product industry (Chapter 10), as well as investment in Burma (Chapter 3), all suggest that the old public relations tactics of deny, delay, divert and dismiss are not effective.

◢ The chapters

The chapters in this book have been written by people from corporations, consultancies, NGOs, research institutes and universities. Consequently, the book is a collection of diverse perspectives on aspects of business–NGO relations and sustainable development. The book is divided into six sections. Part 1 contains three chapters that expand on some of the key themes in this introduction, specifically those driving factors for increasing levels of business–NGO engagement: globalisation and the governance gap (Chapter 1), the decline of traditional means for generating organisational legitimacy (Chapter 2) and the free flow of information because of the telecommunications revolution (Chapter 3).

Part 2 contains four chapters that present examples of business–NGO relations from different industry sectors, specifically the timber, mining, biotechnology and financial sectors. In 'Planting the seeds of change: business–NGO relations on tropical deforestation' (Chapter 4), David F. Murphy and I discuss the myriad of relations between NGOs and companies involved in the timber trade around the globe. The deforestation issue provides one of the best examples of how, when governmental and intergovernmental policy processes fail to deliver significant change, civil society can work with the private sector to provide alternative modes for regulating those practices that are damaging to sustainable development. It is an example of how civil society can make responsible business a market necessity, and, in the Forest Stewardship Council (FSC), we are shown an institution that manages to bring diverse stakeholders together to define, identify and promote responsible practice.

Even when working together, NGOs can have very different values, priorities and objectives. Understanding these differences and how NGOs relate to each other is important for companies seeking to build stakeholder relations. Using case studies from Canada and Australia, in 'Shades of green: NGO coalitions, mining companies and the pursuit of negotiating power' (Chapter 5) Saleem H. Ali describes relations between mining companies, environmental and indigenous peoples groups. He finds that the environmental and indigenous NGOs often had quite different agendas, thereby presenting a challenge to a responsible corporation to build a consensus, or, alternatively, an opportunity to an irresponsible corporation to employ a 'divide and rule' strategy with NGOs. Ali rejects the latter approach, as it does not allow core issues to be addressed, thereby sustaining conditions for future conflict. Instead he argues that:

> NGOs should be supported in various ways to partake in meaningful dialogue and then even negotiation. Companies cannot leave this process to civil society alone, as coalitions of NGOs can marginalise certain issues. Instead, companies

should take a leadership role in helping to support systems of independent consultation, which may include efforts to build the organising and negotiating capacity of affected groups. This is a major undertaking for an individual corporation, and so partnership with other companies, major international NGOs and intergovernmental agencies is advisable (p. 94).

In 'A no win–win situation? GMOs, NGOs and sustainable development' (Chapter 6), I consider an industry that has been plagued by controversy. As the quotation at the start of this introduction illustrated, emotions run high over the development and utilisation of biotechnology for agriculture. After reviewing the potentials and risks of the genetically modified (GM) crops and the reaction from governments, consumers, retailers, farmers, NGOs and the biotechnology companies, I conclude that what is at issue is more than the science. Rather, biotechnology is at the centre of a war of values that is being fought between business, governments and civil society at daybreak on the 21st century. What is at stake is the future balance of power between market, state and civil organisations, between the haves and the have-nots, between human greed and human kindness. The challenges are so great that I argue that companies need to reconsider their role in society and re-evaluate their systems of corporate governance. Therefore I discuss some possibilities for building systems of accountability into corporate governance.

In 'The listening banks: the development of stakeholder relations with NGOs' (Chapter 7), Mike Lachowicz provides a quick-fire tour around developments in the banking sector. He identifies the 1992 United Nations Environment Programme (UNEP) *Statement by Banks on the Environment and Sustainable Development* as a significant step forward on the part of managers in recognising the pivotal position that banks occupy. This recognition has led some banks, such as the Co-operative Bank, to engage with NGOs as part of a process for developing their proactive stance on ethical lending. The NatWest Bank is helping its existing clients to adopt more sustainable practices through an innovative partnership with the World Wide Fund for Nature (WWF). Together they produced the 'Better Business Package' in the form of a video, training pack and CD-ROM which are available at low cost to NatWest business account holders.

Part 3 includes three chapters that home in on the experiences of individual organisations. First, the experience and perspective of a major company that has embraced partnerships with NGOs as a means of furthering its sustainability policies and practices is presented. In 'Meeting social and environmental objectives through partnership: the experience of Unilever' (Chapter 8), Anne Weir summarises the company's involvement with WWF in order to establish the Marine Stewardship Council and its work with local community groups in Germany, Switzerland and Austria on the Living Lakes project. Unilever believes that working with stakeholders and other companies is essential for implementing improvements throughout the supply chains of its products, and this is why it has become an important player in the Tea Sourcing Partnership, which is now a member of the UK-based union, NGO and industry initiative on labour rights, called the Ethical Trading Initiative (ETI).

In 'Working non-STOP for sustainable development: case study of a Canadian environmental NGO's relationship with businesses since 1970' (Chapter 9), Marie-France

Turcotte describes the different ways one NGO has influenced the operating environment of chemical companies. STOP has been involved in many issues such as air quality, water quality, waste management, acid rain and energy over the past 30 years. Turcotte's analysis demonstrates that one NGO can successfully adopt various tactics in its attempt to influence corporate activity—tactics that include lobbying for environmental regulations, opposing business projects, participating in multi-stakeholder initiatives, consulting contracts for business organisations and building 'natural alliances' with some industries.

In 'Bridging troubled waters: the Marine Stewardship Council' (Chapter 10), Simon Heap and Penny Fowler consider whether there is an emerging model for environmental and social certification overseen by councils comprised of multiple stakeholders. The Marine Stewardship Council (MSC) is the second multi-stakeholder council, being based on the original Forest Stewardship Council (FSC). By comparing the separate processes to establish the FSC and MSC they highlight key issues about the potential replicability of the stewardship council model in other sectors such as mining, oil or agriculture. They argue that the FSC was a bottom-up process led by members, while the MSC has been a top-down process led by 'experts', and this difference has meant that the MSC faces more attacks about its legitimacy, especially from Southern NGOs. In addition, from their experience of the way social issues have been downplayed in the development of the MSC, they suggest that, currently, it may be easier to translate environmental issues into a business/financial case for corporate change than it is to translate the social aspects of sustainable development.

In Part 4 we move away from the individual cases to consider some of the cross-cutting management issues that arise from working together for sustainable development. Business–NGO partnerships pose novel management challenges, which have led to a recent proliferation of 'how to' guides such as those from the Prince of Wales Business Leaders' Forum (Tennyson 1998) and the Environmental Defense Fund (EDF 1999). Of course, one of the most important decisions is to pick the right people to work with, and in 'Partners for sustainability' (Chapter 11), John Elkington and Shelly Fennell present a typology to help businesses and NGOs understand each other and choose the right organisation to approach. Their tripartite typology of business–NGO relations, NGO attitudes towards business and business attitudes towards NGOs uses marine metaphors, such as sharks and dolphins, to illustrate the common characteristics of different organisations.

In 'Culture clash and mediation: exploring the cultural dynamics of business–NGO collaboration' (Chapter 12), Andrew Crane adopts a different level of analysis, recognising that organisations are not internally undifferentiated and that individuals are key to relations between businesses and NGOs. Crane looks at the management challenges that arise because of the differing organisational cultures brought together in the implementation of a partnership. He uses a case study of the WWF 1995 Plus Group and describes the role of individuals in the implementation process. Certain individuals, termed 'cultural mediators' played a crucial buffering role in the partnership by translating cultural knowledge between the different sectors and acting as architects of shared meanings across the sectors.

In 'The art of collaboration: lessons from emerging environmental business–NGO partnerships in Asia' (Chapter 13), Christopher Plante and I develop some key themes for the management of partnerships. First, though, we provide some examples of the diverse relations between businesses and NGOs in various countries across Asia, from protest to partnership. For a variety of logistic and linguistic reasons there is a limited amount of work on the state of business–NGO relations in the non-Western world, including Asia. The partnership initiatives we draw on are those supported by the Asia Foundation's NGO–Business Environmental Partnership Initiative. We feature initiatives that have brought benefits and reduced risks to the partners, their communities and the global community, while recognising that this is not typical of the continent as a whole. We re-work the principles of ancient Asian strategic military lore, which have been used by corporations on the commercial battlefield (the 'Art of War'), into an 'Art of Collaboration' which outlines management approaches that contribute to the success of business–NGO partnerships.

In Part 5, three different ways of conceptualising the growing trend for business–NGO partnerships are presented. The opportunity to bring together the complementary resources of civil and private-sector organisations is one conceptualisation developed by Steve Waddell in Chapter 14. He believes that the 'transactional corporate culture' means it is impossible for corporations to achieve the same reflective depth and understanding of society as NGOs, with their longer time-horizons and value orientation. In 'Complementary resources: the win–win rationale for partnership with NGOs', he demonstrates this with concrete examples grouped together into eight areas: risk management; cost reduction and productivity gains; new product development; new market development; human resource development; supply chain organising; building barriers to entry; and stimulating creativity.

In 'Thinking partners: business, NGOs and the partnership concept' (Chapter 15), David F. Murphy and Gill Coleman conceive of business–NGO endearment as part of a wider social trend toward partnership thinking. They explain how partnership is an idea with increasing political power today, in the sense that it invokes positive connotations within society which make people act in novel ways. They explore the meaning of the 'partnership' concept for organisations, before considering policy debates on sustainable development and discussing some examples of the partnership approach between business and civil society. In doing so they locate innovative business–NGO initiatives as part of an emerging global partnership of state, private and civil society organisations at local and international levels, for sustainable development.

It is probable that the growing consensus on the benefits of partnership and on the existence of win–win opportunities are now key drivers in shaping business–NGO relations, alongside the power of the discourses on sustainable development, globalisation, corporate legitimacy and the communications revolution explored in Part 1. The articulation between discourses and social realities has parallels with the debate on the articulation between individual agency and social structure, the topic of Chapter 16. In 'Change the rules! Business–NGO relations and structuration theory', Uwe Schneidewind and Holger Petersen use structuration theory to throw light on the powerfulness of the relationships we deal with in this book. They challenge a typical view in business studies that the commercial, political and societal environment of a company is a given set of parameters. Such a view is dependent on the concept of society as embodying a set of rules and unchanging structures. Instead, they agree with sociologists such as Anthony Giddens that there is an intercourse between social structure and social agency: we, the people, may have certain options open to us because of the way in which our societies are structured, yet we, the people, can change those structures by our actions and thereby influence the actions of others in society. With three examples from Germany they show that companies who collaborate with NGOs are able to change the rules of markets, politics and societies in order to implement a shift toward sustainability.

The concluding Part 6 of the book focuses on the future directions of relations between business and civil society, pulling together the different examples and various strands of thought to describe an emergent civil framework for doing business in the 21st century. In 'New frontiers: emerging NGO activities to strengthen transparency and accountability in business' (Chapter 17), Rob Lake and I discuss emerging trends in civil society, particularly the increasing interest of development and human rights NGOs in the activities of the corporate sector. As campaigners in various NGOs—focused on quite different goals—begin to recognise the common threads of their individual efforts to influence corporate behaviour, and consider the frameworks within which all businesses operate, so we may be on the verge of a powerful new social movement. Broad and Cavanagh (1999) call this the corporate accountability movement, and the key frontiers of this movement relate to corporate transparency, accountability and financing. We argue that the first step for a business toward generating legitimacy is to be transparent—by providing all information that a society considers relevant to its interests, and to make it widely available in an understandable format, with ample time for potential implications and responses to be discussed. Therefore, business and NGOs are engaged in dialogue, through processes such as the Global Reporting Initiative, to define the type of reporting required to deliver meaningful transparency.

A second frontier of business–NGO relations relates to corporate accountability. As the power of corporations to shape society is recognised (Chapter 16), all sorts of civil society groups are calling on businesses to be more accountable to society. The extent to which a company can be both accountable to different stakeholders and its shareholders is a difficult issue, and leads us to consider the issue of corporate governance—who should own the corporation, who should run it, and how. We agree that 'as the 21st century gets into its stride, the make-up and activities of corporate boards will be in the spotlight as never before' (Zollinger and Elkington 1999). Consequently, we discuss some of the options open to corporations seeking to engineer stakeholder accountability into the very systems of corporate governance.

The final frontier of business–NGO relations is finance. As NGO campaigners have begun to understand business more clearly and realise the constraints experienced by managers seeking to maximise shareholder value, so their attentions have begun to turn to the financial community. NGOs have woken up to the fact that institutional investors are the real force and are working on various fronts to make the financial community more supportive of the advances being made by pragmatic NGOs and leadership companies on sustainable development issues. In Chapter 17 we detail some of the new initiatives in this area.

In 'Civil regulation: a new form of democratic governance for the global economy?' (Chapter 18), the material presented in the previous chapters is brought together under a unifying concept called 'civil regulation'. The thesis is this: global business is beginning to be regulated by a global civil society, a situation that provides some promise for a just and sustainable global order in the 21st century, while showing significant shortcomings and posing major political challenges. A key challenge is to bring some order to what is a very anarchic process at present, to build the necessary institutions as quickly as possible, and to ensure that democratic principles are upheld. The United Nations has taken up this challenge with the establishment of the Global Compact. John Gerard Ruggie and Georg Kell, who worked with UN Secretary-General Kofi Annan on creating the Global Compact with business, hope that interactions between the corporate and NGO communities could provide a springboard from which to establish a social basis for global economic activity (Ruggie and Kell 1999).

◢ A personal challenge

Businesses and NGOs are seen by many to be locked in a perpetual war of values and ideologies. What this book demonstrates is that the war has moved on. Today's battles are often fought within companies themselves, as those who understand the strategic importance of sustainability issues and stakeholder relations struggle with those who are not convinced. With the weight of experience, managers who argue the case for their company to deepen their involvement with the sustainable development agenda in partnership with stakeholders will hopefully win out and more companies will make the change. In the end it is down to each individual manager to make the move. This is a theme that seems to resonate from most of the contributions in this book: the role of individual commitment, ingenuity and bravery in stepping outside one's role as manager or campaigner in an attempt to become part of the solution. The ability of individuals to assume new responsibilities and try new ways of working is at the heart of the partnerships described in this book. Such action involves personal professional risk. I just hope for the sake of everyone this risk is taken more often than not.

A WEBSITE AND DISCUSSION LIST PROVIDES AN OPPORTUNITY TO EXPLORE further the issues in this book and keep up to date with developments in this field. The 'Business-NGO-Relations Online Gateway' contains publications available for viewing or downloading, links to organisations working in this area, and to consultancies that are providing relevant services. Messages sent to the discussion group can be browsed or searched. Most of the authors of the chapters in this book are members of the discussion group and will respond to interesting questions. To access the new online gateway, go to: www.mailbase.ac.uk/lists/business-ngo-relations/files/welcome.html.

The editor of this volume, Jem Bendell, can be contacted at jembendell@email.com and can also be found at www.jembendell.com.

PART 1

Driving Factors for Business–NGO Engagement

GLOBALISATION AND THE NEW POLITICS OF SUSTAINABLE DEVELOPMENT*

Peter Newell

Institute of Development Studies, UK

This chapter seeks to provide a broad framework within which to understand the contemporary significance of relations between businesses and NGOs in the environmental area. Different aspects of the process of globalisation are used to provide a way of explaining the growth and dimensions of these relationships. This focus allows us to understand the emergence of conflict and conciliation between companies and NGOs, and the opportunities and constraints they are subject to in an age of globalisation. The process of globalisation has both produced and coincided with strategic changes taking place within businesses and NGOs, which also provide key explanations.

◢ Which globalisation?

The growth in relations of all kinds between businesses and NGOs has taken place within an intensified period of international economic activity, commonly referred to as 'globalisation'. The term is often taken as a byword for any activity extending beyond sovereign borders in the economic, political, social or cultural domain. The fluidity of the term has led to a debate about what really is new about globalisation (Hirst and Thompson 1996). It has been suggested, for instance, that there has merely been a deepening of the trend towards internationalisation which has waxed and waned over the last century, rather than a clear break with previous eras of economic integration. In

---

* This chapter draws on Newell 1999 and Newell forthcoming.

geopolitical terms it is also sometimes argued that the term 'globalisation' is misleading because it describes a trend that is largely confined to the relations between a small number of highly industrialised states and firms operating within the triad (East Asia, North America and Europe). Relations between businesses and NGOs demonstrate, however, that it is a process with repercussions that extend far beyond the power centres of the global economy. International economic processes and social norms penetrate and impact, however indirectly, on the lives of most people, even if the architects of the current system and those who propagate the neo-liberal 'Washington consensus' most vociferously are based in the industrialised world.

The challenges generated by the growth in cross-border economic transactions in trade, production and finance are multiple and operate at the level of international institutions, the state, social movements and the private sector. There is a fear that the imperatives of competing in the global marketplace force governments to prioritise economic objectives at the expense of environmental protection. Deregulation and liberalisation are said to heighten pressures to lower environmental standards. The freedom of mobile transnational capital to locate where environmental regulations are weakest is one of the more vocal of a spectrum of concerns about the negative impacts of globalisation. It was perhaps no surprise, then, that one of the grounds for stalling negotiations towards a Multilateral Agreement on Investment (MAI) was that it would undermine standards of environmental protection by denying local and national government authorities the right to uphold environmental protection as a legitimate basis for discriminating against would-be investors.

There is a sense in this understanding of globalisation that enhanced economic integration creates an institutional crisis in which global economic forces remove the means of addressing the problems they create. In other words, further intensification of current patterns of resource-intensive economic growth may require strong state intervention in order to check the worst excesses of this activity at the very time that the state is said to be in retreat (Strange 1996). On the other hand, the increasing role that private investment is playing in implementing environmental measures suggests that governments are regarded as insufficiently flexible and innovative to make the most of the opportunities offered by responses to the challenge of sustainable development. This is symptomatic of a broader shift towards environmental policy instruments that adopt a market-based approach and rely on co-operation with private-sector actors. Traditional command and control forms of regulation, in particular, are regarded as insensitive to the transformational capacities of the market and are being replaced by an emphasis on initiatives such as eco-taxation and the creation of markets in pollution permits.

It is arguably as a result of this renegotiation of the relationship between state and market that NGOs are increasingly targeting their advocacy at multinational companies— because governments increasingly seem unwilling or unable to regulate the conduct of transnational corporations (TNCs) themselves. Shareholder activism, consumer boycotts and a range of other confrontations between environmental NGOs (ENGOs) and TNCs are indicative of a new politics in which NGOs seek to check the growth in the power of TNCs associated with globalisation. NGOs are actively working to develop international behavioural norms from which companies find it increasingly difficult to escape, wherever they operate. Where traditional forms of state regulation have been reduced, therefore, informal NGO-based regulations are emerging in their place. The objective of this chapter is not to assess the effectiveness of these strategies as mechanisms of governance or civil regulation, as others have done.[1] Rather, it is to provide an insight into the global forces shaping the nature of environmental protest and partnership in relations between businesses and NGOs, as a means of understanding their contemporary importance.

◢ Environmentalism in an age of globalisation

In arguing that these new patterns of conflict and collaboration can be considered a response to changes in political authority at the national and international levels, the point is not that the strategies being adopted by NGOs have not been adopted before in other contexts, but that there has been a resurgence in their use and that they are increasingly important in a contemporary context. There is a long history of the use of strategies such as consumer boycotts (Smith 1990). Shareholder activism and the emergence of multi-stakeholder 'stewardship councils' (see Chapters 4, 10 and 12), as they are applied in the environmental area, however, do seem to be largely new phenomena.

The growth of these new types of relationship is informed by twin developments in global environmental politics and the global political economy. First, on the environmental side, the effectiveness of traditional mechanisms for achieving environmental protection has come under critical scrutiny. International environmental institutions have been criticised as a result of the disappointment felt by many at the outcome of the 1992 United Nations Conference on Environment and Development (UNCED) held in Rio de Janeiro. This disillusionment was heightened by the Rio+5 evaluations of 1997, which demonstrated a lack of progress in implementing the goals of the original conference (Dodds 1997). Often, international agreements are vaguely worded, slow to negotiate and difficult to enforce. The greatest indictment of all is that despite the proliferation of inter-state accords relating to the environment, the rate of environmental degradation in most areas proceeds unabated (Conca 1993).

Against this background, the increased attention of NGOs to TNCs may reflect a frustration with the pace of international, inter-state reform and the prospect of higher direct returns, given that the investment decisions of major TNCs now dwarf those of many states (Korten 1995). In this sense 'Transnational groups want to affect world politics in whatever ways they can; they are not oriented merely towards influencing states . . . [they] engage in traditional state-oriented politics only to the degree and extent necessary to the dilemmas at hand' (Wapner 1996: 46). Declaratory diplomacy based on announcing (commitments) and reporting (progress) is unlikely to remain the subject of NGO attention if it repeatedly fails to deliver on effective environmental protection.

---

1   See Newell forthcoming for more on the governance dimensions of these relations, and Murphy and Bendell 1999 for more on civil regulation.

The 'strategic turn' on the part of some NGOs towards the private sector derives not only from cynicism about the degree of change that can be brought about through international organisations. The growth of more radical groups targeting the corporate sector in more confrontational ways can also be understood as a reaction to the increasing institutionalisation and bureaucratisation of certain parts of the environmental movement. This process was consolidated during the Rio process such that, according to some, many NGOs were co-opted (Chatterjee and Finger 1994; Finger 1993; Sklair 1994). Concern was expressed that NGOs gave more, in terms of legitimacy conferred on the process, than they have received (in terms of concessions to their demands) by being part of the UNCED process. Perhaps related to this, there has been a growth in groups targeting companies directly instead of pursuing change in company behaviour through governments.

Of particular concern, nevertheless, has been the failure of international environmental agreements to regulate companies responsible for ecological degradation. The issue of TNC regulation was conveniently dropped from the UNCED agenda at the insistence of the US in particular (cf. Chatterjee and Finger 1994). Similarly, while Agenda 21 includes recommendations that affect TNCs, it does not take the form of a code of conduct. An international code of conduct to regulate the activities of TNCs has been on the international agenda since the 1970s. The United Nations Centre for Transnational Corporations (UNCTC) was set up in 1973 to perform this task, but, after two decades of failed negotiations, the Centre was closed in 1993 and has been replaced by the Division on Transnational Corporations and Investment located within UNCTAD (the United Nations Conference on Trade and Development). In place of binding commitments at the international level, there has been a growth in voluntary agreements, self-monitoring, and the proliferation of sustainability audits of corporations by external consultants. The best-known voluntary guidelines on the environment are those endorsed by the ICC (International Chamber of Commerce) known as the *Business Charter for Sustainable Development*, a document of 16 principles produced prior to UNCED (Schmidheiny 1992). At the same time, during the UNCED negotiations, TNCs successfully presented themselves as part of the solution to environmental problems, arguing that only they have the necessary capital, technology and expertise to deliver positive environmental change (Chatterjee and Finger 1994). Their role in all of these key areas, necessary for the successful implementation of international environmental agreements, has elevated them to the status of partners alongside governments. The increasing concentration of capital and technology in private hands as a result of globalisation has served to entrench this relationship.

Businesses are, therefore, centrally involved in the setting of standards and targets for environmental protection. The darker side of this special relationship is the significant impact of business lobbying on government environmental policies (Newell and Paterson 1998; Chatterjee and Finger 1994). Business groups are involved in drawing up environmental agreements, and often sit on government delegations at international negotiations. The involvement of the BCSD (now WBCSD) and ICC with the UNCED process is credited by some with derailing previous attempts at regulating TNC activity such as the UNCTC's proposals for a code of conduct (Humphreys 1997a). More broadly, some writers have referred to the 'privatisation' of the United Nations system, a trend towards corporate influence over decisions and activities that are traditionally the prerogative of states at the international level (Lee *et al.* 1997).

Governments' reluctance to impose restrictions on the companies they depend on for investment is heightened in a context of globalisation where capital mobility and the internationalisation of production permit companies greater freedom to choose where to base their business (Newell and Paterson 1998). The structural power of capital over states, therefore, also becomes a disciplinary power which can penalise, through capital flight, governments that propose forms of environmental action that larger businesses disapprove of. This makes it costly for states to adopt unilateral and regional environmental measures in the absence of similar measures by rival states and firms for fear of industry relocation, however exaggerated the phenomenon is. It is important to note also that governments find it convenient to use the threat of economic loss at the hands of competitors as an excuse to justify cutbacks in environmental programmes. The extent to which the process of globalisation, in itself, constrains the ability of states to pursue more far-reaching environmental programmes is, therefore, difficult to assess.

It is not just the failure of environmental agreements to regulate corporate activity that is significant here. There is also a perception among many NGOs that companies are increasingly central to environmental decision-making and resource-use behaviour. This reflects the importance of corporate investment decisions for the development paths pursued by countries, the ecological impact of the volume of trade and transfer of goods around the world that they administer, as well as the ecological impact of production processes. Companies can diffuse best practice along global supply chains with important implications for upgrading. The global scale of sourcing and suppliers has been consolidated by the internationalisation of production and the increasingly positive attitude of many LDCs towards investment from TNCs, a marked change from the 1970s when nationalisation and acquisition of foreign-owned industries was not uncommon (Stopford and Strange 1991).

Concern about the power of TNCs also has to be understood as a reaction to the powers that international agreements confer on multinational enterprises, particularly in the area of property rights. The allocation of trade-related intellectual property rights (TRIPs) to companies through the World Trade Organisation (WTO) TRIPs agreement has shown how patents on biological materials and seeds can affect people's livelihoods in direct and potentially detrimental ways. Recent outcries at the patenting of genetically modified seeds and biological resources, such as the neem tree plant for commercial purposes, indicate the scale of unease about corporate control (Shiva and Holla-Bhar 1993; Inez-Ainger 1999; Martinez-Alier 1997). For some NGOs, governments have further proven themselves unreliable allies by seeking to negotiate a Multilateral Agreement on Investment (MAI), currently stalled, but certain to return. Negotiated amid an extraordinary degree of secrecy, this agreement embodied the right of TNCs to invest anywhere in the world on equal terms with national and local business. The OECD agreement would have allowed TNCs to sue signatory governments for profits lost through laws that discriminate against them (Rowen 1998). The agreement would have been binding for 15 years after withdrawal and a country must give five years' notice that it wants to leave the agreement.

According to NGOs, the agreement would elevate corporations to the status of 'super-citizens' free from the normal obligations of citizens in relation to the environment. Consequently, the MAI negotiations provoked a strong NGO campaign, using the Internet to facilitate global communication and co-ordination, as described in Chapter 3.

The MAI agreement is part of a broader trend in which regional trade organisations also permit companies to challenge governments and local authorities about restrictions on their activities. Within NAFTA (North American Free Trade Agreement) two Mexican authorities are currently being sued by US companies that were prevented from establishing toxic waste dumps in their jurisdictions (Rowen 1998). These developments led Temple to argue that 'in the global commons we find concerted, systematic efforts to transform all relations with respect to resources and the means of production into corporate private property' (1997: 26). In broad terms, these patterns imply a growth in the power of TNCs and a reduction in restraints on the terms of their investment. It can be argued that this creates a 'crisis' of governance where institutions have not kept pace with the demands and needs for new protection to which economic globalisation gives rise. As Vidal argues:

> Corporations have never been more powerful, yet less regulated; never more
> pampered by government, yet never less questioned; never more needed to
> take social responsibility yet never more secretive ... To whom will these
> fabulously self-motivated, self-interested supranational bodies be account-
> able? (1997: 263).

TNCs are said to wield power without responsibility. They are often as powerful as states and yet less accountable. At the same time, because they are simultaneously more anonymous than governments and often more financially powerful, they are increasingly attracting the attention of social activists. For corporations this means 'their own globalism is being actively turned against them by the emerging civil society' (Vidal 1997: 265). Globalisation helps us to understand why it is that NGOs increasingly target TNCs. They perceive power relations to have changed in a way that privileges the position of TNCs to such an extent that they are now equally, if not more, important targets for pressures towards reform.

◢ Towards partnership?

The failure of states and inter-state organisations to regulate TNCs also coincides with a changed context of NGO–TNC relations informed by strategic changes within both the business and NGO communities. The opportunity for more co-operative engagement has been occasioned by a more solutions-oriented approach adopted by many NGOs who have sought to move beyond awareness-raising and engage directly in reform, sometimes by collaborating with TNCs (SustainAbility 1996; Murphy and Bendell 1997a).

The growth in the size of many NGOs (particularly during the mid–late 1980s) also means that they cannot afford the risk of litigation undertaken by companies against their direct actions. They now have sizeable assets that would be threatened by successful court action against them. Hence, despite the ongoing role of Brent Spar-style confrontations, co-operative approaches have become more important for some groups in order to develop credibility among those able to generate reform and to avoid financial loss. McCormick notes, for example, that through the 1980s Greenpeace became 'less confrontational and more inclined to use the same tactics of lobbying and discrete political influence once reserved by the more conservative groups' (McCormick 1991: 158). It is important, however, not to overstate the shift in NGO attitudes towards a less adversarial politics, because for many groups this transition has clearly not taken place. Indeed, SustainAbility note, 'it may prove to be the case that the really limited resource is the availability of credible, skilled and energetic ENGOs willing and able to work alongside business and other partners' (1996: 1).

Business approaches to environmental issues have clearly shown a transition since the late 1980s (Fischer and Schot 1993; Hoffman 1996a). Many have also become more proactive in the debate, rather than merely resisting government-led controls or lobbying against legislation. As Haufler (1997) notes, in order to pre-empt government regulation, firms often seek to develop their own framework of commitments and obligations, often with the help of NGOs. NGOs are coming to be seen as useful partners who can offer not only expertise, as the collaboration between EDF and McDonald's illustrated (Dubash and Oppenheimer 1992; Murphy and Bendell 1997a), but also a degree of public legitimacy given that the public is generally more trusting of NGOs than business. Negotiating voluntary codes or sets of principles such as the Valdez Principles requires businesses to accept only very general principles, a far cry from government-set standards and patterns of enforcement.

An expansion in consumer markets and international trade in goods also brings choice and thereby heightens the power of the consumer to exercise the threat of taking business elsewhere by buying differently (consumer flight). Liberalisation and expansion of consumer markets may therefore create new vulnerabilities to popular pressure exercised through boycotts and the pursuit of ethical consumerism. Consumers, unlike voters in a government election, make a series of votes, often on a daily basis about what they think of a TNC's product and which TNC they will 'vote for'. The repercussions of these choices are felt directly and economically. This has created an extra incentive for companies to engage with NGOs with wide supporter bases that are able to sway consumer choice.

The challenge for NGOs monitoring the global activities of TNCs is to generate norms and expectations by which multinational companies operating in a number of countries feel bound in each of their operations. This has partly been facilitated by technological advances in transportation and communications which have compressed time and space such that flashpoints can spread rapidly around the world. Instead of having to deal with a single and more manageable source of opposition, corporations today have to deal with simultaneous co-ordinated actions of an international nature. The communications technologies that globalisation has brought in its wake have enabled NGOs to organise more quickly and effectively and to extend the reach of their surveillance of TNCs, so that, ironically, TNCs have also provided the means for their own monitoring. Public relations disasters can be ignited easily and with global ramifications. The cases of Brent Spar and Nigeria illustrate how 'local incidents can soon develop into international crises' (Vidal 1997: 240). The boycotts of Shell petrol stations spread quickly across Europe in response to these two incidents. Ken Saro-Wiwa was able to globalise the plight of the Ogoni by drawing in the support, resources and media contacts of Greenpeace International and The Body Shop and in so doing force the oil company to defend its investment practices in the Niger Delta (cf. Fabig and Boele 1999; Rodman 1998; Chapter 2 of this volume).

◢ Conclusion

Relations between NGOs and TNCs provide a useful way of understanding both power shifts in the global economy and the way NGOs perceive and react to them, and the contribution of non-economic actors to the governance of the global economy. The activities of NGOs described in this book are contributing to the reconfiguration of the landscape of global economic affairs by creating new social norms and changing the practice of transnational firms as well as highlighting, as others have done, pockets of resistance to globalisation (Gills 1997; Mittelman 1998).

Not only are new patterns of relations between NGOs and businesses a product of the trends associated with globalisation, they also create a new type of globalisation in which informal rules and norms replace, without compensating for, the absence of inter-ventions on the part of governments and international organisations. While globalisa-tion strengthens the position of TNCs, and governments secure for them unprecedented freedoms enshrined in multilateral agreements on trade and investment, it is important to note that social norms increasingly outstrip the legal requirements imposed on firms (Mitchell 1997). In this sense, NGOs exercise a different form of power over corporations. They use information and images to help expose, cajole, educate and persuade the corporate sector. Theirs is a less coercive power aimed at changing consciousness and creating mechanisms of accountability. They employ informal channels of political engagement, such as norms, moral codes and knowledge, rather than law and forced compliance.

What is particularly notable from a company perspective is that many NGO strategies result from frustration with the formal political process and the incapacity or unwilling-ness of governments to act in defence of the environment. They seek to re-embed the activities of global economic actors within a political and social framework supportive of environmental protection. This is achieved by encouraging companies to exercise restraint, consult those affected by their activities, as well as by using the market as a political vehicle, and market actors as partners in efforts to protect the environment. These strategies may also, however, prompt government intervention to provide an element of uniformity, consistency and public authority to informal practices of regulation, which may evolve into a broader shift towards the re-regulation of the corporate sector.

Clearly then, globalisation is not a one-way street. While there seems to be evidence of a reduction in regulation in formal arenas at the national and international level, a 'double-movement'[2] also develops, manifested by an increase in alternative types of (often informal and voluntary) regulation, and the emergence of norms that bound economic activity. Looking at relations between business and NGOs not only tells us something about the fluidity, complexity and contradictory nature of the globalisation process, but it also tells us something about new forms of environmental and social regulation and, in particular, the importance of informal rules and norms of behaviour, which co-exist alongside the more traditional instruments of regulation and management to which we are accustomed.

There are lessons both for business people and for NGO campaigners. Businesses move fastest when the threat of government regulation looms and this appears to be a key driver for business to engage in partnership with NGOs. In order to maintain business interest NGOs must therefore continue to lobby for government and international-level regulation in order to make business a more responsive partner. The challenge will be to design informal spheres of regulation that build on and supplement state-based regulation rather than undermine it by removing the need for it. Most companies know by now that pressures from NGOs and public expectations about corporate conduct will not go away. Much as some companies may view NGOs as a nuisance to contend with, many recognise that working with co-operative NGOs is a preferable alternative to state-enforced initiatives which are likely to be less flexible and open to negotiation. Companies have nothing to lose; successes may be internalised in government policy, best practice often adopted by other firms or by governments and imposed on competitors, creating obvious first-mover advantages, and failures are part of a valuable learning curve that will shape future patterns of interaction. Clearly, despite the enormous growth in interactions of all sorts between businesses and NGOs, successful partnerships remain a relatively new phenomenon. It is becoming clear, however, that the complex and contradictory processes of globalisation create both opportunities and challenges that will only increase in the future.

2 Karl Polanyi used the term to describe society's movement towards a framework of welfare provision and a more regulated economy following the onslaught of *laissez-faire* economics in the 19th century (Polanyi 1946). Glover (1999) and Mittelman (1998) use this approach to characterise 'micro-counter-globalising tendencies' as 'moves' towards the emergence of a double-movement against neo-liberal global economic forces.

MAKING IT LEGIT

New ways of generating corporate legitimacy in a globalising world

Cheryl Rodgers

University of Portsmouth Business School, UK

The upsurge in interest in corporate social responsibility along with social and environ-mental reporting at the turn of the new century signals a significant change in the perceived role of the corporate institution in today's society. This changing role, coupled with a decrease in the power of the state to regulate and otherwise control the activities of those corporates, as described by Peter Newell in the previous chapter, mean that high-profile companies are seeking new ways of defining their role and defending it to their publics. That is, corporates are facing a crisis in terms of being able to legitimise their operations and their behaviour. 'Legitimacy is a generalised perception or assumption that the actions of an entity are desirable, proper, or appropriate within some socially constructed system of norms, values, beliefs and definitions' (Suchman 1995: 574). Corporate legitimacy has traditionally been conferred, to a large extent, by the state—yet this is eroding.

To date the primary consequence of this 'legitimating vacuum' has been the promul-gation of a new business phenomenon: extended stakeholder management. In order to prevent, at one end of the scale, challenges to their reputations, and heavily publicised accusations of malpractice at the other, corporates are seeking acceptance and endorse-ment of their activities from their major stakeholder groups. Significantly, they are proactively seeking legitimacy from agencies other than the state and the regulators. British Airports Authority (BAA) have described this phenomenon as obtaining and maintaining a 'licence to operate' (*BAA Environment and Community Report* 1997–98), while Bendell (1998: ch. 18) speaks of it in terms of 'civil regulation' and the democ-ratisation of corporations.

One of the most powerful stakeholder groups or 'external influencers' (Mintzberg 1989: 99) in this process is that of NGOs which use their campaigns to challenge any company in any industry. The increasing significance of the NGO stakeholder role is leading to a transition in their relationship with corporates from one of confrontation to one of consultation and even association. Contextual conditions significantly affect the nature of the relationship. For example, the ideology of the NGO is a central factor in determining its stance. Similarly, the extent to which the NGO position is representative of other stakeholders' opinions and/or is a catalyst for wider stakeholder support determines the extent to which an adversarial or advisory stance is adopted. The latter factor also underpins the extent to which NGO endorsement of, or identification with, elements of corporate behaviour confers legitimacy. A natural progression for alert corporates is thus to begin encouraging NGO involvement in order to gain legitimacy within the wider stakeholder audience. As a result, strategic alliances between the two types of organisation are becoming evident. There is, however, a danger that such alliances may lead to 'NGO capture' in much the same way as powerful corporates may succeed in dominating relationships with regulators giving rise to 'regulatory capture'. At this point the objectives and objectivity of the NGO may begin to be compromised, so that the new ways of generating corporate legitimacy will also be undermined.

This chapter discusses the changing role of the corporate and examines the transfer of power from state machineries (scientific endorsement, regulation, acting in the public interest) to the corporate world. It moves on to discuss the role of the NGO in the context of extended stakeholder management and begins to explore the character of the relationships that may exist between corporates and NGOs. The chapter concludes by speculating as to the effects of such relations both on the legitimacy of the corporate and the cause(s) of the NGO.

◢ The changing role of the corporate

There is increasing acceptance that the role of the corporate in today's society, particularly the high-profile multinational, is changing. Its business is no longer simply business but now also includes a responsibility to society that goes beyond engaging only in activities designed to increase its profits. Widespread public expectations of corporates now include environmental and socially oriented projects such as The Body Shop's Easterhouse programme providing work for the unemployed in a deprived area of Glasgow, UK. Also in the UK the Co-operative Bank's ethical policy and other 'ethical investment funds', such as those operated by NPI are adding a financial dimension to these performance criteria. Indeed, one of the main drivers behind social reporting, according to NPI, is to integrate social and financial performance reporting such that a company's evaluation by the City reflects not only economic aspects but also social and environmental ones (O'Connor 1998). Patten, researching the drivers for company disclosures in annual reports, concludes that 'social disclosure is related to public pressure as opposed to profitability' (Patten 1991: 305). Perhaps the epitome of the current reporting trend was Shell's *Report to Society* (1998) which Chairman and Chief Executive, Chris Fay, defended on the basis that:

> the days when companies were judged solely in terms of economic perfor-
> mance and wealth creation have long disappeared. Today, companies have far
> wider responsibilities to the environment, to local communities and to
> broader society (Fay 1998a: 2).

Such change suggests that the mechanisms that direct and legitimise corporate behaviour are in the process of being revolutionised. With regard to sustainability, 'long term success will depend on how markets and corporate governance systems are structured requiring radical reforms over decades' (Elkington 1998a).

◢ Transition of power from the political to the corporate arena

Accompanying the changing role of the corporation is a redistribution of political power as politicians increasingly accede their traditional power either to the corporates themselves (as in privatisation and so-called 'voluntary' regulatory initiatives; see Rodgers 1998) and/or to an increasing range of NGOs. The argument that globalisation is changing the relative roles of government, private and civil society sectors, as described in Chapter 1, is supported by NGO campaigners. The director of Greenpeace UK identified three trends underpinning the transfer of power:[1]

1. **The increased deregulation of 'domestic' business by the state and, where new regulation is being developed, an increased emphasis on voluntarism.** EC Directives on waste management, for example, invoke the principle of 'pro-ducer responsibility' which advocates voluntary initiatives within industry sectors.

2. **Freer world trade.** As international markets become increasingly accessible to a greater number of firms, regulation often needs to operate at a supra-state level. While a number of bodies do function at this level, such as the Conven-tion on Biological Diversity (CBD), their lack of regulatory authority means that much of the control of international corporate behaviour passes to the firm itself.

3. **The increasing influence of global corporations.** Some global and multi-national firms now report turnover levels beyond those of some countries' GNPs. The balance of power between the boards of such companies and the

---

1   Drawn from discussions with Peter Melchett, Director, Greenpeace UK, 1998.

governments of the host state may thus be weighted in favour of the firm. This is particularly the case where 'first-world' companies are operating in developing countries.

As a result of these three trends, the 'legitimising capability' of the state *vis-à-vis* its 'domestic' industry is being eroded. Traditional forms of legitimisation for corporate behaviour have been derived from the state machineries of regulation, legislation and government's role as representative of public opinion. The loss of public faith in the state's ability to manage issues of significant public concern contributes to the erosion of legitimacy. One of the most high-profile areas is environmental management and, 'given scientific uncertainty and previous policy failures, scepticism about the ability of governments to influence environmental problems is surely understandable' (Jacobs 1997: 56). Such scepticism gives rise to greater demands on companies to manage these issues as the decreasing effectiveness of state mechanisms transfers political power to the firm and other non-state agencies. 'Given the weakening of formal political institutions, corporations will have to increasingly accept the role of a political actor' (Grolin 1998: 214).

Corporates are judged quarterly (at least) by the finance markets and daily by their consumers; politicians are judged by their publics typically only every five years. The argument follows that firms are more vulnerable to consumer pressure than are politicians to public pressure. As regulation adapts to a more industry-led approach, increased levels of voluntarism are occurring whereby the responsibility for achieving and even establishing targets is allocated to industry. Currently this appears to be effective. The power and pressure brought to bear by consumers means that changes demanded in corporate behaviour are occurring far more rapidly and are more widespread than those that could be forced by the command-and-control style[2] of legislation. Indeed, 'there appears to be mounting recognition in a number of large companies of the need no longer to assume that the government's appraisal methodologies are robustly grounded, and to begin instead to engage more directly with broader social currents of concern' (Grove-White 1997: 115). That is, there is now a burgeoning acceptance that a wider body of agencies, beyond the state and its regulatory agencies, can confer legitimacy on the firm.

◢ Extended stakeholder management

Extended stakeholder management is now a recognised phenomenon in strategic literature (Lynch 1997; Johnson and Scholes 1999) and, as stakeholders proliferate, they are being defined according to issue-based interest groups: 'green stakeholders' for

---

2 Command and control is one of the main approaches to legislation. It operates essentially by the regulator imposing standards, e.g. emission standards, with which companies must comply or be subject to regulatory penalties.

example. As the demands on the transparency of the organisation and its activities increase (see Chapter 17), the question arises as to the extent to which all stakeholders should be kept informed. Despite the fact that 'the multiplicity of legitimacy dynamics creates considerable latitude for managers to manoeuvre strategically within their cultural environments', it is clear that 'no organisation can completely satisfy all audiences' (Suchman 1995: 585). Apart from the direct and overhead costs of attempting such mass communication, stakeholders are likely to 'start suffering from terminal cases of dialogue fatigue' (Fay 1998a). More sophisticated stakeholder dialogue processes are required and NGOs such as the Environment Council now advise companies as to 'appropriate' stakeholder dialogue.

The change in establishing corporate legitimacy is not only in the new audiences but also in the information that is deemed 'reliable'. The implications of scientific data appear to be particularly prone to debate and this has been acutely apparent in the debate over Shell's planned dumping of the oil platform Brent Spar in the North Sea and the concerns over the safety of beef after the outbreak of BSE in cattle. A comment derived from the Brent Spar case raises an important (if here phrased misogynistically!) question: 'Arguing with Greenpeace is like arguing with your wife: what have the facts got to do with it?' (Shell executive quoted in Greenpeace 1998: 101). However, 'facts' derived from a Western rationalistic perspective are often elusive and cannot be sufficiently corroborated to hold sway. In their place, expressions of values are becoming significant inputs: 'what people believe and what they care about need to be factored into the assessment of what is important' (Osborn 1997: 131). This opens the way for the value-driven NGO to enter the debate from a position of strength. During the Brent Spar incident, scientific data presented both by Greenpeace and Shell UK were challenged and in some cases dismissed by third parties. The value-driven nature of the Greenpeace cause, however, expounded in slogans such as 'Shell—if you dump that rig, then we'll dump you' (C. Evans quoted in Greenpeace 1998: 101), was supported and sustained momentum throughout the battle.

◢ The primary role of the NGO

As a result of trends such as the decreasing ability of states to confer legitimacy to corporations and the questioning of our traditional deference to technology, scientific knowledge and 'expert advice', NGOs are becoming increasingly important to large corporations. Often they occupy a central position in the corporate/stakeholder dialogue process and can affect a corporate's legitimacy in either of two ways:

1. As a facilitator—that is, they advise the company on a specific issue or issues. This role may or may not be publicised by the corporate.

2. As a lead stakeholder and/or a stakeholder catalyst.

Many NGOs are often not sufficiently strong or financially influential to impose criteria on individual corporations. However, they are becoming adept at mobilising other more powerful stakeholder groups to take up their position: that is, they are operating as stakeholder catalysts. Consumer boycotts, media pressure and moral outrage are but a few techniques being employed to incite stakeholders to 'take up arms' against specific corporate activities. Greenpeace, for example, aims to win its campaign by getting corporates 'to do what it wants', but in order to do so it 'identifies the players who are potential allies'[3] and co-operates with or supports them, typically bringing more pressure to bear on the corporation.

Two facets of the business–NGO relationship are key: first is the perceived gap in objectives between the NGO and the corporate; the second is the scope of the issue under scrutiny along a spectrum of broad to narrow. These facets often determine the type of relationship likely to ensue between the two organisations. Where the relationship between NGO and corporate is characterised by focusing on a narrowly scoped issue (such as a specific incident) and a high perceived gap in objectives exists between the two organisations, the relationship between NGO and corporate is likely to be one of conflict. There is little congruence in opinions and objectives *vis-à-vis* the issue under scrutiny and an adversarial relationship is likely to develop. The Shell–Greenpeace Brent Spar issue is one example. Where the scope of the issue under scrutiny is narrow, the adversarial stance is reinforced because the NGO can run a targeted campaign against one 'event' and/or against a single corporate. This allows both the incident and/or the company to become isolated and incites public interest. Claims of precedent setting can also be levelled, as was the case with the dumping of the Brent Spar rig, and this raises the political profile of the issue. Greenpeace purposefully selects scenarios of potential conflict on which to target its campaigns. It elects issues on which to focus using three criteria:[4]

1. International scope

2. Relevance to historical/geographical strengths of Greenpeace

3. Existence of a 'real conflict'

Consequently Greenpeace has been at the forefront of European civil society response to the commercialisation of genetically modified organisms (GMOs), as this issue fulfils all three criteria. With the GMO issue it appears that the possibilities for Greenpeace adopting a role as facilitator does not arise (see Chapter 6). However, the environmental group is also active in what Peter Melchett, its UK director, characterises as a 'joint initiative'[5] with BP concerning solar developments, and its colleagues in Germany have worked with the refrigeration company, Foron, to produce a CFC-free refrigerator (Hartman *et al.* 1999). Thus its position is more complex than a single stance defined by its ideology. However, some NGOs' ideologies may preclude taking an adversarial stance. If this is the case, the NGO will be unlikely to target a specific issue because of the problems of 'naming and shaming' individual corporates. NGOs in this position prefer to address

3 Drawn from discussions with Peter Melchett, Director, Greenpeace UK, 1998.
4 *Ibid.*
5 *Ibid.*

industry-wide issues and adopt an advisory stance—possibly establishing an industry forum in which to debate the problem. The World Wide Fund for Nature (WWF)'s stance on forestry, working with industry to establish the Forest Stewardship Council is one example that has been tremendously successful (see Chapters 4 and 12).

Where the perceived gap in objectives between the organisations is low, such as where a company seeks assistance in developing its environmental report, the NGO may take an advisory role. As this type of relationship becomes more sophisticated, it inevitably moves towards a consultancy arrangement and organisations such as the Environment Council are beginning to overtly adopt this approach. The changing dynamics of the relationship between NGOs and corporates, such as a successful joint outcome or proactive behaviour by an industry sector, may move the relationship towards a closer alliance. For example, in the WWF initiative on forestry, the gap in objectives between the industry sector and the NGO was narrowed as progress towards well-managed forestry was achieved (see Chapters 4 and 12).

A second imperative may be for the NGO to achieve a broader impetus: that is, to widen the argument from the specific to the general. Because of the dynamics of NGO campaigns and the vagaries of public interest and opinion, the relationship may begin with a relatively narrow scope, as in the Brent Spar campaign. However, as that campaign progressed, the scope of the issue broadened to include all similar rigs in similar situations with the issue of precedence being used to Greenpeace's advantage. If the aims of the NGO and the corporate or industry being targeted converge across a broad scope, the two organisations will move towards a form of 'strategic alliance'. This convergence in the aims of NGOs and corporates is seen by some as a foregone conclusion:

> whether we are the chairman of a major British company, or the representative of an environmental pressure group I believe that all of us now share a common starting point. The successful company of the future will need to demonstrate year on year progress toward greater openness and the involvement of key stakeholders (Fay 1998a).

◢ The implications for corporate legitimacy and the NGO cause

It has already been noted that Shell's *Report to Society* (1998) was something of a watershed in corporate social responsibility, acknowledging as it does the requirement for companies to report to their various publics on a broad spectrum of issues. It marks an increasing acceptance of the notion that stakeholder and corporate objectives are compatible:

> It is fair to say that even two or three years ago, a Shell UK *Report to Society* would have been met with widespread cynicism and even disbelief from a wide range of our stakeholders. But today, I believe that constructive dialogue and positive

criticism have replaced hostility and point scoring on both sides. And that's an entirely positive development (Fay 1998a).

Such 'positive developments' can be welcomed but there is an inherent danger that potentially adversarial stakeholders may be manipulated by large corporates seeking better relations with them. As corporates seek the endorsement of those NGOs that are perceived by the public to be 'good and worthy causes', financial or other corporate support may be offered in return. Even where corporates do not seek to manipulate, the cause of the NGO may be compromised as a result of such transactions. Murphy and Bendell (1997a) recognise that a similar problem may also arise as NGOs work with companies on selective issues:

> . . . single-issue partnerships may prevent environmental groups from pub-
> licly criticising their business partner on other social or environmental matters.
> The worry, therefore, is that partnering groups may lose their edge as industry
> watchdogs.

It is in the interests of both the corporates and the NGOs to prevent forms of 'NGO capture', where the causes or interests of the NGO are compromised and in consequence the public perception of the NGO is damaged. Once the NGO has lost its legitimacy as a 'value broker' in the eyes of the public, it will be unable to confer 'legitimacy by association' on corporates. In this way corporations will have returned to a situation where it is difficult to build reputation and re-produce legitimacy. Whether this breakdown is inevitable is open to debate, but what is certain is that, in order to prevent it, NGOs need to address their own systems of accountability to wider civil society. Strategies might include operating in a more transparent manner and involving members or beneficiaries of the NGO directly in the governance of the NGO. In addition, Murphy and Bendell (1997a) suggest that:

> Accountability also depends on ongoing critical monitoring of the process
> by . . . other parts of the wider green movement. For business, this critical
> monitoring ensures that the partnership is deemed to be credible in the public
> eye.

Businesses could help to support efforts at maintaining NGO independence and reputation by preferring NGO partners with wide networks and demonstrable accountability to constituencies in society. Meanwhile, adversarial campaigns will continue to have an important role and, far from moving NGO–corporate relationships towards strategic alliance, there may be significant merit in maintaining the potential for conflict. Ideally, the map of corporate–NGO relations should show populations at different points along the spectrum of relationship types with dynamism provided by the introduction of new issues following the resolution, either by adversarial or advisory relationships, of the old.

◢ Conclusion

It is now clear that 'deeper societal changes reflecting the emergence of a late–modern risk society imply that business can no longer rely on government approval and scientific expertise as primary sources of corporate legitimacy' (Grolin 1998: 213.) Instead, corporates must seek approval from an ever-widening body of stakeholders with disparate interests and levels of power with which to affect the company. Moreover, the defence of corporate activities and reputations, particularly in social and environmental contexts, must now draw on different instruments and more qualitative data sets. As with environmental policy-making, it needs to be recognised that 'the rationalist approach . . . based on scientific analysis and risk assessment is a tool, not a total solution' (Osborn 1997: 131). NGOs in both adversarial and advisory relationships with corporates are increasingly becoming primary agents in the stakeholder dialogue process and are able to significantly affect the perceived legitimacy of corporate activities. The Brent Spar incident illustrated that, with mass public support and media attention, this can even be achieved in the face of 'state-approved activities'. The implications of 'a CNN world' (Elkington 1998b) are becoming ever more apparent to high-profile corporates. The pervasiveness of incidents such as Brent Spar, the BSE crisis and GMO protests mean that traditional structures and legitimacies are being challenged:

> The growing range of interactions, and even of prospective coalitions, between particular industrial actors and NGOs across previously unbridgeable divides, boosted by reflection on the Brent Spar episode, appears itself to hint at modest but potentially significant reconfigurations within civil society (Grove-White 1997: 120).

The increasing importance of the NGO role signals more significant changes in the corporate–societal interface and the challenge for managers directing companies through these changes will increase sharply in the next few years. The effects may ultimately transform corporate–state–civil society relations.

WEB WARS

NGOs, companies and governments in an Internet-connected world*

John Bray

Control Risks Group, UK

> Knowledge itself is power.
>> *Francis Bacon (1561–1626)*

Questions of power and accountability lie at the heart of the debate between companies and non-governmental organisations (NGOs). Advocacy NGOs point to the sheer size of today's major international companies. For example, multinational companies are said to account for 51 out of the world's largest 100 economic entities, with the remaining 49 being countries (*Understanding Global Issues* 1997). Groups campaigning on issues such as the environment and human rights therefore seek to ensure that companies use their power responsibly. In contrast, business people tend to question the real extent of their power and the scope of their responsibilities.[1]

The Internet is a medium, not a message. The technology does not of itself change the quality of the arguments presented on either side. But, by making certain kinds of information more widely available, the Internet changes the balance of power between NGOs, companies and governments. In particular, the wider distribution of information puts greater pressure on companies to explain their activities in countries and regions that previously were considered obscure; and it makes it more difficult for companies and governments to conduct confidential negotiations on issues such as trade and investment.

---

* This paper develops ideas from an earlier article, 'Web of Influence', *The World Today* 53.8–9 (August 1997), and a presentation on 'The Role of the Internet' at a conference on *Multinational Investment and Human Rights* (Royal Institute of International Affairs, 20 April 1998).

1 These issues are discussed in greater detail in Control Risks Group 1997.

This chapter begins with a broad analysis of the strategies employed by NGOs in their use of the Internet, and companies' responses. It focuses on two case studies: the international human rights campaign for Burma (Myanmar), and the NGO campaign against the OECD's proposed Multilateral Agreement on Investment (MAI). The chapter concludes with a general discussion of the changing relationship between companies, governments and NGOs, and the implications for the wider debate on the environment, human rights and sustainable development.

◢ NGOs and the Internet

NGOs have been swift to make full use of the Internet. Increasingly, the mainstream press and broadcasting media are dominated by governments, conglomerates and 'moguls' because of the large investments and operating costs involved. In contrast, anyone with a computer and a modem can set up a website at minimum cost: the medium lends itself to 'network guerrillas' (Jonquières 1998). These 'guerrillas' have used the Internet first as a source of information but, secondly—and more importantly—as a means of co-ordinating their activities regionally, nationally and internationally.

A source of information

The Internet both supplies NGOs with greater information on their campaign issues and allows them to spread information on those same issues, whether these relate to countries, companies, or both.

Information on countries

Internet sources on Tibet—a country that was formerly a byword for remoteness and obscurity—demonstrate both the medium's strengths and its limitations as a source of information. Specialist information sources include: World Tibet News (WTN), a free e-mail cuttings service;[2] the non-partisan London-based Tibet Information Network (TIN);[3] and the Free Tibet Campaign (FTC),[4] which explicitly campaigns for Tibetan independence. In addition to these specialist news sources, information on current events in Tibet may be found on academic sites and the websites of other organisations with broader mandates, such as the BBC World Service or Amnesty International.

The range of readily available information on Tibet is therefore unparalleled in comparison with any previous period in the country's history, but there are still limitations. All these different sources need to be read critically: the Internet may be neutral, but information providers are not. Moreover, Chinese censorship is still effective within

2   Subscription details are posted on www.snowlion.com.
3   www.tibetinfo.net
4   www.freetibet.org

Tibet: it is very difficult to get 'the whole picture' from any source or combination of sources.

So far, few mainstream Western companies have shown a serious interest in Tibet: Holiday Inn formerly managed a hotel in Lhasa, but became the target of a FTC campaign and has now withdrawn. No mainstream Western company could expect to operate in Tibet—however remote it may seem—without its activities being closely monitored.

Information on companies

Advocacy groups are alert to the Web's potential as a source of information on the activities of large companies. For example, the Washington-based Environmental Resources Information Network (ERIN) publishes an activist's guide to resources for researching corporations on its website.[5] ERIN's objective is to help smaller environmental groups improve their access to information so that they are on a more equal footing both with larger, national environmental organisations and—on the other side of the fence—with companies from the extractive industries. ERIN points to a range of different sources, including both on-line and printed business publications, academic libraries—and the websites of NGOs such as Corporate Watch[6] that specialise in monitoring multinationals.

A campaign tool

The Internet facilitates many existing NGO activities, such as organising petitions, as well as making it easier to share information between allied groups and their supporters. The new technology also makes it possible to conduct new kinds of campaign, such as 'electronic direct action'.

Spreading the message

The Web provides NGOs with a 'shop window' from which to advertise their own existence, explain their arguments and recruit new members. NGOs have often displayed great imagination in their website designs, making full use of the medium's capacity to display images and sound, as well as text.

For example, the World Wide Fund for Nature (WWF) offers viewers a video library, art and photo galleries and a section entitled 'Just for Kids', as well as information on its latest campaigns on climate change, forests and the seas.[7] In early November 1998, the Greenpeace UK site[8] offered live broadcasts of six Greenpeace activists conducting a six-day protest on the Piz Buin glacier in the Austrian Alps to draw attention to the consequences of global climate change. Greenpeace offers viewers the chance to become 'cyber-activists'; join mailing lists; or become citizens of 'Waveland' ('a global country situated on the World Wide Web').

5   www.enviroweb.org
6   www.corpwatch.org
7   www.panda.org
8   www.greenpeace.org

These and similar NGO sites almost always contain 'links', cross-referring readers to the websites of other organisations who are interested in similar issues.

Letters and petitions

Since its foundation in the early 1960s, Amnesty International has been calling on its supporters to write letters to government officials on behalf of prisoners of conscience. Similar letter-writing campaigns have been used by other groups campaigning on environmental and other issues. New technology now makes it possible to send such 'letters' by fax or e-mail. For example, over a three-day period in early December 1998, Norwegian students sent some 200,000 e-mail messages to leading politicians in protest over a rise in interest rates on student loans (*Independent* 1998).

Many NGOs make this form of protest even easier by including direct links from their websites to the e-mail or fax addresses of their 'targets'. For example, several US sites include the e-mail addresses of members of Congress, while the UK-based World Development Movement[9] invites readers to write to the chairman of Rio Tinto. Readers have only to click on to the relevant addresses, write and 'sign' their messages—and send them off. By way of literary variation, the Rainforest Action Network (RAN) website until recently invited readers to get in touch with their 'inner poets' and send a *haiku* to the president of Mitsubishi Corporation to protest against the company's timber operations.

Organising

In the 1970s and 1980s, anti-apartheid activists operated complicated telephone networks to spread urgent messages: individual activists undertook to ring, say, three others to inform them of forthcoming demonstrations or other protests. The Internet makes it much easier to advertise and co-ordinate campaigns. For example, in the UK, protesters involved in the movement against road-building—'Reclaim the Streets'—send information to each other about where and when to meet for forthcoming protest marches. The ability of e-mail to help a disparate group of activists to organise is one of the main reasons why the Free Burma Campaign (FBC) boycott of goods made in Burma has proved so effective (see below).

'Electronic direct action'

For a minority of activists, the Internet provides scope for various forms of 'electronic direct action'—the electronic equivalent of sit-ins and graffiti-writing. A common method is to send a flood of e-mail messages—in some cases from pre-programmed computers—in the hope of causing the recipient's computer to crash.

One group that specialises in this approach is the so-called Electronic Disturbance Theater, which originated as a US-based support group for Zapatista rebels in Mexico

9   www.wdm.org

(who have their own website[10]). Recent targets for the theatre's software attacks have included Mexican President Ernesto Zedillo and the US Defense Department (Harmon 1998). Stefan Wray, one of its founders, says that he sees such tactics as 'a form of electronic civil disobedience . . . transferring the social-movement tactics of trespass and blockade to the Internet'. He seeks to rally like-minded activists with the slogan, 'The revolution will be digitalized!'

Other groups have broken into their targets' websites to add their own messages. In June 1998, shortly after India's nuclear explosion, British and Dutch students claimed credit for breaking into the website of India's major nuclear centre and imposing the image of mushroom-shaped cloud. A few months later, activists broke into an Indian government website promoting tourism in Kashmir; they wrote 'Save Kashmir' on the opening screen, and included pictures of alleged victims of the Indian army's Kashmir counter-insurgency campaign (Harmon 1998). Companies are potentially at risk from the same sort of direct action.

◢ Company responses

In early 1998, a report by Fletcher Research, a specialist British management consultancy, commented that companies tended to 'miss the point' of the Internet (Kuper and Mackintosh 1998). Many simply post annual reports and other standard printed material on the Web, without making any attempt to modify the design for a different medium or a wider audience. In particular, they often ignore the Web's interactive qualities, which make it possible to receive messages as well as transmit them. This 'collective lack of imagination' has resulted in lost commercial opportunities.

Similar criticisms have applied to companies' responses to NGO debates, at least initially. Rather than taking the initiative to put forward their points of view, companies have either ignored controversial issues on their websites, or reacted defensively. As a result, they may come across as remote, uncaring and—in some cases—arrogant. It is only relatively recently that companies have begun to adopt a more sophisticated approach, acknowledging different points of view and using the Internet as a means of soliciting opinions rather than simply conveying counter-propaganda.

Freeport McMoRan

Freeport McMoRan, the US-based mining company, uses its website[11] to defend itself from criticism concerning its mine at Grasberg in the Indonesian province of Irian Jaya (also known as 'West Papua'). The mine is one of the world's largest, and it is sited in a previously remote highland region with little previous economic development. The

---

10   www.ezln.org
11   www.fcx.com

project has attracted fierce criticism from groups such as the UK's World Development Movement (WDM), both on account of the environmental repercussions and the social impact on indigenous peoples.

Freeport's website acknowledges the complexities of Grasberg's problems, and it includes an extract from an independent social audit report calling for the company to demonstrate greater 'vision and drive in social and cultural development'. However, the overall tone is uncompromising. People who disagree with Freeport's position are dismissed as 'anti-mining activists', a designation that apparently leaves little room for honest disagreement.

Monsanto

Monsanto, the US-based life sciences company,[12] adopts contrasting approaches in its US and UK websites, and these reflect differences in the political and social environment in the two countries although—of course—both sites can be viewed worldwide.

Over the last ten years, Monsanto has embarked on a billion-dollar research programme to develop genetically modified crops, including a new variety of maize which is resistant to corn borer insects. US consumers appear ready to trust companies to undertake biotechnological experiments. In contrast, in Europe, consumers have been sensitised by problems such as the UK's 'mad cow disease' (BSE) affair, which suggest that 'interference with nature' can have dire results. Greenpeace and other NGOs have conducted a high-profile campaign against the company's plans.

The website of the US parent company[13] discusses the company's biotechnological innovations, boldly asserting that it will help feed the world's expanding population. However, there is no substantive discussion of the potential risks. Similarly, the website of the South African subsidiary[14] is clearly addressed to farmers rather than consumers: 'Now you have the opportunity to make your corn production more profitable over the long run . . . '. The text says that turtles 'carry complete protection against natural enemies' throughout their lives, and argues that maize deserves the same privilege. To underline the point, the text concludes with a picture of a small turtle cheerfully waving its head. The site includes a section entitled 'Social Responsibilities', but this refers to corporate good works, such as school sponsorship, rather than the impact of its own products.

The website of Monsanto's UK subsidiary[15] is much more forthright in acknowledging alternative points of view. It affirms the company's own position, which is that the new technology is socially beneficial as well as financially profitable, but it also explains that many disagree. Food is important, and readers have a right to know all the arguments, so the website helpfully provides links to critics such as Greenpeace, Friends of the Earth and the 'Iceland' supermarket chain (whose proprietor opposes genetically modified foods). The tone of its website suggests that the company has learned to treat its critics

12   See footnote on p. 14.
13   www.monsanto.com/monsanto/default.htm
14   www.monsanto.co.za
15   www.monsanto.co.uk

with respect while still hoping to win the long-term argument and—most importantly—the approval of consumers. This may prove to be a long battle.

Royal Dutch Shell

Royal Dutch Shell's website[16] is highly sophisticated, both in the style of its presentation and in its contents. The website repeatedly stresses the company's willingness to listen and respond to contrary points of view from NGOs and individuals.

This approach is a considered response to past controversies. In 1995, Shell was embroiled in a vigorous Greenpeace campaign on account of its plans to dispose of the Brent Spar offshore platform by sinking it at sea. In November 1995, human rights activists accused the company of collusion with the Nigerian regime following the execution of Ken Saro-Wiwa, a dissident leader from the oil-producing region of Ogoniland. These two events prompted the company to review the way it operated. Shell Group Managing Director Cor Herkströter acknowledged that the company might have been 'excessively focused on internal matters' (Herkströter 1996). As a result, it had proved sensitive to changing attitudes outside the company—and the Brent Spar and Ogoniland controversies caught it by surprise. The company's website is designed both to express the company's point of view to the outside world, and to provide an early warning system of similar controversies in the future.

Shell's *General Business Principles* are published on its website. These include commitments to contribute to sustainable development, and to 'express support for human rights in line with the legitimate role of business'. However, the company acknowledges that putting these principles into practice may not be straightforward. Under the heading 'Issues and Dilemmas', the company lists six problem areas: dealing with industrial legacies; renewables; sustainable development; human rights; globalisation and the role of multinationals; and operating in politically sensitive regions. Under each heading, the company includes a space for readers to type their own views, and a 'Shell Ballot Box' where readers are invited to register their views on questions such as: 'Should business use their influence with government to address broader issues of human rights?'

To judge by the number of people responding, the site has been a success. Between 1996 and 1998 it attracted nearly six million visitors, and received nearly 26,000 e-mails. In November 1998, Shell launched a new, completely redesigned website and it promised that this would evolve continuously with the help of feedback from readers. Information on public opinion gathered via the Internet contributes to company policy-making. However, consultation via the Internet is not a panacea. Shell rightly emphasises that international companies face dilemmas to which there may be no consensus answers.

16   www.shell.com

◢ Internet activism for human rights and sustainable development in Burma

The international controversy over the future of Burma illustrates how companies may be caught up in wider international debates where there are no obvious solutions. In the last ten years, Burma has emerged as a *cause célèbre* among human rights activists because of its history of political repression. Between the 1960s and the late 1980s, the country adopted an isolationist policy, preferring to develop an indigenous 'Burmese Path to Socialism'. During that period, internal political developments were scarcely reported in the outside world. In contrast, in the 1990s, Burma's internal affairs have been vigorously debated abroad, and the Internet has played a key role in facilitating the debate.

The international debate has focused on Burma's poor record on civil and political rights, but it is impossible to separate this from other issues, such as environmental management and the prospects for equitable economic development. Burma's military leaders argue that an authoritarian government is well placed to take the tough decisions that are needed to accelerate the country's economic expansion. In contrast, the regime's opponents point out that a regime that lacks democratic accountability is more likely to serve the interests of a narrow group of supporters—in this case the army and its commercial allies—rather than the country as a whole. Many of the government's decisions—for example, the granting of logging permits to Thai companies in the early 1990s—have been associated with severe environmental damage.

Western businesspeople working in Burma typically acknowledge the country's many problems, but argue that their own companies operate to the highest labour and environmental standards. As this case study will show, NGO critics insist that this view of corporate social responsibility is far too narrow.

International policy dilemmas

It is almost universally agreed that the present state of affairs in Burma is unsatisfactory. The military regime has been widely condemned for its refusal to enter into dialogue with the main opposition party, Aung San Suu Kyi's National League for Democracy (NLD). The NLD won a two-thirds majority in the 1990 national elections, but the new parliament was never allowed to convene. Aung San Suu Kyi's movements remain restricted, and many of her followers are in prison.

Every year since 1991, the UN General Assembly has passed consensus motions condemning the country's human rights record, but there is no international consensus on the best means of influencing the ruling State Peace and Development Council (SPDC; previously known as the State Law and Order Restoration Council [SLORC]). Governments, companies and NGOs each face their own variations on a common set of dilemmas:

☐ Governments have to decide whether confrontation or 'constructive engagement' is more likely to promote reform. The US government has opted for confrontation by implementing unilateral sanctions on new investment in

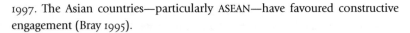

1997. The Asian countries—particularly ASEAN—have favoured constructive engagement (Bray 1995).

☐ Companies—and their critics—have had to grapple with similar questions: would investment and trade help support a pariah regime? Or would increasing commercial contact with the outside world help to promote reform? To what extent would companies' presence in the country be associated—directly or indirectly—with human rights abuses such as the government's use of forced labour to build roads or railways?

☐ Development NGOs have been involved in a similar debate. There is no doubt of the need for development assistance, but NGOs have had to ask to what extent they can operate independently in Burma. Does their presence help support the regime? Or does overwhelming human need override all other considerations?

Opposition leader Aung San Suu Kyi has consistently favoured international confrontation with SLORC/SPDC rather than 'constructive engagement' and has called on investors to avoid Burma as long as the present regime is in power. As a Nobel Peace Prize winner, she has immense moral authority, and Burma human rights campaigners across the world have tended to follow her line.

The role of the Internet in the Burma debate

A source of information

The Internet has provided a rich source—or rather a set of sources—of information. The BurmaNet news group sends daily bulletins of news free of charge to subscribers. These mainly consist of articles from the international press—particularly from Thailand—with occasional editorial comment. It also includes reports from NGOs working with Burmese refugees in Thailand. BurmaNet is run from Bangkok by an enthusiast who operates under the pseudonym 'Strider'.

Meanwhile, NGOs, governments and companies each discuss current Burmese affairs on their websites:

☐ Notable Burma human rights campaign groups include the US-based Free Burma Campaign.[17]

☐ The Burmese government has responded by creating its own website.[18] This includes extracts from the official newspaper, *The New Light of Myanmar*.

☐ International companies operating in Burma discuss their activities on their own sites. The quality of the information they provide varies enormously. The

---

17 www.sunsite.unc.edu/freeburma/index.html
18 www.myanmar.com

US petroleum company Unocal[19] discusses the progress of its project, and ancillary social development schemes, in some detail. However, Premier Oil (UK) has only just recognised the need to have a website at all. The website[20] contains only the scantest references to Burma.

There are still significant gaps. Burma remains a closed society. Diplomats in Rangoon complain that they are forced to rely on rumour rather than more reliable sources of information on a notoriously secretive regime. Reliable information on areas outside the capital is scarce. The Internet is not available within Burma except to a handful of privileged international agencies.

A campaign tool

The Free Burma Campaign (FBC) in America is a powerful example of a pressure group's use of the Internet. In the early stages, the leading figure was Zarni, a Burmese PhD student at the University of Wisconsin (he has now received his doctorate), who was said to spend some 15 hours a day in front of his computer. The FBC argues that Burma is the 'South Africa of the 1990s'. Using the Internet, the FBC has been able to co-ordinate more than 120 local support groups in schools and colleges across the US. It also works with like-minded groups internationally. Its British counterpart is the Burma Campaign (formerly the Burma Action Group).

The FBC's strategy has been first to call on consumers to boycott the goods of companies operating in Burma. Secondly, it has pressed US city and state administrations to introduce 'selective purchasing legislation', whereby they would refuse to do business with companies operating in Burma. The state of Massachusetts has introduced such legislation, as have a dozen cities including Berkeley (California) and San Francisco.

The impact on business

These campaigns have affected companies in different ways, and the precise impact depends in part both on the industry and on the country of origin.

Consumer goods

Producers of consumer goods are most vulnerable to boycott campaigns, and the Internet has made these campaigns all the more effective. A succession of clothing companies have withdrawn contact with suppliers based in Burma. The first such company was Levi Strauss in 1992 and it has been followed by a series of others, including Liz Claiborne, Macy's department store and British Home Stores.

Similarly, Heineken and Carlsberg withdrew from Burma in 1996, followed by Pepsi in 1997. Shortly before Pepsi announced its withdrawal, it lost a $1 million contract with Harvard University as a direct result of the FBC campaign.

19   www.unocal.com/myanmar
20   www.premier-oil.com

Tourism

The Burmese authorities declared 1996/97 to be 'Visit Myanmar Year', but have had much less success in attracting foreign tourists than they had hoped. The new international-style hotels which have been built in Rangoon since the early 1990s are said to be running with occupancy rates of 15%–20%. Burma support groups in the West have been calling for a boycott on tourism in Burma, and the Internet apparently helped them get their message across.

Oil and gas

The impact on the companies engaged in offshore gas exploration has been more mixed. There are two principal offshore gas projects. Total (France) is the lead operator in the Yadana field and works in a joint venture between Unocal (US), the Petroleum Authority of Thailand (PTT) and the state-owned Myanmar Oil and Gas Enterprise (MOGE). In 1997 Premier (UK) replaced Texaco (US) as the lead operator in the Yetagun field in association with PTT, Petronas (Malaysia) and Nippon Oil (Japan).

From a human rights point of view, the petroleum companies' presence is particularly sensitive. First, the gas will ultimately provide one of the main sources of income to the government. Second, the main export pipeline runs through an area that has suffered from a long-running insurgency involving the Mon and Karen ethnic minorities. The operating companies ultimately depend on the protection of the Burmese army, which is not renowned for its adherence to human rights principles. Third, the government has reportedly used forced labour to help construct a railway line running south from the town of Ye towards the pipeline terminus. The companies have denied that the railway line is linked to their project, or that they will benefit from it, but many of their critics have been reluctant to accept this. A fourth concern voiced by NGOs is the environmental impact on forests on both sides of the Burma–Thailand border.

Texaco's decision in 1997 to sell its share in the Yetagun field was ostensibly based on a commercial judgement. However, it is widely believed that the US government's decision to impose sanctions on new investment in Burma exercised a significant influence, even though Texaco—as an existing investor—was exempt from the sanctions.

The other petroleum companies have proved more robust. This is partly because of the nature of their investments. Investments in the oil sector are much larger and demand a longer lead time than investments in the clothing or drinks sectors. Additional factors may include the fact that Unocal scaled down its downstream activities in the US, and to that extent is less exposed to consumer boycotts. Total is less exposed to consumer pressure in France than Unocal is in the US because the Burma human rights campaign movement is less developed there. Similar considerations apply to the partners in the Yetagun field. Premier does not have significant downstream operations, while neither Petronas nor Nippon Oil faces major Burma campaigns in its own country.

However, while the international partners in the Yadana and Yetagun fields are determined to continue their operations, they are nonetheless sensitive to the impact of Burma human rights campaigners on their reputations. Alongside their main commercial activities, they have helped fund development projects in the pipeline area and, in

Premier's case, in Rangoon and the Inle Lake region. Some of these projects are described on the Unocal websites and provide evidence to support the companies' argument that their presence in Burma benefits the wider population and not just the ruling élite. The debate continues—both on the Internet and in other media.

Implications for the wider human rights debate

The Burma case study shows that the impact of NGO pressure—with or without the Internet—varies according to the industry in which specific companies operate, and their country of origin. Companies producing consumer goods are more susceptible to pressure than those in the petroleum sector. Petroleum companies are more susceptible if they have significant downstream operations, and in particular if they operate in the US.

The Burma case study also points to two broader issues:

☐ First, when is 'engagement' with an outcast regime 'constructive'? To many Burma human rights activists, 'constructive engagement' has been synonymous with 'appeasement'. However, as noted above, some development NGOs as well as companies have decided that the benefits of operating within the present system in Burma outweigh the disadvantages. From a human rights point of view, what forms of 'engagement' are constructive? And in what circumstances?

☐ More importantly, who decides? Both Japan and the European Union have denounced Massachusetts's selective purchasing legislation discriminating against companies operating in Burma. Critics have suggested that Massachusetts is—in effect—conducting its own foreign policy. Is this legitimate? Are mere state legislators qualified to judge complex international issues?

However, critics of Massachusetts's 'foreign policy' may be missing the point. In the future, a Western company's human rights standards will be judged not so much by governments—whether national or regional—as by ordinary consumers. The Internet will play an important role in shaping their views.

◢ The campaign against the Multilateral Agreement on Investment (MAI)

NGOs affect companies directly, when their campaigns focus specifically on the companies' own activities, as well as indirectly when they lobby governments on proposed new legislation or international treaties. The successful NGO campaign against the Multilateral Agreement on Investment (MAI) provides a particularly powerful example of the influence on both government and business of the new on-line civil society. The MAI is—or was—a draft international treaty drawn up by the 29 member countries of the

Organisation for Economic Co-operation and Development (OECD). Negotiations began in May 1995, and at first attracted little publicity outside a narrow circle of specialists. However, in early 1997 the draft MAI came to the attention of advocacy groups in North America and Western Europe. They argued that the treaty would give too much power to transnational corporations—not least because it would undermine governments' rights to regulate the environment within their own jurisdictions.

The NGOs used the Internet to co-ordinate an anti-MAI campaign involving several hundred groups across the world. Largely as a result, the OECD's discussions on the MAI were suspended in April 1998, and there is no immediate prospect of a resumption. This case study therefore illustrates both the role of the Internet in facilitating such campaigns, and the wider debate about the role of transnational corporations in the global economy.

The case for the MAI

The MAI was intended to establish a liberalised framework for international investment, complementing the work of the World Trade Organisation (WTO) on trade matters. The OECD points out that international investment has made a major contribution to economic growth, particularly in the last 50 years, and is an 'essential agent of economic growth, employment, sustainable development and rising living standards' (OECD 1998a). However, the multilateral system lacks a comprehensive and coherent framework of 'rules of the game' for investment. The MAI therefore aimed to provide:

> a level playing-field with uniform rules on both market access and legal security. It aims at eliminating barriers and distortions to investment flows, promoting a more efficient allocation of economic resources and thereby achieving higher economic growth, more jobs and increased living standards (OECD 1998a).

The agreement was to include disciplines in three key areas: investment protection, investment liberalisation, and binding dispute resolution. The core concept of the MAI was non-discrimination: government signatories were to commit themselves to treatment of foreign investors and their investments 'no less favourably than they treat their own investors' (Drohan 1998).

The agreement was to be a free-standing international treaty open both to OECD members and to non-member states. Signatories were to commit themselves to its terms for a minimum of five years. Even if they subsequently decided to withdraw from the agreement, foreign investors who had entered a host country while the MAI was in force would continue to enjoy its privileges for a minimum of 15 years.

The campaign against the MAI

The most striking aspect of the NGO campaign against the MAI was its international reach. This would have been impossible without the Internet. As the chair of the NGO Council of Canadians commented:

> We are in constant contact with our allies in other countries. If a negotiator says something to someone over a glass of wine, we'll have it on the Internet within an hour, all over the world (Drohan 1998).

In early 1998, the Council of Canadians used the Internet to publish a joint statement on the agreement which was endorsed by 560 organisations in 67 countries.[21] These ranged from the national branches of major 'multinational' NGOs such as Friends of the Earth (FoE) to much smaller organisations such as the Area Clamdiggers' Association (Canada), Green Osijek (Croatia) and the Tartu Student Nature Protection Group (Estonia). The signatories criticised both the way that negotiations had been conducted, and the substance of the draft agreement.

First, they argued that the OECD was not an appropriate forum within which to discuss a treaty with global ramifications. The OECD, which is often described as a 'rich man's club', represents industrialised rather than developing economies. However, the overwhelming majority of transnational companies are based in the OECD. If developing countries wanted to retain access to international investment, they would face intense pressure to sign the MAI without having been involved in the negotiations.

Second, the NGOs accused the OECD of conducting the negotiations in a secretive manner, to the extent that many government ministers were poorly informed of its implications, even in OECD member states. Lori M. Wallach of the Washington-based Public Citizen Group compared the MAI with Dracula: it would not stand up to public scrutiny of the 'light of day' (Wallach 1998).

Turning to the substance of the treaty, the NGOs pointed out that the MAI was wholly unbalanced: it concentrated on the rights of investors and not on their obligations. In particular, it did not devote adequate attention to environmental safeguards. They argued that companies could use the treaty to override government environmental regulations initiatives, such as the governmental promotion of local production and trade. Moreover, citizens, indigenous peoples, local governments and NGOs would not have access to the dispute resolution system established by the MAI, and therefore could not hold international companies accountable for their operations.[22]

The NGOs scored points in the MAI debate by the way in which their arguments were presented, as well as the arguments themselves. The OECD has now set up its own MAI website,[23] but this comes across as staid and colourless in contrast with the NGOs' counterblasts.

The initial OECD reaction to the NGOs has been bemusement and even bewilderment (Jonquières 1998). The NGOs have clearly demonstrated their collective power, but in official circles there is little understanding of their motives and methods.

At a meeting in Paris on 22 October 1998, senior representatives of OECD member countries reaffirmed the need for and value of a multilateral framework of rules for investment. However, they also acknowledged the concerns that had been raised about issues of sovereignty and safeguards for the environment and labour rights. They

21   www.canadians.org
22   www.canadians.org
23   Within www.oecd.org.

therefore recognised that there was a need for further discussions with representatives of civil society, including NGOs (OECD 1998b). In early December, there was an OECD meeting with representatives of trade unions and NGOs: there was a useful exchange of views but no specific outcome. The issues still remain on the international agenda, but there is no clear programme to find a means of addressing them.

◢ Beyond the Web war of words?

From the NGOs' point of view, the MAI affair vividly demonstrates the negative implications of globalisation—the growing power of transnational corporations with different views on sustainable development—but it also points to some positive aspects. New communications technology has made it possible for like-minded groups of activists to co-ordinate their activities internationally in a way which previously would never have been possible. Greater public access to information via the Internet has helped change the balance of power between companies, NGOs and consumers. In an Internet-connected world, companies are coming to realise that there is no hiding place for poor performance on environmental and social issues. Today's business leaders are having to discuss complex issues of sustainable development and corporate responsibility much more openly than in the past.

However, criticism from NGOs and defensiveness from business will not be enough to achieve the much-cited goal of sustainable development, or consensus on human rights and other controversies. Both the Burma and the MAI campaigns have been essentially 'negative', in the sense that they have sought to prevent companies and governments from pursuing particular policies, rather than seeking to identify solutions to complex problems.

There are significant cultural obstacles on both sides. All too often, senior business and government leaders have tended to dismiss NGO critics as ill-informed trouble-makers. The NGOs have responded with counterblasts that tend to caricature big business, rather than seeking a more nuanced understanding of the way decisions are made.

The Internet will not solve these problems, but it does offer a tool that can be used for constructive debate, as well as polemic. A recent example is an Internet discussion group for practitioners and researchers interested in business–NGO relations and responsible enterprise, hosted by the Mailbase server of Newcastle University in the UK.[24] Some companies, such as Shell, have shown how to move beyond a Web-driven war of words and harness the Internet as a tool to promote discussion rather than suppress it—and to learn from the results. It is a lesson that needs to be much more widely learned—by governments as well as companies.

24   www.mailbase.ac.uk/lists/business-ngo-relations

PART 2

*Examples from
Industry Sectors*

PLANTING THE SEEDS OF CHANGE
Business–NGO relations on tropical deforestation*

Jem Bendell and David F. Murphy

New Academy of Business, UK

In this chapter we discuss the myriad of relations between NGOs and companies involved in the timber trade, around the globe. The deforestation issue provides one of the best examples of how, when governmental and intergovernmental policy processes fail to deliver significant change, civil society can work with the private sector to provide alternative modes for regulating activities that undermine sustainable development. The mobilisation of civil society to combat deforestation has helped make business responsibility for sustainable forest management a market necessity. This chapter describes the emergence of one of the first *civil regulation* initiatives to promote business responsibility for sustainable development at the global level. The Forest Stewardship Council (FSC) represents an institution that has successfully brought together diverse stakeholders to define, identify and promote responsible business practice in the world's forests.

◢ Deforestation and the timber trade

Deforestation arrived as a significant international policy issue and major Northern media story in the mid-1980s (Humphreys 1997b). Since that time the rates of forest

---

* This chapter is an expanded version of a section from the previously published United Nations Research Institute for Social Development (UNRISD) discussion paper, No. 109 by David F. Murphy and Jem Bendell (1999) entitled *Partners in Time? Business, NGOs and Sustainable Development*.

degradation have shown little evidence of slowing. Despite lengthy consultations among governments, and rising activist and consumer concern reaching a peak at the 1992 Rio Earth Summit, deforestation has increased dramatically in recent years. Tropical forests are disappearing at the rate of nearly 1% per year, with the annual deforestation rate in the Brazilian Amazon increasing by 34% since the Rio Summit (United Nations 1997). Located in Southern countries, the rapidly diminishing tropical forests serve a variety of economic, environmental, social and cultural purposes at local, national and international levels.

Economically, forest lands are major revenue generators for national governments and international business. In 1990 the global timber harvest was estimated at 3.43 billion cubic metres, up from 2.93 billion in 1980 (Viana *et al.* 1996). There are also coveted assets beneath forest lands—oil, metals and aggregates. Indonesia currently receives its highest tax receipts from companies mining in forested regions such as Irian Jaya. Forests are also attractive places for land-hungry settlers and those seeking a profit from agricultural practices such as cattle ranching.

Environmentally, forests provide essential climatic functions and can either alleviate or contribute to climate change at regional and global levels, depending on human impact. They are also species-rich, with rainforests purported to contain between 50 and 90% of the world's creatures. Extinction of mass species as a result of mining, logging and drilling for oil are common (Myers 1992).

The variety of economic, social, environmental and cultural functions of forests are inseparable for those for whom the forest is both home and livelihood. There are some 300 million people who live in close association with tropical forests, many of whom are threatened by rapidly degrading and shrinking homelands (Colchester 1993).

The uses for forests we describe here give some suggestion as to the causes of their degradation. Logging, mining, iron smelting, cattle ranching, cash cropping, dam construction, road building, housing and hotel development, shifting agriculture and fuel-wood collection are some of the causes. In this chapter, we are concerned with causes that directly involve Northern countries and their companies, and specifically the international timber trade. Robert Repetto and Malcolm Gillis argued that commercial logging was the main agent of deforestation, opening up rainforests to other commercial threats (Repetto and Gillis 1988).

◢ Government and industry initiatives for rainforest protection

For much of the 1980s and 1990s, governments and various international bodies attempted to respond to the worldwide concern about tropical deforestation. The first international instrument for tropical forests came with the 1983 International Tropical Timber Agreement (ITTA), which provides a framework for co-operation and consultation between tropical timber producers and consumers on a range of issues. Then in May

1991, members of the International Tropical Timber Organisation (ITTO) approved a 'Year 2000 Target' for sustainable forest management.[1] This official decision committed 'ITTO members to progress towards achieving sustainable management of tropical forests and trade in tropical forest timber from sustainably managed sources by the year 2000'. The general NGO feeling is that the ITTO has been too complacent about tropical defor-estation in that it has avoided challenging 'the destructive activities of the timber industry' (FoE-UK 1992: 5).

At the regional and national levels in the South, some governments have introduced new policy instruments to monitor logging company activities. The South Pacific Forum Code of Conduct for Logging of Indigenous Forests sets minimum standards for the preparation and implementation of work programmes by concession holders. Similarly, the Forestry Commission of Guyana has introduced a code of practice for forestry operations in natural forest concessions. The Commission has developed an associated monitoring procedure to evaluate compliance with the Code. It includes a qualitative checklist of standards, including roads, reserves, harvesting, chemical use, health and safety as well as quantitative measurements of harvest levels and damage to the residual stand.

At the international level, in the mid-1990s the World Business Council for Sustain-able Development (WBCSD) commissioned an independent study of the pulp and paper industry by the International Institute for Environment and Development (IIED). The Institute recommended that the industry 'consider introducing the equivalent of [the chemical industry's environmental code of conduct] Responsible Care . . . [including] sector-wide monitoring of performance and guidance to companies' (WBCSD 1996).

The first global certification system for well-managed forests, however, was set up in 1993 by civil society working in partnership with business. This scheme, with a variety of NGO and industry members from the North and South is called the Forest Stewardship Council, to which we will return later. The reasons why companies in the timber trade have collaborated with NGOs can only be understood by examining the role played by civil society in shaping the deforestation issue since the mid-1980s.

◢ Civil society protest in the South

> The 1980s were a bloody decade [in Amazonia]: ten years of violence against
> the unions and rubber tappers had started in July 1980, when Wilson de Souxa
> Pinheiro, a union activist and rubber tapper was shot dead by hired *pisterleiros*
> [assassins]. Pinheiro's crime had been to organise a demonstration which had

---

1 Defined by ITTO as 'the process of managing permanent forest land to achieve one or more
   clearly specified objectives of management with regard to the production of a continuous flow
   of desired forest products and services without undue reduction in its inherent values and
   future productivity and without undue undesirable effects on the physical and social environment' (International Tropical Timber Council Decision 6(XI), Quito, 8th Session, May 1991).

> stopped the chain-saw gangs cutting down the forest. It was the first real
> assassination of the land wars in the 1980s and it set a gruesome pattern for
> the decade (Rowell 1996: 212).

One of the major stages for deforestation and conflict in the 1980s was Amazonia. The problem was particularly acute in Brazil where the military junta was trying to 'flood the Amazon with civilization' by facilitating billions of dollars of subsidies and tax breaks for entrepreneurs to buy up land and 'develop' the forest (Revkin 1990). Unions of rubber tappers led the fight against cattle ranchers and loggers. For years they had struggled with national businessmen in order to secure better pay and escape debt-bonded labour. Now even their meagre livelihoods were being threatened as the rubber barons realised they could make more money cutting down the trees and grazing cattle. The rubber tappers therefore staged *empates* whereby chainsaw gangs were confronted and asked to leave the land they were clearing. These protests raised the attention of the international media so that:

> By the mid-1980s . . . indigenous groups and tappers were considered legiti-
> mate participants in the debate. Their persistent resistance to expropriation and
> to felling the forest, combined with their links to national and international
> organisations, converted them from pariahs to legitimate actors in the unfold-
> ing drama (Dore 1996: 15).

One protester who rose to international fame was the leader of the Xapuri Rural Workers Union, Francisco Alves Mendes Fiho, known as Chico Mendes. He soon became a symbol of the human dimension to the deforestation issue:

> With Mendes' involvement with the rubber tappers, the authorities could no
> longer dismiss efforts to save the rain forests as foreigners interfering with
> Brazilian affairs (Rowell 1996: 214).

The *empates* protests worked as a tactic: by December 1988, some three million acres of the Amazon had been saved (Hecht and Cockburn 1990). After one particular protest, the authorities bought out the prospective rancher so that his plans could not proceed. In revenge, the rancher ordered the killing of Mendes. In December 1988 Mendes was the ninetieth rural activist to be murdered in Brazil that year (Hall 1996). After his death the world's news media reverberated with headlines and leading stories on the rubber tappers and deforestation. Following the international condemnation that followed Mendes's murder, the new civilian administration of President Sarney proceeded to establish a new environmental control agency (IBAMA), promote a new environmental policy (Nossa Natureza) and set up several protected extractive reserves (Hall 1996).

Therefore grass-roots action by Southern unions backed up by international concern did bring some specific successes. Indeed the combined protests of civil society groups in the tropical forests of Africa, South-East Asia and Latin America in the 1980s began to shape a new international policy debate. In the 1970s and 1980s cattle ranching and logging were almost universally promoted as the best way to develop tropical forest regions. By 1990 they had become a symbol of destruction.

◢ Civil society protest in the North

The profile of environmental issues climbed political and consumer agendas in most Northern countries in the late 1980s. As the struggles of indigenous peoples against tropical deforestation became known, the role of the timber trade became a key consumer concern. A wooden product such as a mahogany table bought in the high-street stores of London, Amsterdam or New York could now be associated with the murder of forest dwellers. At this time, local rainforest action groups in North America, Europe and Australia, some informally affiliated with the Rainforest Action Network, were set up. Rainforest Action Groups (RAGs) in Australia organised emotional protests, blocking ships with timber imports. RAGs later mobilised trade unions: the Victoria branch of the Building Workers' Industrial Union, which covered all building projects in Melbourne, refused to use tropical timber.

In Great Britain, beginning in the spring of 1991, various RAGs started to take direct action against wood-product retailers. These groups organised mock chainsaw massacres outside do-it-yourself (DIY) and furniture stores with protesters dressed as loggers graphically depicting the destruction of the world's rainforests. Protesters leafleted customers and delivered anti-tropical timber pledges to store managers. The most extreme protests included setting off smoke bombs inside some stores. The intention was to encourage customers to boycott tropical timber.

Later in 1991, local FoE-UK groups built on the initial RAG protests. On one November weekend, there were over 100 demonstrations, including 25–30 demonstrations outside the stores of leading DIY retailer B&Q alone. Subsequently, on 11 December, FoE-UK claimed in a press release that its protests had prompted dramatic policy developments at B&Q and two of its main competitors, Texas Homecare and Homebase, who were now committed to 'stop selling environmentally damaging tropical rainforest timber' (FoE-UK 1991). B&Q's version of the protests differs, with B&Q having tried 'to establish a constructive dialogue with FoE to discuss their concerns' at an earlier date but without success (Knight 1992: 15).

No matter what the interpretation of the story, there is little doubt that the anti-DIY demonstrations proved to be highly successful and garnered considerable media and public attention. Customers began to write letters to the retailers and to confront store managers and employees with tough questions about timber sourcing. For the most part, the companies took both the protests and customer letters seriously.

Meanwhile, the World Wide Fund for Nature International (WWF) was itself beginning to turn to industry, having become disillusioned with protracted international negotiations on a global forest convention and other international policy initiatives. WWF had already announced its own 1995 target for the world's timber trade to be sustainable. At the June 1992 Rio Conference, governments could only produce 'a non-legally binding authoritative statement of principles for a global consensus on the management, conservation and sustainable development of all types of forests'. WWF-UK's Francis Sullivan believed 'you can't just sit back and wait for governments to agree, because this could take forever', and felt certain it was right to try to work with people and companies who might be able to get things done.

◢ The emergence of timber industry–NGO partnerships

For many of the DIY retailers and suppliers, WWF-UK appeared to be a solution to a mounting business problem. Following WWF-UK's forest seminar in December 1991 (entitled 'Forests Are Your Business'), ten companies committed themselves to reaching the WWF-UK 1995 target and launched the 1995 Group. The cumulative effects of different forms of environmental campaigning seemed to have firmly taken root in the private sector. The 'chainstore massacre' demonstrations and resulting consumer awareness were instrumental, as was the catalytic role of WWF-UK at its forest seminars. Internally, directors of the targeted companies were worried about the public relations and commercial implications of the protests, customer letters and media coverage. Other pressures from investors, insurers and lenders were on the horizon.

To join the 1995 Group, the companies had to agree to phase out, by 1995, the purchase and sale of all wood and wood products not sourced from well-managed forests. In pursuit of this target they had to provide WWF-UK with a written action programme detailing how the company would reach the target and then submit regular six-monthly reports on their progress. It soon became apparent, however, that the participating companies needed a credible system for defining good forest management and for ensuring that products were from such forests.

What was needed was a standard-setting body with a system for verifying product claims. Following 18 months of preparatory work, the Forest Stewardship Council (FSC) was launched in 1993. The founding group consisted of environmental NGOs, forest industry representatives, community forestry groups and forest product certification organisations. Both WWF-International and B&Q provided financial and logistical support, among other organisations.

The first FSC board included two representatives from the private sector and seven from NGOs, certifiers and individual experts. The FSC mission statement commits members to 'promote management of the world's forests that is environmentally appropriate, socially beneficial and economically viable'—language consistent with the principles of sustainable development. The FSC accredits certification bodies to ensure that they adhere to FSC principles and criteria when certifying forests as well managed (see Box 4.1), and allows them to issue the FSC logo once a chain of custody has been recorded from the forest to the company that packages the final product.

By the end of 1995, commercial support for the FSC had spiralled. The WWF-UK 1995 Group had reached 47 members, accounting for about a quarter of the UK consumption of wood products. Although many of the companies did not reach the targets set by WWF-UK, a significant number had purchased certified timber and had specified from where most, if not all, their timber was coming. Therefore the group was extended with the target that member companies would make all their purchases from certified forests in 2000. There are now over 90 members in the renamed WWF-UK 1995 Plus Group.

In the Netherlands, there is a similar story of partnership following protest. Launched in early 1992 the *Hart voor Hout* (Heart for Wood) campaign co-ordinated direct action protests against DIY stores. After a second wave of protest, the largest store, Intergamma,

1. **Compliance with laws and FSC principles.** Forest management shall respect all applicable laws of the country in which they occur and international treaties and agreements to which the country is a signatory, and comply with all FSC principles and criteria.

2. **Tenure and use rights and responsibilities.** Long-term tenure and use rights to the land and forest resources shall be clearly defined, documented and legally established.

3. **Indigenous peoples' rights.** The legal and customary rights of indigenous peoples to own, use and manage their lands, territories and resources shall be recognised and respected.

4. **Community relations and workers' rights.** Forest management operations shall maintain or enhance the long-term social and economic wellbeing of forest workers and local communities.

5. **Benefits from the forest.** Forest management operations shall encourage the efficient use of the forest's multiple products and services to ensure economic viability and a wide range of environmental and social benefits.

6. **Environmental impacts.** Forest management shall conserve biological diversity and its associated values, water resources, soils and unique and fragile ecosystems and landscapes, and, by so doing, maintain the ecological functions and integrity of the forest.

7. **Management plan.** A management plan—appropriate to the scale and intensity of forest management—shall be written, implemented and kept up to date. The long-term objectives of management, and the means of achieving them, shall be clearly stated.

8. **Monitoring and assessment.** Monitoring shall be conducted—appropriate to the scale and intensity of forest management—to assess the condition of the forest, yields of forest products, chain of custody, management activities and their social and environmental impacts.

9. **Maintenance of natural forests.** Primary forests, well-developed secondary forests and sites of major environmental, social or cultural significance shall be conserved. Such areas shall not be replaced by tree plantations or other land uses.

10. **Plantations.** Plantations shall be planned and managed in accordance with principles and criteria 1–9, and principle 10 and its criteria. While plantations can provide an array of social and economic benefits, and can contribute to satisfying the world's needs for forest products, they should complement the management of, reduce pressures on and promote the restoration and conservation of natural forests.

Box 4.1 **FSC principles of forest management**

signed a declaration of intent to stop selling tropical timber products, with the exception of tropical timber that is sustainably produced. Five years on and *Milieudefensie* (FoE-NL), WWF-NL and the development NGO Novib, were overseeing a group of 252 municipalities, 10 state departments, 72 real estate developers, 139 housing associations and the three largest DIY retailers, who account for almost 70% of the Dutch DIY market. Eric Jan Schipper of the leading Dutch DIY chain, Intergamma, has become a champion of the partnership approach:

> The NGOs are not telling us what we shouldn't do but are discussing with us what we could do for the environment. They are not easy on us. They are telling us that there are a lot of things we do wrong in their eyes but we're on a working level with each other. They think with us and they see where our problems lie and what we can do about it and what we can't do, and what we are trying to do (quoted in Murphy 1996b: 65).

Partnerships between the timber industry and NGOs are growing in other countries. There are groups of timber buyers and producers committed to the FSC (so-called forest and trade networks) in Austria, Australia, Belgium, Germany, France, Switzerland, Sweden and seven other countries. In the USA, a group has been designed in close co-operation with future members rather than being predetermined by one environmental group or a coalition of NGOs. Participants include companies such as The Gap, Home Depot and Starbucks, as well as NGOs, namely WWF-US, the Natural Resources Defense Council (NDRC) and the Rainforest Alliance. Despite ongoing efforts by WWF-International to encourage the development of forest and trade networks in Japan, Hong Kong, Brazil and South Africa, the international network has yet to extend beyond Western Europe and North America.

Northern forest and trade networks are, of course, driven by Northern consumers, campaigners, corporations and NGOs. However, members of Southern civil society also have a voice in the process, through the FSC. Representatives of NGOs such as the Foundation of the Peoples of the South Pacific (Papua New Guinea), Kenya Energy and Environment Organisation (Kenya) and SKEPHI (Indonesia) participated in the FSC as either board representatives or members of specialist working groups. At the national level in the South, FSC working groups have been established to ensure that the global principles and criteria are adapted to the local context (e.g. Brazil, Cameroon). Although only 25% of current FSC members are from the South, the organisation is supporting efforts to increase this number. Furthermore, a special working group on social aspects of certification is attempting to find ways in which the social performance of the FSC could be improved. The Social Working Group is drawing particular attention to land tenure rights, indigenous peoples' rights, worker welfare and greater participation by all affected groups.

Before the partnerships between timber companies and environmental NGOs, there was no functioning mechanism whereby consumer power in industrialised countries could be captured to promote sustainable forest management around the world. By early 2000, almost 20 million hectares of forest had been certified worldwide.

Key driving forces

The natural question is, therefore: Why have such large sections of the timber trade been interested in partnership with NGOs? The absence of a significant number of partnership initiatives in the South suggests that many of the driving forces behind greater responsibility in the timber industry are peculiar to Northern countries.

It is clear that NGO efforts to change forest management practices via protest and dialogue were key factors in the emergence of forest and trade networks in Western

Europe in the early 1990s. Protecting corporate image and reputation in the face of a financially powerful, well-informed consumer base with a choice of companies to buy from was obviously a key factor. For companies in the public eye, having a good environmental reputation has the potential to bring competitive advantage in the long term. Green marketing is central to a business strategy based on environmental responsibility. In order to attract and maintain consumer support, a green marketing strategy must go beyond product promotion to encompass 'integrated and effective environmental information systems' (Welford 1995: 173). The green company also has the potential to attract committed workers and to manage risk more effectively.

No matter whether the company is high-profile or not, there are other benefits from above-compliance performance. In research by Jem Bendell and David Warner (1996), many managers of WWF-UK 1995 Plus Group companies stated that they felt employee motivation had been beneficially affected by the company policy. The hands-on management of purchasing and supply required to implement the timber policy also led to more stable relations with key suppliers.

Collaborating with a well-known environmental NGO also promised additional benefits to those to be gained by internal environmental management initiatives (Bendell and Warner 1996). Mike Inchley of the UK DIY company Do-It-All explains that 'we needed guidance and one way of getting that guidance is to join up with people who know what they're talking about'. The group provided a forum for companies to share their experiences and jointly target key suppliers. It therefore allowed companies to combine their efforts to fight what was seen as a threat to the entire industry. In addition to help with getting the job done, significant public relations benefits could be gained from collaborating with NGOs.

Recent research undertaken by the New Academy of Business on forest and trade networks (Murphy and Carey 1998) revealed the following primary motivations for company collaboration with WWF and other NGOs:

☐ Competitive advantage

☐ Environmental values

☐ Corporate leadership

☐ To do the right thing

☐ Gain customer trust

The findings suggest that companies have joined forest and trade networks for a mix of commercial and altruistic reasons. The prominence of factors such as 'environmental values', 'corporate leadership' and 'to do the right thing' may reflect growing business recognition of the important link between profits and principles in the marketplace. While it could be argued that such responses merely reflect what companies think NGOs want to hear, they may indicate that corporate values are indeed being influenced by their active engagement with the environmental movement. The integration of environmental and commercial values is captured by one of the company respondents: 'We actually do believe that maintenance of the world's forests is not only ecologically vital, but also commercially extremely important'.

There appears to be a great deal of scepticism, nevertheless, among the public over the environmental performance and claims of companies (WWF 1991; NCC 1996). Although not always the case, alliances with NGOs often help to assuage that scepticism, giving consumers confidence in the environmental information with which they are provided.

◢ Criticism of timber industry–NGO partnerships

Notwithstanding the progress to date, there is considerable criticism about the role and contribution of the FSC scheme. A number of environmental groups have expressed concern with initiatives such as FSC certification and labelling. Some have challenged the use of market mechanisms for rainforest conservation by arguing that such schemes fail to address the underlying causes of deforestation and the infringement of indigenous peoples' land rights. Stephen Corry, of Survival International, criticises the use of market mechanisms for forest conservation:

> Consumers can consume even more, companies can make profits, forest communities can make an income, the environment is saved . . . No one and nothing is criticised. The causes of rainforest destruction and the invasion of tribal peoples' lands are not addressed. This is not a panacea, a placebo or even a quick fix, it is just slow poison (Corry 1993: 9).

Other groups express concern not with the concept of certification but with how its operation may become unduly affected by commercial interests. The German NGO, *Rettet den Regenwald*, has suggested that 'the certification process might go ahead faster than the situation in the forest justifies just because there is pressure from the market' (Murphy and Bendell 1997a: 111).

Meanwhile, not all companies in the timber trade support the FSC form of certification. On a practical level, some argue that producer certification would be too expensive and bureaucratic to implement across the whole of the industry. Others argue that focusing on performance standards does not allow for progress over time and so they prefer assessing forest management systems under the auspices of established international bodies such as the International Organization for Standardization (ISO) or national agencies such as the Canadian Standards Association (CSA). Both of these organisations have strong government and industry links. Given its strong NGO membership base, the FSC is not considered by many of its critics to be a legitimate standards body. A number of companies have difficulty with forest certification in principle, suggesting that non-governmental bodies do not have the authority to 'regulate' a company's management practices. This, they argue, is the role of sovereign governments or intergovernmental organisations (Harris 1996).

Some critics in government, business and civil society argue that the championing of forest certification by Northern NGOs and companies at the international policy level is another example of the industrialised North imposing its perception of environmental problems and remedies on the rest of the world. Whereas the social, political and cultural contexts in many Northern countries have produced a concerned retail trade and an impetus for certification, the situation in the East and South is different.

Japan, the largest importer of tropical timber and timber products in the world, has not yet become an advocate for a sustainable timber trade. An ITTO report states:

> The Japanese trade, industry and consumers have not exerted any pressure upon their suppliers for certified timber of whichever species. Consumers are not well organised and have not been the same force in the debate as seen in Europe and the USA. Accordingly, the wood products manufacturers and the Japanese import trade have had no incentive to respond (Wadsworth 1996: 44).

Although WWF-Japan has reported some interest in the FSC within the Japanese business community, this has yet to translate into substantial commercial demand for certified products.

The rise of consumer concern and business response in most other Northern countries, therefore, may just serve to shift international trade patterns, with certified timber going to Europe and North America and non-certified timber going to Japan and, increasingly, South-East Asia. The movement of companies from countries such as Malaysia, Thailand and Indonesia into the tropical rainforests of Latin America, the South Pacific and the Congo basin is worrying:

> Facing dwindling timber stocks and tighter environmental regulations in overcut forests at home, an army of Asian timber companies is plunging into the world's remaining rainforests (Ito and Loftus 1997: 1).

To illustrate, in Papua New Guinea, Malaysia's largest logging company, Rimbunan Hijau, now controls at least 60% of the government's 21.5 million-acre forestry concession area through more than 20 subsidiaries (Ito and Loftus 1997). Despite recent attempts to introduce codes of conduct, the prospects for influencing these concessions through legal or market mechanisms appear bleak. Faced with national debt and a need to attract foreign direct investment (FDI), most governments of tropical forest countries appear to be locked into a 'race to the bottom' of environmental regulation.

◢ New tools and tactics for forest protesters

In response to the apparent inability of governments to curb the ongoing destruction of tropical forests, civil society organisations, both North and South, are developing new tactics and using new tools to influence corporate behaviour. Helen Collinson (1996) and Barbara Rose Johnston (1997) document environmental resource battles across the South at the close of the 20th century. Many of the protests they describe are aimed at the international timber, oil and mining industries. The protests differ from those in the 1980s in two significant ways. The first relates to the use of information technology and the second to a new focus on Northern markets. Together, these developments are leading to a new level of North–South co-operation in civil society.

The role of electronic information technology in Southern forest struggles first gained major significance during the Zapatista uprising in the forested Chiapas region of Mexico in 1994. Protesters could send their complaints, including those about the environmental degradation of the Lacandon Biosphere Reserve, around the world by e-mail. Journalists and activists on the appropriate e-mail lists accordingly received immediate accounts of the events unfolding: it was the first 'on-line revolution' (Stea *et al.* 1997: 218). Communication technology is also helping forge new alliances between local, national and international groups. The local environmental group in Chile, Defensores del Bosque Chileno, is communicating with NGOs in Australia, New Zealand and Argentina in order to campaign for a 'Southern Hemisphere Gondwana Forest Sanctuary' which would protect temperate rainforests 40° south (Hoffman 1997b).

The second dimension to Southern group campaigning is an increasing focus on Northern markets. Defensores del Bosque Chileno has also begun collaborating with Japanese environmentalists to launch an education campaign to help curb the woodchip trade between the two countries (Hoffman 1997b). The struggle of the Guarani and Tupinikim Indians in Brazil against the paper and pulp company, Aracruz Cellulose S/A, is another example of such a strategy.

Aracruz Cellulose S/A is the world's leading producer of bleached eucalyptus market pulp (ITTO 1997). In Brazil, the Aracruz land-holding covers 203,000 hectares of which 132,000 hectares are planted with eucalyptus. The Guarani and Tupinikim Indians have been contesting the Aracruz operations on their traditional lands for many years. When the government announced that Indians could lay claim to their traditional lands, there was hope that the Guarani and Tupinikim would benefit. In 1993 the executive commission of the two tribes submitted an application to annex 13,274 hectares. However, in 1996 an adjustment to the law meant that prospective logging companies could appeal against the claims of forest dwellers. Aracruz Cellulose did so and the Guarani and Tupinikim became concerned that FUNAI (the National Indian Foundation) would reject their claim. In response they began an international campaign to raise awareness of their cause.

In early 1997, representatives of the tribes, together with Dutch campaigner, Winfred Overbeek, visited Norway and Great Britain to put their case to the customers of, and investors in, Aracruz Cellulose. In Norway, the group tried to talk with Aracruz shareholder, Den Norsk Bank (Bank of Norway), and also the Lorentzen Group, which holds 28% of Aracruz's ordinary shares. 'Den Norske Bank did not want to talk with the indigenous representatives', explains Overbeek. Consequently, the representatives took their case to the government—the Bank's major shareholder—and the media. Questions in parliament and reports on television and radio followed. In response, the Minister of Trade and Commerce stated that there was no way for the Norwegian government to define how Den Norske Bank applies its money. The international campaign also included meetings with members of the WWF-UK 1995 Plus Group, the FSC-accredited Soil Association and the Paper Federation of Great Britain. The companies and organisations agreed to examine closely the decision on the demarcation of the disputed lands.

Meanwhile, in the South there appears little mileage in establishing communication with the Aracruz management. Against a history of violence—an activist for the tribes, Paulo Cesar Vinha, was murdered in 1993—one Guarani chief does not believe dialogue with Aracruz is possible: 'They have taken our land without talking to us. They have shown us no respect; so we do not want to talk to them—we don't see how this would help.'

Indeed, the international campaign of the Guarani and Tupinikim appears to have generated a retaliatory public relations campaign, not dissimilar to the tactics of anti-environmentalist 'Wise-Use' groups in the United States (Rowell 1996). Overbeek explains the Indians' concern that Aracruz has contracted Burson-Marsteller, the largest PR company in the world, to curb growing support for their international campaign:

> A probable example of Burson-Marsteller's work here is that the trade union of Aracruz employees, SINTICEL, which is supporting the indigenous land struggle has run into trouble. Since they denounced Aracruz handling of the affair in Norwegian newspapers, Aracruz has begun a campaign of its own— with a letter signed by company employees [indicating] that SINTICEL does not have the support of its own members. Despite this, LO, the biggest confederation of trade unions in Norway and CUT, the Brazilian confederation of trade unions, are both supporting SINTICEL's stand.[2]

Thus the response of Aracruz Cellulose appears to be the antithesis of many other companies in the forest industry around the world, who are engaging constructively and openly with civil society in order to help reduce deforestation.

◢ The seeds of change?

This case study has described varying degrees of corporate responsibility for tropical deforestation and a range of tactics employed by NGOs. It appears that some companies are either unable or unwilling to embrace environmental concerns. Further research is needed to reveal the variety of financial, political and cultural factors that enable some companies to engage civil society on the deforestation issue while others avoid, undermine or perhaps even kill their critics. For those companies that have moved forward with civil society, progress appears to have been the result of individual commitment—beyond the call of managerial duties. WWF-International's Francis Sullivan explains:

> Success has boiled down to the commitment of individuals and the support that senior management has given to those individuals . . . You have some companies that are not particularly committed themselves, but you have got an individual in there who is unbelievably committed to actually getting the thing sorted out.[3]

The support that these individuals have received in different companies, organisations and countries illustrates how the boundaries of corporate social and environmental responsibility have been shifting dramatically, alongside rapid developments in the tools

2 Personal communication with J. Bendell, July 1997.
3 Personal communication with D.F. Murphy, November 1994.

and tactics of NGOs. We have observed the role of protest, North and South, in raising public and consumer awareness about adverse effects of tropical deforestation. At the same time, market leaders have responded to this pressure as an opportunity to maintain leadership in a changing marketplace. This in turn has cleared the way for some of the more cautious competitors to follow, thereby planting the seeds of change in the timber trade.

SHADES OF GREEN

NGO coalitions, mining companies and the pursuit of negotiating power

Saleem H. Ali

Massachusetts Institute of Technology, USA

An appreciation of the dynamics of relationships between different types of NGO within civil society is important for those companies pursuing enhanced systems for corporate accountability—and thereby seeking to consult with NGOs. Consequently, this chapter explores the effect of strategic NGO coalitions on their respective relationships with the business community. The focus is alliances between environmental NGOs (ENGOs) and indigenous rights NGOs (INGOs) in their dealings with mining companies. The relationship between these two types of NGO is particularly intense in the developed world where both groups are seeking remediation and rehabilitation of past injustices. In this chapter I question the assumptive alliance between the green movement and the indigenous rights movement in negotiations with a corporation. Although engaged in strategic alliances to increase their negotiating power with the mining industry and governments, the evidence shows that NGOs do not always have a united and unifying agenda, and coalitions can actually marginalise the interests of certain constituencies in civil society.

The implication for corporations is that, by working with certain NGOs and coalitions of NGOs, they may actually marginalise other interest groups. At first glance this may appear a sensible approach for managing external pressure, and ways of co-opting potential opponents have already been discussed in some of the management and sociology literature (see e.g. Moorhead and Griffin 1992). In this chapter I question this approach, for two reasons. First, it does not allow core issues to be addressed and thereby sustains conditions for future antagonisms. Second, at the personal level, it is an alienated and manipulative approach for a manager to adopt.

The scene for the chapter is the mining industry. Modern society relies fundamentally on mining as a primary source of raw material and fuel for production at all levels of industry. Mining companies are thus powerful entities that can wield considerable influence with government and the population at large. They also have the resources to bring a sudden surge of development in otherwise remote and impoverished parts of the world, which are often inhabited by indigenous tribal populations. These indigenous groups have limited resources and in most cases feel relatively powerless in negotiating with a large corporate entity. There is frequently an ambivalence regarding the prospect of development on their land. Economic incentives may attract one segment of the population while traditional leaders may oppose the project on grounds of ecological disturbance or cultural and spiritual association with the land.

In such cases environmental organisations aimed at protecting and preserving eco-systems have generally felt a strong sense of sympathy for indigenous groups throughout the world. The enduring theme of natives living in harmony with their natural environment has led many non-governmental organisations to think of native concerns as part of their own agendas. European colonial repression of indigenous communities in the 'New Worlds' of America and Australia was particularly severe and persistent. Unlike regions such as India or most of Africa, the settlers in America and Australia have become a permanent and overwhelming majority of the population, often displacing the indigenous peoples from their environment and instituting resource-intensive enter-prises, such as mining, in their place. Environmental groups in Australia and the Americas have thus felt a particular degree of contrition towards the native cause.

The past few decades, particularly since the United Nation's involvement in indige-nous people's issues, has brought forth a need for 'atonement' in these countries.[1] This sense of retribution is similar to the congruent need for remediation efforts in the environmental realm, as exemplified by laws such as the Superfund legislation in the United States.[2] There has thus been a confluence of interests between the indigenous rights movement and the environmental movement at the macro scale, which may occlude the latent conflicts in interest between the two movements at other levels of analysis. The common perception is that the native people of the world are inherently environmentalists because for so long they have led relatively sustainable lifestyles.

The value of natural resources in monetary terms is often at odds with their intrinsic worth to certain communities. In most modern economies, the primary agent of change in a resource-rich ecosystem is usually a profit-driven entity, such as a private corpora-tion, for which ecological considerations are generally economic externalities. The inertial forces in the same system are often indigenous groups, and non-profit organisa-tions and individual activists, for whom environmental change is unusually traumatic. Uranium mining presents a perennial imponderable for ENGOs since their environ-mental motives are often at odds with the aspirations of the native groups. While both ENGOs and INGOs would like to see each other as allies, the following two case studies from Australia and Canada show that alliances have become increasingly tenuous.

---

1   The United Nations presented a draft declaration on the rights of indigenous peoples in 1994. This document is being amended for ratification. The European Union and the Organization of American States have similar declarations. The most important legally binding convention in this regard is the International Labour Organisation's Convention 169.
2   Superfund is the common name for the Comprehensive Environmental Responsibility, Compensation and Liability Act of 1980.

◢ Olympic Dam mine in South Australia

In 1961, a team of geologists from the Western Mining Corporation (WMC) began to explore the vast expanse of the South Australian desert in search of minerals. Large-scale surveys ten years later indicated a number of coincident gravity and magnetic anomalies west of Lake Torrens, near a small irrigation pond known as Olympic Dam. An exploration licence was granted by the South Australian government in May 1975, and by July drilling had begun. In 1979, WMC joined forces with the British Petroleum Group (BP) to sink an exploration shaft.

An INGO called the Southern Lands Council called for a moratorium on further exploration. However, there were other Aboriginal groups who felt mining would bring much-needed income to their impoverished communities through compensation agreements. One such group called the Andamooka Land Council, based in a town about 15 km from Olympic Dam, began to seek an agreement with the WMC. Meanwhile, Friends of the Earth and several regional ENGOs, with a strong opposition to all forms of uranium mining, quickly started a movement against the project. Soon the Aboriginal opposition movement and the environmental movement came to be heard as one voice.

However, an Act was passed by the South Australian parliament that overrode other laws regarding Aboriginal heritage. Consequently, the mine was established, in spite of vehement protests, including pleas from some Aboriginal groups and ENGOs at the international level. Full production of copper and uranium ore began in 1988 with 45,000 tons per annum of refined copper, and over 830 tons per annum of uranium oxide (WMC Annual Report, 1996).

In 1993, the WMC acquired full ownership of Olympic Dam and soon thereafter announced plans for an expansion of the existing mine. These plans were held back under the Labour government during the early 1990s but this changed after the 1996 election when the Conservative John Howard became Prime Minister. Howard pledged to improve the economic plight of Australia by renewing investment in mining development. Encouraged by the new government's policy on mining, in July 1996, the WMC board commissioned a detailed design study of an expansion to 200,000 tons/annum (t/a) of copper and uranium. In October 1996, an agreement was reached between the WMC and the State government on the expansion to 350,000 t/a of copper and associated products. At this time, the negotiations were entirely bilateral.

Once the environmental impact assessment was commissioned—that is, when the consultation process began formally—public announcements were made regarding the intention to expand mining operations. Anthropologists were hired by the company to identify appropriate tribes with whom consultation should take place. Meanwhile, the Australian parliament in Canberra published a report in May 1997 on 'Uranium Mining and Milling in Australia' and exonerated the WMC of any serious environmental damage in its past operations. The concerns of the environmental groups were raised but summarily dismissed as not being of much validity: 'The Committee has had only limited opportunity to assess the accuracy of matters raised by the Conservation Council and the Friends of the Earth but it notes that only a limited amount of supporting evidence has been tendered' (Parliament of the Commonwealth of Australia 1997: 132).

Around the same time, Australia was embroiled in a major legal debate over the rights of Aborigines to claim title to land after a revolutionary supreme court decision. The case in point is *Mabo v. Queensland* (175 CLR 1, 1992) in which the High Court of Australia for the first time recognised the prior land rights of Australian Aboriginal people. Soon after this decision, the Native Title Act was passed in 1993 to give a systematic process to land title claims. The Act provides a regime for determining whether native title exists over a certain area of land or water. The Act was to be administered by the National Native Title Tribunal, essentially a negotiating and mediating body whose decisions were not binding. Provision is made in the Act for contested claims to be determined by the federal court. Although a number of cases after *Mabo* have not favoured Aboriginal groups,[3] one important case in New South Wales commonly referred to as *The Wik* verdict, stated that native title is not necessarily extinguished by a pastoral lease. Since then the post-1996 Australian government has been continuing a concerted campaign to limit the extent of Aboriginal land claims.

The main environmental groups that were opposing the Olympic Dam expansion— Friends of the Earth, the Australian Conservation Foundation and the Conservation Council of South Australia—campaigned against the government's attempts to reduce the impacts of the court rulings and the Native Title Act. The ENGOs saw the native land rights issue as a means of halting rapid industrial projects and protecting sensitive ecosystems. Their opposition to mining was voiced on this platform as mining companies were lobbying for limited Aboriginal claims and increased discretion. The Aboriginal groups began to seek alliances as well. Protection of their sacred and significant sites was of immense concern to them but their opposition to mining was certainly not as unequivocal as the ENGOs. Some of the INGOs decided to ally with the mining company to try to get immediate compensation, while others felt that in the long run their interests were more adequately met by alliances with the environmental groups. The dilemma that they faced was not too different from that faced by their distant peers several thousand miles away across the Pacific.

◢ McArthur River Uranium Mine in Saskatchewan, Canada

Saskatchewan has been called 'The Saudi Arabia of the Uranium Industry'. Collectively, the province contains the largest known reserves of uranium in the world, with over five active mines within an area of about 200,000 km^2. Chipewyan Inuit, Dene and Cree Nations comprise 80% of the 30,000 inhabitants in this region, mostly centred around the shores of the numerous lakes that punctuate the landscape.

---

3   Some of the cases are: *Western Australia v. Commonwealth 1995; Mason v. Tritton 1994; Walker v. New South Wales 1994; Coe v. Commonwealth 1993; Pareroultja v. Tickner 1993.*

In the early 1980s Eldorado Nuclear (now part of Cameco Corporation) entered into an agreement with the provincial government of Saskatchewan to begin mining activities in the vicinity of Wollaston Lake. The Saskatchewan Mineral Development Corporation was thus formed to organise the mining activities. The native communities of the region felt that their subsistence lifestyles of hunting and fishing would be threatened by water pollution from the mining development. Their opposition was partly because of the past experience of affected communities in Uranium City (one of the first uranium mining regions in Canada).

In the late 1980s, the Saskatchewan government deregulated the uranium mining industry and largely divested its own interests to form a publicly traded company named Cameco. This would soon become the largest uranium mining company in the world with control over two-thirds of the world's largest, high-grade uranium mines at Key Lake and Rabbit Lake in Saskatchewan. The 'best' was yet to come. The McArthur River ore body was explored extensively in the early 1990s after a governmental environmental review for underground exploration. The highest-grade deposits (as much as 50% of U_3O_8) were discovered 550 m beneath the surface soon thereafter.

The Environmental Impact Statement for the project was prepared in May 1995 and circulated for public comment. Cameco and its partners, Uranerz Exploration and Mining and Cogema Resources Inc., proposed to mine the ore-body underground; crush and grind the ore and render it into a slurry suitable for pumping; thicken the slurry into a paste, and transport it 80 km south-west to the Key Lake operation for milling. The wastes would be disposed of at the existing Key Lake Deilman tailings management facility. The environmental impact of this project would thus be spread across two sites and raised many concerns for environmental groups, most of whom were based in southern Saskatchewan.

The development dichotomy is quite stark between northern and southern Saskatchewan. Unlike common development discourse, 'The North' in this case is the impoverished and underdeveloped region, while 'The South' is considered the more affluent and developed part of the province. More than two-thirds of the residents of northern Saskatchewan claim aboriginal ancestry. In Canada, there are two different categories of aboriginal lineage: (1) registered Indians and Inuits; and (2) Metis (or mixed-blooded aboriginal). There are different treaty obligations for the two groups, though they often present a united front when dealing with issues of development in the north. Nevertheless, surveys conducted by the company had shown that a majority of the people in the north supported uranium mining.[4]

The environmental groups in this case were mostly regional organisations, such as the Inter-Church Uranium Committee and the Saskatchewan Environment Center. Greenpeace had been involved in lobbying efforts in the 1980s but had since withdrawn for financial reasons. The activist movement had been given considerable publicity in the late 1980s with the publication of a book on the Wollaston Lake Community by Miles Goldstick (1987). The main thrust of that book had been the aboriginal resistance to

---

4   These surveys were conducted for Cameco by independent consultants (personal communication with Jamie McIntyre, Saskatoon, 21 March 1998).

mining—it was subtitled 'People Resisting Genocide'. Here, too, the aboriginal rights issues were presented in complete congruence with environmental ideals. The tenacity of this alliance was largely unspoken and a challenge to research inquiry.

◢ The comparative outcomes

After reading about the outcomes of these cases, one may wonder what the point was of offering this comparison when in both cases the companies attained their desired objectives. Both companies were eventually able to get approval for their mines and are currently mining ore as planned. Is this simply a case of different approaches to community relations depending on different legal contexts? Indeed, law has not figured prominently in my exposition because in my opinion legal recourse should be a means of deterrence but not a process for dispute resolution at the corporate/community level. While my analysis clearly favours the approach taken by Cameco, the study does not espouse a 'good-versus-bad player' dichotomy. Indeed, many of the decisions made by the WMC were in good faith and worked out in terms of short-term strategic planning. Long-term community relations were, however, not considered and may come to haunt the project in the future. Issues of social responsibility *vis-à-vis* a private corporation are clearly at stake. While companies cannot assume the role of a social welfare entity, they clearly have certain responsibilities when operating in a remote area in which they have a monopoly over economic opportunities for the population.

The ENGOs in both the Australian and Canadian cases were not successful in satisfying native demands nor were their approaches too dissimilar. My research has revealed that, even though ENGOs often aspire to meet the demands of native groups and appear to lobby on their behalf, the strategic alliances are at best tenuous and usually destructive to both causes.

In summary, even though the outcomes in both cases may appear to be similar (see Table 5.1), there are some distinct differences in the way the companies approached the negotiations and these are likely to lead eventually to a difference in the long-term viability of the projects. Some of the key differences that were found at various tiers of the process are highlighted below, using a model of negotiating power and perceived leverage.

◢ Analysis using the sources of power model

The experience of NGO coalition building on their relations with the mining companies can be analysed in terms of power relations. Sociological and political analyses of 'power' are varied, drawing on thinkers such as Emerson (1962) or Lukes (1974) to consider what it is, what it does, who or what it involves and how we can tell if it is there. In this chapter

	Australia	**Canada**
Corporation	WMC Mining: ☐ Annual revenues: A$2.2 billion ☐ Transnational; HQ: Melbourne, Australia	Cameco Corporation: ☐ ~Annual revenues: C$642 million ☐ Transnational; HQ: Saskatoon, Canada
Surrounding indigenous community (within 150-mile radius)	Aboriginal (mainly Kokotha and Arabanna): ☐ Originally hunter–gatherer ☐ Population: ~1,500 (estimate)	Dene and Cree Nations (various N. Saskatchewan bands): ☐ Originally hunter–gatherer ☐ Population: ~2,000 (estimate)
ENGOs	☐ Conservation Council of SA ☐ Friends of the Earth ☐ Australian Conservation Foundation	☐ Inter-Church Uranium Committee ☐ Saskatchewan Environment Society
Legal regime	☐ Based on British Common Law ☐ Native title doctrine originally based on *terra nullus* ☐ Native title accepted in 1993 under the Mabo decision	☐ Based on British Common Law ☐ Several treaties with natives (except in parts of British Columbia and Newfoundland)
Government authority	☐ Environmental regulations largely under state (not federal) authority ☐ Federal authority over certain aspects of uranium industry	☐ Environmental regulations largely under provincial authority ☐ Federal authority over certain aspects of uranium industry
Environmental concerns	☐ Water extraction from Great Artesian basin ☐ Radiation exposure ☐ Aesthetic and cultural appeal of resources	☐ Water quality concerns and loss of fisheries ☐ Radiation exposure ☐ Aesthetic and cultural appeal of resources

Table 5.1 **Profile of cases**

I use the model of bargaining power developed by Fisher (1983). He identifies seven attributes or aspects of power for parties to negotiations: the power of skill and knowledge, of a good relationship, of a good alternative to negotiating, of an elegant solution, of legitimacy, of commitment and finally the power of a process.

Figure 5.1 shows the various stakeholders in the conflict, and their domains of interest and power, as Venn diagrams. The key to the various loci in the diagram are shown in Table 5.2. The size of ellipses indicates the relative bargaining power of each group. The magnitudes of power that I have attributed to each stakeholder ensue from a qualitative

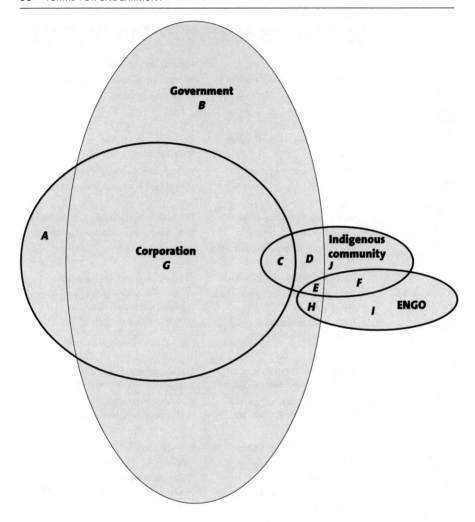

Size of ellipses indicates the relative bargaining power of each group

Figure 5.1 **Venn diagram showing loci of interest for various players in both disputes**

evaluation of the economic resources of each entity and also their potential contributions to the decision-making process.

In the following sections I discuss whether, for each of Fisher's attributes of power, the
alliance between the ENGOs and the INGOs had any effect on the bargaining power of
either group of NGOs as they interacted with the mining companies. I consider whether
there was any 'empowerment synergy' in the interactions between the two.

Venn diagram regions	EXPLANATION WITHIN THE CONTEXT OF THIS CONFLICT AND THE COUNTRY IN WHICH IT IS BEING PLAYED
A	Corporate interest only: Maximising profits from operations beyond this country
B	Government interest only: policies of importance to constituencies outside this dispute
C	Common interests between community and corporation: employment and labour benefits. A portion of the community that feels that the compensation being offered by the company is adequate. Potential for splinter group within community.
D	Common interests between the government and the community only (excluding corporate or ENGO interest): welfare benefits, political representation
E	Common interests between ENGO, government and community (excluding corporate interest): environmental protection through state-level economic analysis
F	Common interest between ENGO and community (excluding government or corporate interest): environmental protection based on normative concerns (value-based)
G	Common interests between corporation and government: strategic economic development concerns for the state, exogenous to the region
H	Common interests between ENGO and government (excluding community and corporation): other environmental lobbying efforts in which the ENGO is involved outside this conflict area (but within the country) that the government endorses
I	ENGO interest only: based on a broader vision of the ENGO's charter. Accountability to international headquarters and to the resolution of other disputes outside this country.
J	Indigenous group interest only: issues of sovereignty, cultural importance and tribal leadership

Note: There is no region of common interest between the ENGO and the corporation (at least from the information currently available for these cases).

Table 5.2 **Explication of loci in Venn diagrams**

The power of skill and knowledge

The technical skill, which some of the ENGO representatives possessed, was shared with the INGOs but no formal effort at training or education was made. The responses to the environmental impact statement, particularly in the Australian case, exemplify the strong scientific backing that the groups possessed. A leading member of the Conservation Council of South Australia was a tenured Professor of Chemistry at Flinders University and several others were well-educated professionals. Friends of the Earth, the Australian Conservation Foundation and the Conservation Council of South Australia collectively submitted 185 comments to the environmental impact statement for the expansion of the Olympic Dam mine, whereas no formal comments were registered from the Aboriginal groups. Out of the 185 comments registered by the ENGOs, five were specifically aimed at addressing Aboriginal concerns. According to Joan Wingfield, a member of the Kokotha tribe and an official at the Australian Heritage Commission, skill and knowledge are the most significant contributions that ENGOs can make to the Aboriginal cause.[5]

In the Canadian case, the federal and provincial government convened a panel to review uranium mining activities in Saskatchewan in 1991. This panel submitted comments on various proposals for mining and also held a protracted series of hearings in 1996 in which all the environmental groups participated actively. This was the main forum for informational exchange between ENGOs and native groups. The panel itself comprised four members, a mining engineer, a biologist, an industrial hygienist and the Chief of the Prince Albert Grand Council, John Dantouze.[6] The skill and knowledge exchange in this case appeared to circumvent the ENGO route since the native groups were being given technical feedback directly from the academics on the panel. Just before the panel was to issue its report, Chief Dantouze and the industrial hygienist Dr Annalee Yassi resigned. The environmental groups considered this a sign of victory and a reflection of the dissatisfaction with the environmental situation. However, the statement of the Chief and correspondence between him and Dr Yassi reveals that the main reason for their dissatisfaction with the panel was the issue of revenue sharing and not environmental concerns.[7] The skill and knowledge that the ENGOs may have been able to offer in this case would probably have had little influence because of existing academic expertise on the panel and the overarching concerns regarding economic development.

The power of a good relationship

Environmental groups have a long history of opposition to the mining industry and therefore their relationship with most mining companies has been largely antagonistic. The mining companies appear to harbour a strong degree of suspicion of any group that may be affiliated with environmental causes. Therefore native groups who were allied with the ENGOs were particularly ostracised from interactions with the mining company in both cases. Since the ENGOs had some interests that were exogenous to the direct aspirations of the community (namely their own agenda of anti-uranium campaigning), the negotiation process was confounded and possibly widened disagreements within the Aboriginal communities. In the Australian case, an Aboriginal splinter group, which was more amenable to the mining company's offers for monetary compensation, was formed. Even though a majority of the community representatives favoured the ENGO's opinions on environmental impact, the fact that they were being represented by an external entity in some ways legitimised the corporation's refusal to talk to them. They were branded as the ENGO's cronies and so the mining company was able to get away with limited communications, only involving a small splinter faction that did not have

5   Personal communication with Joan Wingfield, Australian Heritage Commission, Canberra, 15 January 1998.

6   *Report of the Joint Federal-Provincial Panel on Uranium Mining in Northern Saskatchewan* (Hull, Quebec: Canadian Environmental Assessment Agency, February 1997).

7   Press Release from John Dantouze, Prince Albert Grand Council, Saskatchewan, 3 October 1996.

the 'activist' label. The rivalry between the two Aboriginal groups led to a stand-off in 1995 in which one person was killed (by the Aboriginal group supporting the environmental cause).

In Saskatchewan the ENGOs did not foster any positive relationship with the mining companies because, as far as they were concerned, there could be 'no consensus on uranium mining'.[8] Media appearances by the ENGOs representatives were replete with accusations of impropriety aimed at the Cameco corporation. The groups also alienated themselves from a lot of government agencies, by 'removing themselves from the environmental assessment review process' and sending their documentation after the 30-day review period as a mark of protest.[9]

The power of a good alternative to negotiating

Negotiation theorists have articulated the need for a negotiated settlement in terms of opportunity costs. They argue that, at the outset, both sides should estimate their Best Alternative to a Negotiated Agreement (BATNA). 'However unsavoury the other side, unless you have a better BATNA, the question you face is not whether to negotiate, but *how*'.[10] The BATNA of the indigenous groups *vis-à-vis* the mining companies is clearly much lower than it is for the environmental groups. For the former, mining investment may be a matter of economic survival, whereas for the latter it is a value-based cause which would not have any direct short-term impact on their means of survival.

In most public disputes, the BATNA is largely related to the amount of power and authority the government is willing to give to the various stakeholders. Mining is critical to the economies of Saskatchewan and South Australia. In both cases the government receives large royalties from the mining because mineral resources are constitutionally owned by the state. Therefore the government has accorded considerable power and respect to the mining companies in the region. Though the federal government technically has ultimate authority over uranium mining, the devolution of power in both cases is such that the federal authorities largely defer action to their state or provincial counterparts. The Canadian situation with regard to the separatist movement in Quebec has made federal involvement in provincial affairs particularly sensitive. In Australia, the current federal government has stated a policy of encouraging mining and limiting Aboriginal land tenure. Previous attempts at a purely confrontational approach, such as the Wollaston Lake episode in Canada or the initial Olympic Dam project in Australia, have largely been unsuccessful. Given this dynamic, the native groups have no choice but to negotiate: the alternative to negotiating would be to have a relatively austere mining establishment in their midst with minimal regulatory considerations for their welfare.

8   Personal communication with Neil Sinclair, Inter-Church Uranium Committee, 25 March 1998.
9   Prairie Media Watch. Phillip Penna (Inter-Church Uranium Committee), radio interview transcript, CBK, La Ronge, Saskatchewan, 6 May 1997.
10 Fisher *et al.* (1992: 161). In their work, Fisher and associates answer a resounding 'Yes' to the question: 'Should I negotiate even with terrorists?' They cite the example of the Kuwait Airways hijacking in 1988, where a negotiation saved many lives and led the way to a general decrease in hijackings.

On the other hand, the ENGOs are more interested in making a value-based statement of opposition and registering their dissent. Their alternative to negotiation is thus a series of confrontational protests which they have staged in both regions.[11] In Australia, members of the Arabanna and Kokotha people did attend the protest and a nationally televised documentary was made by one of the private television stations highlighting the concerns of these groups. The presence of a strong alternative to negotiation for the ENGOs should have conferred them power at the negotiating table, more than that of the INGOs. However, the ENGOs did not want to enter dialogue in forums that they felt were organised by governments to further the interests of companies, so we did not witness this power in action.

The power of an elegant solution

As far as the ENGOs were concerned, the only acceptable solution to the problem would be no uranium mining whatsoever. The native groups felt that if implemented properly the mining could be a possible solution to the problems of economic development in their region. Interestingly enough, the solution proposed by the ENGOs in both cases to the concerns regarding economic development was to institute means of promoting eco-tourism. This was of course an alternative rather than a solution to the existing negotiation process.

Revenue sharing was the 'elegant solution' proposed by the communities in the Canadian case. This has been the major bone of contention in the negotiations as well. The native groups feel they deserve a larger share of the pie than the company is willing to offer. A remediation model was developed by the community (without ENGO involvement) during the initial working group meetings between the mining company and the native communities. Such simple solutions to potential conflicts, when backed by a commitment, can be an important source of power.

In Australia, the company felt no obligation to present any solutions *per se* but rather to simply comply with government regulations.[12] In any event, the ENGOs did not try to find some amicable solution to the existing situation of economic deprivation. Joan Wingfield of the Australian Heritage Commission felt that the ENGOs should contribute monetarily towards Aboriginal development if they were to use their platform as a means of advocating the environmental cause.[13] Though many of the individual members of the ENGOs have tried to help the Aboriginal people financially, there has not been an institutional effort to accord them a financial assistance package.

11   In Canada most of the protests have taken place at the corporate headquarters of Cameco in Saskatoon, whereas in Australia the protests have taken place at the mine site itself.
12   Personal communication with David Stokes, Community Relations Officer, Western Mining Corporation, Port Augusta, South Australia, 22 January 1998.
13   Personal communication with Joan Wingfield, Australian Heritage Commission, Canberra, 15 January 1998.

The power of legitimacy

The ENGOs in both cases are largely represented by urban inhabitants who are far removed from the plight of the native communities.[14] In the Canadian case, the most prominent members of the Inter-Church Uranium Committee had never actually visited the mining communities in northern Saskatchewan.[15] There was no native person who was formally a member of this organisation. The native groups in Canada could be seen to have a very legitimate concern because most of them were residing in close proximity to the mine and the relative isolation of these communities and their adherence to subsistence-oriented lifestyles based on hunting and fishing was well documented.

In the Australian case, the issue of legitimacy loomed large for both native and green groups. While Canada has a category for multi-racial individuals, known as Metis, Australia does not have such a categorisation. Therefore the mining company was resentful of 'white-looking' people who were claiming Aboriginal ancestry and hence compensation. Because of the hunter–gatherer nature of Aboriginal society, it is also very difficult to delineate tribal domain over areas of land. Indeed there was no formal system of property rights in Aboriginal society and hence anthropologists have struggled to demarcate ancestral lands for mining projects. The legitimacy of certain native claims were therefore subject to scrutiny from anthropologists who had widely differing views. Archaeological evidence was the primary means that the company used in its determination of Aboriginal claim. The ENGOs attempted to present anthropologists that could perhaps legitimise the claims of the Aboriginal groups who were supporting their cause. However, since very few of the Aboriginal people were actually living near the mine itself (and were themselves residing in nearby cities), the claims were difficult to defend. Some notable anthropologists did, however, challenge the mining companies' assertions but were largely ignored. The urban background of the ENGOs also made matters more difficult to defend. The community relations officer for the WMC referred to many of the ENGO representatives as 'kids from the garden suburbs of Melbourne on holiday from universities'.[16]

The power of commitment

Mining ventures by their very nature are relatively ephemeral, usually not lasting for more than 50 years. Therefore, gaining a commitment from the company to decommission the mine and remediate afterwards is the most critical dimension of any such agreement. The company in return could also want a series of commitments to reach an amicable settlement. However, in development disputes of this kind it is not easy to identify the

14 There are of course a few exceptions. Jan Whyte, a member of Friends of the Earth, Australia, has lived with the Arabanna Aboriginal community for the past few years. However, even in such cases, there is always a choice to go back to the life in the city and hence the BATNA generally remains unchanged.

15 Personal communication with David Greenfield and Neil Sinclair, Saskatoon, 25 March 1998.

16 Personal communication with David Stokes, Community Relations Officer, Western Mining Corporation, Port Augusta, South Australia, 22 January 1998.

benefits the company can attain through a formal commitment from the community. The tacit commitment that the company would seek is positive relations with the community so that there would be no hindrance to their activities in terms of protests or sabotage. However, according to the mining executives, the protests that the ENGOs staged were not of much consequence and they would not need any commitments from the environmental groups.[17] The clearest means of gaining commitment in such cases is to involve legal terms and conditions for a settlement. Lawyers are inevitably involved in such cases. The ENGOs in both cases were not staffed by any lawyers nor were they able to hire any legal professionals to this end.

The Aboriginal groups in Australia were partly represented by the Australian Legal Rights Movement, which is not affiliated with any specific environmental cause. In the Canadian case, there was no direct legal involvement as most of the native grievances were addressed through the public hearings held in various parts of the province. An Impact Management Agreement is proposed to be the legally binding document in this case. The governments in both cases are responsible for monitoring compliance with any agreements reached.

The power of process

In both cases the ENGOs did not want to directly negotiate with the mining company. Most communication between the ENGOs and the mining company was carried out through government channels. Environmental Quality Committees were set up by Cameco in northern Saskatchewan to try to garner opinions of native groups regarding environmental management. The Athabasca Working Group comprised the respective chiefs of Hatchet Lake, Black Lake and Fond du Lac and the mayors of the hamlets of Wollaston Lake, Stony Rapids, Uranium City and Camsell Portage, and had regular meetings from March 1993 onwards. It held several public meetings as well but there is no record of ENGO involvement in this process. The Working Group came up with an 'Agreement-in-Principle on Environmental Protection and Compensation' on 31 January 1998.

Various consultative committees were organised in the Australian case as well. The ENGOs believed that most of these entities were moulded by the mining companies to fit their interests and hence they did not participate in any of their activities. Though the credibility of some of these groups, particularly the Dieri Mitha Council, is highly questionable, the inability of the ENGOs to engage the company in any process of reconciliation with the native groups is nevertheless a matter of some concern. A conference was also organised by WMC in which various ENGO representatives were invited. Amnesty International was the only international NGO that agreed to participate in this session and it did so for human rights concerns rather than environmental causes. Though the divisions within the Aboriginal community were often attributed by the

17 Personal communication with Steven Green, Environmental Manager, Western Mining Corporation, Olympic Dam Mine, 23 January 1998, and with Elaine Kergoat, Manager for Public Relations, Cameco Corporation, 24 March 1998.

environmental community to a corporate neo-colonial policy of 'divide and rule', it is important to recognise that the factionalisation made the situation considerably more complex for the mining company as well. In order to alleviate this problem, the company initiated a process of mediation between the Andamooka Land Council and the Kokotha Peoples' Committee. An Aboriginal person from the eastern states was hired to be the mediator.

◢ Competing interests and the corporate objective

The INGOs and ENGOs represent stakeholders with a variety of interests and values that are not shared and thus any alliances that may form are usually strategically opportunistic and can be divisive. This is not to doubt the sincerity of each group towards the other but rather a manifestation of differing world-views about development that are not easily reconcilable. Uranium mining exemplifies these differences most acutely because the ENGOs advocate a permanent moratorium on uranium mining, while most of the native groups do not share this stance.

An important lesson is the relationship between culture and power (Lund and Duryea 1994). In both cases the indigenous groups have similar hunter–gatherer lifestyles and hence share certain anthropological traits in terms of their perceptions of the natural world, their values and their conceptions of power. How well an ENGO, INGO or business is able to 'empower' the community or place things in perspective for all sides is dependent on their understanding of this cultural divide. The Canadian company was clearly able to proceed more successfully in its negotiations with the indigenous communities because they provided forums such as the Athabasca Working Group which gave the communities a feeling of empowerment and respect.

Differences in bargaining power can often lead to disillusionment with the process of negotiation. Indeed, there is sometimes a perception that the mere process of negotiation is perhaps a concession to the other side. This has been the case in many ecological disputes, particularly those involving ENGOs.[18] However, a closer analysis reveals that such intransigence usually leads to long-term adversarial relationships among stakeholders, thereby undermining the interests of all sides. Negotiations particularly become important when there is no legal recourse or the expense involved in seeking an adversarial alternative is unacceptable.

Several models of negotiations have been proposed by economists, sociologists and lawyers. In economics, for example, 'game theory' has been used on negotiations discourse ever since Thomas Schelling wrote *The Strategy of Conflict* (1960). However, conceptualising the particular negotiating circumstances in these uranium mining cases requires a broader appreciation for various approaches to dispute resolution. The cases

18   James Crowfoot and Julia Wondolleck have compiled a volume (1990) on environmental disputes with several case examples on how appropriate mediation and negotiations strategies have been more effective than conventional modes of social resistance.

under discussion are not zero-sum games and therefore require more than just a static model of possible outcomes. A more dynamic analysis involving anthropological and qualitative approaches to personal and organisational behaviour is helpful (Susskind and Field 1997).

Positive outcomes from negotiations may be difficult to envisage or attain. Economists such as James Cobbe (1979) have argued that there are essential characteristics of mining companies and the nature of the global mining economy that can cause breakdowns in negotiations.[19] These characteristics result from the relative monopoly over economic development that resource extraction companies have in remote regions. Like all cases of monopoly power some form of external intervention, such as government mediation, may help to move the process forward.

Even without government intervention, existing interactions between businesses and NGOs, both indigenous and environmental, could be improved, and the long-term viability of a project could be considerably enhanced, by appreciating the various sources of negotiating power that have been highlighted in this chapter. The business community needs to understand the dynamics of strategic coalitions between NGOs more closely, and to try to cultivate negotiating power for consensus movements, so that they do not have to rely on opportunistic and divisive activities. We all need to be aware that NGOs may form coalitions in an opportunistic fashion which can mask differences, thereby making the coalition unaccountable to certain interests and concerns. As this case shows, one NGO can be interested in corporate activity because of the impact on a specific issue of ideological concern, and another can be interested because of the affect of a corporation's activity on a group of constituents. This is an important consideration for business because of the increasing concern with accountability.

From the arguments of Cheryl Rodgers (Chapter 2) and Rob Lake and Jem Bendell (Chapter 17) in this volume, we are able to say that many companies today are seeking effective systems for demonstrating their accountability to society, given the breakdown of traditional means of maintaining corporate reputation and legitimacy. Consequently, for a corporation to use divisions between different NGOs to further immediate goals is short-sighted and ultimately counterproductive. Instead, the different interested and affected parties and their representative NGOs should be supported in various ways to partake in meaningful dialogue and then even negotiation. Companies cannot leave this process to civil society alone, as coalitions of NGOs can marginalise certain issues (Wapner 1996). Instead, companies should take a leadership role in helping to support systems of independent consultation, which may include efforts to build the organising and negotiating capacity of affected groups. This is a major undertaking for an individual corporation, and so partnership with other companies, major international NGOs and intergovernmental agencies is advisable. Thus the mining industry may have

---

19   Smith and Wells (1975) also undertook a detailed study of negotiations involving mining companies and governments of developing countries. The dynamics of such talks may, however, be quite different, given the nature of 'the state' in many parts of the world. The 'bargaining hypothesis' is also tested in some detail by Kobrin (1987), though in the context of the manufacturing industry.

something to learn from initiatives such as the World Commission on Dams or the Forest Stewardship Council (see Chapters 4 and 12).

As far as business interactions with conflict-oriented NGOs are concerned, the doors should always remain open for negotiation. Keeping in mind the other stakeholders' BATNA helps us to appreciate the reasons for resistance. In the final analysis there will always be some degree of value-based resistance between certain sectors of the NGO world and the business community. However, by being more discerning about the reasons for conflicts and going beyond a zero-sum game, we can at least endeavour to disagree without being violently disagreeable.

A NO WIN–WIN SITUATION?
GMOs, NGOs and
sustainable development*

Jem Bendell

New Academy of Business, UK

From reading much of the literature on business and sustainable development you could be forgiven for thinking that the only things preventing businesses from behaving sustainably are organisational inertia and a lack of management knowledge. A widely shared view is that there are an abundance of 'win–win' opportunities, where managers can take action that is both good for business and for sustainable development (Rappaport and Flaherty 1992). The concept of 'eco-efficiency', where novel systems for saving energy and reducing waste can deliver financial benefit as well as reducing a company's environmental impact, has guided many managers in their conversion to environmentalism. Beyond eco-efficiency, success stories of environmental marketing, where a company has successfully sold its products on the basis of environmental criteria, reinforce the idea of a win–win world (Hartman *et al.* 1999). Discussions of the corporate benefits of high staff morale, good community support, and sustained interest from high-calibre applicants, which arise from trust in a company's leadership position on sustainable development, broaden the win–win paradigm (Fukuyama 1995). Good relations with all of a company's stakeholders is understood to be beneficial by ensuring the company has an ongoing exchange of knowledge that can lead to beneficial innovation (Zadek 1999). On the flip-side, bad relations with stakeholders can create risks to corporate reputation, which, ironically from a win–win world-view, means that good corporate performance on sustainable development is effective risk management (see Chapter 2). The win–win world-view is not restricted to environmental issues and has been mentioned in the context of labour standards and human rights; 'win–win–win' has even been mentioned in this context, to emphasise the inclusion of social considera-

* I would like to thank Rene Rivera (FUNDE, El Salvador), who asked me to work on GM crops, and Rupesh Shah (University of Bath) and Simon Heap (INTRAC) for their contributions to the business-NGO relations discussion group, which stimulated my thinking for this chapter.

tions (Elkington 1997b). Indeed, the revived concepts of 'corporate social responsibility' (CSR) and 'corporate citizenship' assume that ours is a win–win world (McIntosh *et al.* 1998).

Much of my work until this time has been in the win–win paradigm, identifying the corporate case for sustainability management beyond narrow eco-efficiencies—by discussing the important role of NGOs in a corporation's operating environment (Murphy and Bendell 1997a, 1999). To generalise too far beyond specific examples is misleading, however. The reality we need to remind ourselves of is one where not everything that is right to do pays, and not everything that pays is right to do. As I hope to show in this chapter, the commercialisation of genetic modification (GM) technology by a few major transnational companies is one case where the win–wins seem illusive. In such cases where there are limited win–win opportunities, we need to consider whether concepts of voluntary environmental management, stakeholder dialogue, corporate social responsibility or corporate citizenship really have anything to offer. We need to consider what can be achieved through adhering to a win–win paradigm, or whether acceptance of the possibility of a 'win–lose' scenario could be the most just and sustainable way forward.

In this chapter I outline the issues surrounding the commercialisation of GM crops, including environmental, economic, sociocultural and political aspects, the response from NGOs and the effect that this has had on retailers, farmers, regulators and investors, before considering the new strategy from the biotechnology transnationals: specifically their call for a win–win dialogue with civil society. I consider what should be up for discussion and where, and conclude that the issue at stake is not only the science, but also the role of business in society. Consequently, the win–win paradigm is considered inappropriate because the key issue is changing the power relations in our society. I conclude that concepts of CSR and corporate citizenship are not necessarily helpful in this case as corporate accountability is the issue; consequently, the best option for biotechnology companies is to relinquish some power and control, and by doing so allow a redefinition of the future utilisation of biotechnology. The only other option would appear to be an attempt to co-opt, divide and infiltrate critical groups, which could lead to violence, unjust and unsustainable economies, without generating long-term value for shareholders.

◢ What are GMOs, how widely are they used and who are the key players?

The debate centres on a technology that can borrow a genetic code from plants or animals and transfer it to a plant to give it a desired characteristic. For example, plants can be engineered to lengthen the shelf-life of their fruits, to withstand saline soils, to contain more vitamins, to resist pests, and even to produce traditionally non-agricultural products such as vaccines and plastics (see Box 6.1). Genetic modification is a very different process from traditional plant breeding: it involves techniques that modify DNA and recombine genes between species that have little or no probability of exchanging genes in nature: fish and tomatoes, for example.

Chemical resistance. Crops can be engineered to be resistant to particular herbicides, so that farmers can apply them to cultivated areas without damaging the crop. This is the main area of development at present.

Pest resistance: continued development of virus- and pest-resistant crops. For example, *bacillus thuringiensis* (Bt) is a naturally occurring soil bacterium which produces a protein that kills a range of common insects once it is ingested. The Bt gene has been isolated and inserted into crops including maize, soybean, cotton, rapeseed, potato, tobacco, rice and tomato.

Ripening and appearance: further development of fruit and vegetables in which the production of ethylene is suppressed so that they take longer to ripen. GM avocados, bananas, pineapples, mangoes and tomatoes are among those that already exist. There is also work on the improvement of flavour and texture.

Nutritional qualities: modification of oils, fats and starches to improve processing or dietary characteristics, and the improvement of vitamin content. DuPont has announced that it will release a soybean with a 'heart-healthier' oil profile in 2000. Other new soybeans have improved protein profiles and lowered levels of indigestible carbohydrates.

Unwanted compounds: the elimination of genes for toxic substances and allergens, or for narcotics. For example, *New Scientist* (21 March 1998) reported that the master gene for caffeine production has been isolated. The first caffeine-free coffee plants were to be planted in Hawaii during 1998.

Hardiness: identification of genes controlling salt tolerance, resistance to drought, flood and extreme temperatures, and response to day length. There are also GM crops that fix nitrogen with greater efficiency, thereby reducing the need for fertilisers.

Medicines: GM plants that produce vaccines or therapeutic agents. A diabetes vaccine in tobacco and potato plants is showing promise, as well as potatoes engineered to provide immunity to cholera. According to a report in *Nature Biotechnology* (27 February 1998), the cholera vaccine is unharmed by cooking the potatoes. Work is under way to develop edible *e. Coli* vaccines in bananas.

Raw materials. GM biodegradable plastics grown in plants such as oilseed rape could begin to replace plastics from fossil fuels within a decade. Reuters (25 March 1998) reported that the process has been patented by Monsanto. In November 1997, Dow Chemical and Cargill announced a new joint venture company, Cargill Dow Polymers, that will manufacture biodegradable plastics from corn and sugar beets.

Pollution control: GM plants for bioremediation, that is, removing toxic chemicals and agrochemical residues from the soil.

Box 6.1 **Current and future development and application of biotechnology**

Although based on a fairly recent technology, the development and uptake of some genetically modified crops has been rapid. In 1999 20%–45% of US corn and soybeans were grown from seed engineered to produce its own insecticidal toxin, and those crops are now used in many processed foods (RAFI 1999b). Globally, GM crops were grown commercially on around 30 million hectares of agricultural land worldwide in 1998.[1] Soybean is the most extensively cultivated of the transgenic crops, accounting for 54% of the total acreage. Corn (28%), canola (rapeseed, 9%) and cotton (9%) are the other three

---

1   ISAAA (International Service for the Acquisition of Agri-Biotech Applications) figures quoted in *The Washington Post*, 9 October 1999.

major crops. The world market for GM seeds is projected to grow to US$6 billion by 2005 (RAFI 1999b).

In recent years some of the world's largest chemical companies have been involved in hectic take-over activity to acquire biotechnology companies and thereby position them-selves as the developers and distributors of GM seeds. At the time of writing this new 'agroscience' industry was dominated by five companies, Monsanto[2] and DuPont from the USA, and Novartis, AstraZeneca and Aventis from Europe (Hilary 1999). Until the end of the 1990s the strategy of these companies had been to commercialise gene manipula-tion in a manner compatible with their existing agrochemical product lines of pesticides, herbicides and fertilisers. For example, herbicide tolerance was the transgenic trait in around 70% of GM crops grown in 1998, up from 23% in 1996, when virus or insect resis-tance accounted for 77% of crops grown (James 1997, 1998).

Opinion is divided over the potentials and pitfalls of GM crops for sustainable development. On the one hand companies describe:

> modern biotechnology as a safe, sustainable tool for farmers and an impor-tant contributor to the future success of agriculture in meeting the world's needs for food and fiber. The technology has already brought important benefits to growers and the environment after just a few years of commercial application (Bob Shapiro, CEO, Monsanto [Shapiro 1999b]).

On the other hand, NGOs such as the World Development Movement (WDM) argue that 'GM crops will be the mechanism for domination of poor farmers by some of the world's largest corporations' (Hilary 1999: 1). In the following section I summarise the differing opinions on the implications of GM crops for the environmental, economic, socio-cultural and political aspects of sustainable development.

◢ Environmental implications

There is an increasing volume of literature on the intended and unintended conse-quences of GM crops. Much of it is inaccessible to non-geneticists given its specialist nature, some using the results of experiments, others deducting probable future out-comes from genetic theory. From this literature it is possible to identify five areas of posi-tive or negative environmental impact: chemical pollution, genetic pollution, ecosystem disruption, biodiversity and food quality.

First, there is the issue of chemical pollution. The companies argue that advances in biotechnology, specifically the ability of plants to produce their own pest toxins, mean that the use of pesticides and herbicides will be less necessary and thus chemical pollution will be reduced (cited by Shapiro 1999b). Some scientists dispute this, arguing that the constant exposure of pest populations to a poison throughout the life of the GM crop creates conditions for pests, which are resistant to that poison, to breed the most successfully and consequently for their resistance to become a common characteristic of the whole pest population (Jenkins 1998). For example, research at the University of

2 See footnote on p. 14.

Hawaii has shown that insects that survive the Bt toxin transmit genetic resistance to their immediate offspring (Spinney 1998). In consequence, in a matter of only a few years, new pesticides would be required. One quite separate area where GM crops might be able to help with chemical pollution is with the decontamination of land, as crops can be engineered to be resistant to and absorb toxic substances from the ground and therefore clean polluted land.

Second, there is the issue of genetic pollution. GM crops have opened the door on this novel concept of environmental pollution, where transgenes spread beyond the intended plants and places. As with chemicals, genes in the wrong place could do a lot of damage. Non-GM plants could be fertilised with a GM variety, passing on the GM characteristic to other farmers' seeds (unless the GM variety was engineered not to be able to do this). This would be an immediate concern if the non-GM crop farmer was selling his produce as GM-free or if he was an organic grower. This impact would be greater if the GM crop carried a gene that rendered the crop unproductive unless a particular biotech company's chemicals were applied to it. This is called 'traitor technology', and AstraZeneca has already patented a gene along these lines, where the crops are designed to fail without application of the requisite chemical (RAFI 1999a). In addition, GM plants might be able to fertilise non-cultivated relatives of the plant which grow naturally. In 1994, research scientists in Denmark reported strong evidence that an oilseed rape plant genetically engineered to be herbicide-tolerant transmitted its transgene to a weedy natural relative, *Brassica campestris ssp. campestris* (cited in TWN 1996). Thus there is the potential for wild varieties to become resistant to herbicides; these are known as 'superweeds'.

A certain degree of genetic pollution may lead to a significant disruption to an ecosystem, yet, leaving the possibility of pollution aside, there are other ways in which ecosystems might be disrupted by GM crops. GM crops are expected to be more competitive because of the incorporation of pest and herbicide resistance genes, as well as genes for resistance to other environmental poisons. This may increase the plants' ability to compete outside of the cultivated area, so they effectively become new weeds, adversely affecting ecosystems (TWN 1996). Likewise, the toxins produced by GM crops could affect non-target organisms. Therefore, researchers from Oregon State University have stressed that the effects on the whole ecosystem must be understood, not just isolated portions, because biotechnology products will have a range of impacts much greater than just the engineered organism. If other organisms in the food web are affected to the point that nutrient recycling, plant growth or important plant growth processes are altered, then the risk is significant (TWN 1996).

A further issue is biodiversity. The growth in biotechnology should create an economic interest in the preservation of natural biodiversity as a source of future commercially useful genes. However, the involvement of biotech companies in conservation is currently minimal. Instead, there are concerns that the genetic pollution, described above, may adversely affect the biodiversity of natural habitats, as might the processes of ecosystem disruption also described above.

A final area of environmental debate is food quality. In the future GM crops could improve various aspects of our food. First, biotechnology can be used to put vitamins and nutrients directly into common grains and vegetable oil, in order to deal with problems of malnutrition in large parts of the world. Second, biotechnology can be used to improve the qualities of the oils that are found in our crops for better cardiovascular health. And, third, biotechnology can be used to create novel pharmaceuticals using plants as factories for producing them (Shapiro 1999b). However, there is concern that consumers of GM crop produce could experience allergenic effects stimulated by novel chemical balances and proteins. Field workers exposed to insecticidal transgenic crops could also develop allergies. The dozens of deaths and the crippling of hundreds of people in 1989 by eosinophiliamyalgia syndrome (EMS), which were linked to a batch of synthetic L-tryptophan produced by a genetically engineered strain of *bacillus amyloliquefaciens*, indicate the unpredictability of genetically engineered food products (TWN 1996).

To conclude this discussion of environmental implications, it is helpful to remember that 175 countries signed the Convention on Biological Diversity (CBD) and thereby committed to the 'precautionary principle', namely that the lack of scientific proof of negative effects on the environment is not a reason for inaction when the theoretical hazard is high. This was agreed because it was recognised that, unlike a scientific test, with the planet you cannot throw away the test tube and start again. The precautionary principle was restated in the Cartagena Protocol on Biosafety, agreed in January 2000.

◢ Economic and sociocultural implications

Carl Feldbaum of the Washington-based Biotechnology Industry Organisation (BIO) said GM crops are 'desperately needed if the world's growing population is to be fed in coming decades' (quoted in Weiss 1999). Whether this is the case depends not only on the ability of the GM crops to grow faster and larger, but for them to benefit the economies of less-industrialised countries. Hence, the economic implications of GM crops are discussed here in terms of productivity, costs and food security.

The main reason why farmers are interested in GM crops is because of the potential for increased production. The idea is that, if crops are better protected against pests and competing weeds then they will produce higher yields. Despite this, higher yields have not been realised in a number of cases in the USA, where crops of cotton and soya failed in 1996 and 1997, with the biotech companies paying compensation to farmers (Spinney 1998). It is important to remember, however, that GM crops may allow the cultivation of lands previously unsuitable. This is because the crops can be engineered to withstand low nutrient levels, low pH, high salinity or low moisture content in the soil. In addition, given the potential of climate change to adversely affect existing agricultural lands, the use of these types of GM crop might prove compelling.

Another reason for interest from the farmers is that GM crops might actually reduce their costs by reducing the amount of agrochemicals needing to be applied. The problem with this is that the chemical companies control the technology and do not intend to commercialise GM crops that will lead to a decline in income from their existing trade in agrochemicals. Meanwhile, increased production and reduced costs are not helpful if there is no market, and in 1999 the market for GM crops shrunk dramatically as consumers, retailers and increasingly governments rejected the new technology.

Improving food security is an important consideration. The report of the Nuffield Council on Bioethics points out that in developing countries the ability to grow vitamin A-enriched rice and salt-resistant or drought-resistant crops could make a vital impact in combating hunger and malnutrition (Nuffield Foundation 1999). They comment that GM crops might produce more food, or more employment income with which to obtain food, for those who need it most urgently. The report takes the view that the possibility that GM crops will make a substantial contribution to food security provides a sound reason for undertaking GM crop research. However, they argue there is an urgent need to direct more GM research at the food staples of developing countries, such as white maize or cassava, rather than just at Western crops.

The argument that GM crops could help avert future world hunger is disputed by organisations such as the World Development Movement:

> Far from being the answer to world hunger, GM crops actually threaten the food security of millions in the poorest countries of the world. Hunger is universally acknowledged to be an issue of access and poverty, not production; concentrating control of the world food system in the hands of a few large corporations is the last thing the poor need (Hilary 1999: 8).

Food security could be undermined as farmers forgo a stock of seeds for replanting. Currently, 80% of crops in the developing world are grown from seeds saved from the last harvest (Hilary 1999). However, biotech companies require their customers not to store and re-use seed, including this as part of their contracts and even hiring private detectives to monitor compliance. Already 100 farmers have been forced to destroy their crops and pay compensation to Monsanto (Christian Aid 1999). The problem is that, if a harvest fails and farmers do not have the capital to buy new seeds, then the lack of an existing store of seeds could prove disastrous. Equally risky are the potential consequences of genetic pollution, described above, such as the creation of superweeds or the spread of a 'traitor' gene which would mean crops need the application of a particular chemical in order to grow well.

The sociocultural implications of GM crops for rural communities have not been fully considered, largely because of a lack of experience of their use in society. However, predictions could be made based on some of the impacts of the green revolution. Further integration into the cash economy, with the associated growth in consumption of manufactured products and services and a diversification of the local economy is one probable outcome of the widespread uptake of GM crops. This could bring benefits in terms of new job opportunities and access to helpful, or novel, consumer products. However, this can also affect the position of certain social groups, such as women, who for a variety of reasons are not as able or likely to borrow money and begin GM cropping. In addition, women's or children's utilisation of non-cultivated plants could be hampered by an increase in monocultures of herbicide-resistant GM crops. The potential psychological impacts of further integration into the cash economy and the effects on social and gender relations should also be considered as part of the impact of this technology. More work needs to be done in this area and policies developed to mitigate any adverse sociocultural impacts of the uptake of GM crops.

◢ Political implications

The development and commercial application of GM crops has implications for the power relations between corporations, governments, communities as well as relations between the West and less-industrialised countries of the world. The key word here is patenting. With it, corporations are extending their private rights into the collective domain, appropriating both indigenous traditional knowledge and genetic materials.

Companies argue that they must be able to make a profit in order to invest in the research and development of new crop varieties. This means that they need legal protection so that they receive payment for when 'their' products are used. However, the products are derived from existing crops which are shared by anyone who wants to use them. Indigenous or traditional knowledge does not lend itself easily to patenting, at least not by those who live indigenous or traditional lifestyles. Researchers often patent crop strains that rely on the stewardship of generations of people, whose descendants do not benefit financially from the patent. The irony is that farmers then end up paying royalties on the products of their own ancestral knowledge, even products on which they rely for survival: half the known plant species in Brazil have already been patented by corporations (WFAFW 1999).

Currently, there is little international protection of the intellectual property of communities in less-industrialised countries. The WTO's TRIPs agreement and the International Convention for the Protection of New Varieties of Plants (UPOV) recognise patenting only for 'novel' plants: where novel plants are those considered to exhibit 'new' characteristics. Some experts believe that farmers' varieties need individual protection in the form of an agreement on international property rights. However, this gives rise to problems of benefit sharing and how to define the 'community', especially the size of the community that was involved in generations of breeding a certain plant. Others believe that open access to shared knowledge is the best thing for agricultural biodiversity: 'The biological world cannot be owned or controlled by corporations, or any other interests, as it is a collective resource that has evolved and been generated over centuries', said Tewolde Egziabher, the Ethiopian delegate to the 4th conference of the parties of the Commission on Sustainable Development (quoted in Spinney 1998).

◢ The response from civil society

The powerful lobbying by commercial interests, which delayed agreement on the Cartagena Protocol on Biosafety, illustrated the cumbersome progress of governmental and intergovernmental agencies in regulating GM crops. Consequently, NGOs turned their attention to the biotechnology companies themselves. The activities of NGOs to influence the policy of biotechnology companies has been almost exclusively confrontational, because of the defensive stance taken by companies and because of most NGOs' fundamental opposition to the technology.

In Asia, protest against biotech companies is widespread. On 28 November 1998 and again on 2 December, contingents of Indian farmers in the Karnataka region, chanting 'Cremate Monsanto' and 'Stop genetic engineering', uprooted and burned genetically engineered cotton fields in front of a bank of television cameras and news reporters. NGOs, including the Karnataka State Farmers' Association, have called on the biotechnology company Monsanto to 'get out of India', and for the government to ban field tests and imports of genetically engineered seeds and crops. In Manila, later that year, under the slogans of 'Stop the terminator seeds' and 'Put a face on the enemy', the South-East Asia Regional Institute for Community Education and 12 other NGOs organised a militant mass demonstration outside Monsanto's corporate offices. As Professor Nanjundaswamy argued in the opening quotation of this book (p. 14), the intention of these direct actions was not only to stop the distribution of GM seeds in the South, but also to undermine investor confidence in the technology around the world.

In the West, NGO action has also included direct action to prevent field trials of GM crops. A group calling themselves the Bolt Weevils claimed responsibility for damaging a field of corn in Goodhue County, USA, being grown for research by Novartis Seeds Inc. They released a statement saying that the action was to 'prevent another day of profiting off the dirty business of genetic engineering' (Bioengineering Action Network 1999). Given rising public concern, the Consumers' Union, the largest consumer group in the US, called for the universal labelling of products made with GM ingredients.[3] In Europe, direct actions increased to the extent that police in the UK said they were unsure if they would be able to protect 75 new crop test sites from demonstrations.[4] Philippe Roch, director of the Swiss Agency for the Environment, Forests and Landscape, called for a moratorium on genetic engineering for at least ten years while research is carried out on possible side effects (Danker 1999).

Protests have also been directed at those institutions that appear to serve the interests of the biotechnology companies. The Mayor of Seattle, Paul Schell, called a 'state of emergency' in Seattle on 30 November 1999 after 50,000 protesters managed to prevent the opening ceremony of the World Trade Organisation's so-called 'Millennium Round' of talks. The fact that agreements affecting the regulation of GM crops were on the agenda of the Seattle talks helps explain why it suffered the greatest level of protest against an intergovernmental meeting in years.

The response by retailers, processors, suppliers, farmers and investors to the concerns of civil society has been varied. Under pressure from NGOs and consumers, large retailers across Europe decided to eliminate genetically modified ingredients from their brands. These included: J. Sainsbury and Marks & Spencer in the UK; Carrefour in France;

---

3 M. Suzman in *Financial Times*, 25 August 1999, cited in a UN Foundation e-mail update, John Cohen, 25 August 1999.
4 ITN World News/PBS report, 16 August 1999.

Effelunga in Italy; Migros in Switzerland; Delhaize in Belgium; and Superquinn in Ireland (ENDS 1999). In turn, some food processors who supply these retailers responded by eliminating GM foods from their product lines. Unilever stated its intention to stop using genetically modified ingredients in its Birds Eye and Van der Bergh brands and Nestlé UK Ltd announced it would ensure that the 'vast majority' of its products were GM-free or labelled otherwise (Weiss 1999).

Given the negative market reaction, farmers had second thoughts about using GM crops. For example, the American Corn Growers' Association urged its members to consider using non-GM seeds in 2000. 'We're sure as hell not going to grow a product the customer doesn't want', said the association's chief executive, Gary Goldberg (*Los Angeles Times* 1999, quoted in Corporate Watch 1999). The emerging negative reaction at the retail end of the supply chain, and the concern that this has sparked in growers means that investors in the biotechnology industry are beginning to reassess their predictions. Frank Mitsch, an industry analyst at Deutsche Bank, told the *New York Times* (Barboza 1999) that 'Clearly everyone in the biotech industry is concerned . . . to some extent the year 2000 is . . . a lost year for them, and we're trying to see the order of magnitude.'

Government responses to concern over biotechnology have been varied. Some governments banned GM crop cultivation, some banned their sale, some mandated labelling of products, some established new committees, while others have done nothing. In April 1999, Switzerland prohibited the release of genetically modified maize and potatoes into the environment. In rejecting the proposed test crops, the federal environment office cited concerns over the inadvertent spread of altered genes.[5] In 1999, the EU had an import ban on GM corn which was estimated to cost the US about $200 million annually in lost sales to Europe (*International Trade Reporter* 1999, quoted in Corporate Watch 1999). Meanwhile a federal judge in Brazil decided to ban sales of Monsanto's Roundup Ready soybean seeds until the government set biosafety rules—a decision that enraged farmers (Epstein 1999). Japan will mandate labelling of some GM foods by April 2001 (Nomura 1999) and, in November 1999, federal lawmakers in the United States introduced legislation that would require labelling of food made with GM crops (Barboza 1999). The Australian government set up a new watchdog agency that has the power to freeze GMO research if it is believed to pose a potential threat to public health, safety or the environment.[6]

◢ New approaches from the biotechnology companies

In response to the campaigns and concerns in civil society, and their effects on the market and regulatory environments, the biotechnology companies began to act. One observable impact of the NGO campaigns was Monsanto's decision not to commercialise the 'terminator technology' which makes seeds sterile, so that farmers would have to buy seeds every year. Their CEO, Bob Shapiro, announced that:

5 Reuters/PlanetArk e-mail, 19 April 1999.
6 *Ibid.*

> You should know that we reached that decision after extensive consultation and dialogue with people in groups around the world who had a variety of points of view, especially in the developing world (Shapiro 1999b).

This decision is part of a broader reconsideration of strategy by the biotechnology companies, who have adopted a conciliatory tone towards critics. For example, DuPont's chief executive, Charles Holliday Jr, admitted that:

> Unfortunately, many in the industry have been reluctant to address concerns about the risks of biotechnology. But we have to listen to the people who are now raising alarms. We don't have all the answers and to pretend we do, or to brush off concern as unfounded, is to be arrogant and reckless (quoted in the *New York Times* [Barboza 1999]).

Monsanto's Bob Shapiro echoed these sentiments in a speech to a conference of the environmental group, Greenpeace, in October 1999, and called for dialogue with critics of the industry:

> Our confidence in this technology and our enthusiasm for it has, I think, widely been seen—and understandably so—as condescension or indeed arrogance. Because we thought it was our job to persuade, too often we forgot to listen . . . We're now publicly committed to dialogue with people and groups who have a stake in this issue. We're listening, and we'll seek common ground whenever it's available and to the extent that it is available. We'll seek solutions that work for a wide range of people.[7]

This is reminiscent of the oil company Shell's transformed approach toward its critics after widespread protest over its plans to dump the oil platform Brent Spar in the North Sea, and its activities in Nigeria where anti-Shell protesters were being executed by the government (Murphy and Bendell 1997a). Shell's then President worked toward the company replacing its 'technological arrogance' with a more co-operative approach, which recognises that environmental issues are 'social and political dilemmas' with 'a range of possible answers' (Herkströter 1996: 9). The results of this strategic conversion, in terms of business–NGO relations and sustainable development, are still being assessed (see Chapter 2).

For biotechnology the question is: where is the common ground between companies and NGOs? Can dialogue really deliver a win–win? If so, what needs to be discussed and where? And what could be decided?

◢ Dialogue and the win–win world-view

The first hurdle for biotechnology companies to overcome is widespread scepticism from NGOs. The validity of Bob Shapiro's call for dialogue with civil society is questioned by some. Simon Heap of the International NGO Training and Research Centre (INTRAC) had this to say about the Monsanto director's speech to the Greenpeace conference:

7   Personal communication with S. Heap, 2 December 1999.

> Just watching this gaunt man sat in his easy-chair reading his speech to us on a video-conference link twenty feet high seemed somewhat comical if not incongruous . . . [I]nstead of being around to field questions, [there was hardly any time] . . . before the link was cut . . . [After this, Monsanto's] Head of Stakeholder Dialogue['s] answers to some very fair questions from the audience would have made even the most hardened tight-lipped politician blush, in that she gave such generalised, non-committal, vacuous, replies . . . So much for dialogue! (Heap 1999).

Commitment to the outcome of dialogue is essential: it is a 'ground rule' of dialogue. Another ground rule is not to rule anything in or anything out, yet the biotechnology companies do not appear comfortable with this idea:

> The underlining premise of dialogue is pretty straightforward. In this case, it is that there are both real benefits to the use of biotechnology and at the same time there are real concerns about its use. If you don't believe that there are real benefits, then there is no room for dialogue (Shapiro 1999b).

Setting the rules in this way is unworkable. Given the risks outlined earlier, many in civil society do not believe there are any net sustainable development benefits to be gained from biotechnology. A win–win resolution appears elusive. One possibility is the engineering of generational transgene obsolescence, where the introduced trait cannot be passed on to future generations of the plant. If successfully done, this would protect the environment from some aspects of the hazard of genetic pollution, and allow the companies to profit from year-on-year sale of GM seed, if there was market demand. However, even this is not a simple win–win scenario. The concerns over consumer health would still remain, and therefore the market demand for the produce would be restricted. If there was market demand and farmers continued to want to buy the seed, then there would still be the problem of agroscience companies acquiring a very powerful role in society. In addition, knowledge of how best to cultivate the original varieties would be eroded and cropping biodiversity reduced. In this way, even those NGOs that might recognise the potential of biotechnology could dispute the potential of its application in the hands of companies seeking rapid commercialisation and profit maximisation. The issues that need to be discussed are therefore probably broader and more complex than the industry would initially desire, such as finding commercially viable alternatives to patenting life-forms and the need for a moratorium on current commercialisation of GM crops.

There are fundamental political problems which need to be resolved in any dialogue. The bottom line for the biotechnology companies appears to be that their stock valuation is based on the investors' belief that the companies will increasingly control the system of food supply in a biotech future worth billions. The bottom line for NGOs might just turn out to be democracy: a belief that no one organisation or group of organisations should have the final say over our future (see Chapter 18). The 'dialogue' should not be over biotechnology then, but the role of business in society. Some within the industry, such as Monsanto's Martina Bianchini, recognise this dynamic:

> . . . we have a societal problem which is much deeper than biotech . . . The deeper question is how should this technology be introduced in society and

what role should the consumers/NGOs/stakeholders etc. play in its introduction and policy making? This leads to the question: what role should
companies play in society and what does society expect from companies? [8]

If the dialogue moves toward the issue of the role of business in society then two
concepts that are likely to be mentioned are corporate social responsibility and corporate
citizenship. These terms describe the ability of corporations to act as ethical institutions,
and thereby exhibit social responsibility or citizenship qualities in their operations. Both
concepts assume a win–win world-view, and in this way would appeal to the companies
who seek dialogue as a means of securing a win–win solution to their current
predicament:

Debating is a zero sum kind of process. It's a win/lose process, in which the
antagonists defend their positions and attack the positions of their opponents
. . . Dialogue, on the other hand, is a search . . . for common ground; for
constructive solutions that work for a wide range of people (Shapiro 1999b).

The problem with this is that GM crops and sustainable development might be a 'no
win–win' situation, in which case the win–win paradigm and associated concepts of
win–win dialogue, CSR and corporate citizenship will fail. This is because both CSR and
corporate citizenship concepts place the onus on the corporation to take action on social
and environmental issues as it is both a good thing to do and beneficial for the company.
The agency is with the company, not the people. The power to do the right thing is
assigned to the company, not the people. Because the CSR and corporate citizenship
concepts assume a win–win world, no conflict is seen to exist between corporate interests
and those of civil society. At most, conflict is seen as a process issue, an outcome of
paradoxes that should be managed carefully (see Chapter 16). Therefore the win–win
paradigm papers over fundamental political concerns about human rights and justice.
CSR and corporate citizenship do not deal with the rights of individuals over the
commercial institutions in society. Is it a human right for one group of people not to
have their future health, environmental and economic security potentially threatened by
institutions working for the profit of another group? If so, then it is essential for
institutions with this power to be accountable to society. In other words, it is essential
for corporations with this power to be less powerful.

At the heart of a meaningful dialogue about the future of GM crops must be corporate
accountability and the mechanisms by which civil society can assume more power in
shaping the commercialisation of biotechnology. This may be the answer while at the
same time being, in terms of power, a win–lose situation. What must be avoided is a
situation where the pure existence of dialogue is regarded as a win: a win for companies
because the NGOs are listening and therefore might change their approach, and a win
for NGOs as the companies are listening and might change theirs. If the existence of
dialogue is, by itself, seen as a win–win, then none of the core issues will be resolved.

---

8   Personal communication with M. Bianchini, 6 December 1999.

◢ Conclusion

It appears that either the biotechnology companies will reassess their accountability to civil society, and examine ways in which NGOs can be accommodated into systems of corporate governance, or biotechnology will be the site of future battles. If companies accept the need to develop corporate accountability, then there are a number of policy options. In Chapter 17 Rob Lake and I discuss recent debates concerning accountability and corporate governance. In light of this, biotechnology companies could undertake the following activities to build accountability through systems of representative and participatory democracy:

☐ **Corporate governance and representative democracy.** The biotechnology companies could work with a civil society observatory organisation which would accredit NGOs so they could have a vote in elections for the non-executive directors of the company's board. Employees could have a parallel process to elect directors. Candidates could be nominated by employees and accredited NGOs.

☐ **Corporate governance and participatory democracy.** The biotechnology companies' various strategic planning committees could be opened up so that representatives of interested NGOs could participate in their discussion on an ongoing basis (confidentiality issues would need to be addressed).

☐ **Building the capacity for effective participation.** The biotechnology companies could work with each other and an intergovernmental organisation or an international NGO to build the capacity of non-participating groups, in less-industrialised countries for example, so the systems of participatory and representative democracy are more effective.

☐ **Establishing an independent council.** Biotechnology companies could facilitate dialogue on the establishment of an independent multi-stakeholder council that could oversee patenting, and perhaps even certify that specific crop varieties and their associated retailing systems are acceptable in terms of sustainable development criteria.

These are just initial policy ideas and there are, of course, other activities that companies could undertake to build accountability. There is an alternative course of action open to biotech companies, a course of action without moral foundation. Companies could seek to co-opt, divide and infiltrate their critics in civil society. To do this companies could:

☐ Set up more front groups to give a sense of independent pro-GM sentiment in civil society

☐ Seek NGO partners that can be convinced of the benefits of current GM crop commercialisation strategies (perhaps targeting specific under-resourced and unrepresentative development NGOs)

- ☐ Establish stakeholder 'talking shops' that champion the existence of dialogue as evidence of success

- ☐ Continue to depict the relationship between business and sustainable development as inherently win–win and dialogue as win–win, so that corporate social responsibility and corporate citizenship are sufficient solutions to public concern

- ☐ Monitor anti-GM NGOs in an attempt to pre-empt their campaigns

- ☐ Infiltrate anti-GM NGOs in order to discredit them by peddling 'junk science' or by turning their peaceful protests into violent ones

It appears that there are value-based and value-less options for the corporation. For the individual, though, there is also the option of quitting. If the company one works for is not proceeding in a direction where one can be part of the solution then quitting is probably the best option. After all, making a life is just as important as making a living.

THE LISTENING BANKS
The development of stakeholder relations with NGOs

Mike Lachowicz

SERM Rating Agency Ltd, UK

Why do banks need to talk to non-governmental organisations (NGOs)? Aren't banks just deposit takers and money lenders? Yes, they are, but because of this function they occupy a central position in most societies and therefore have a responsibility for the state of those societies. In this chapter I describe the extent to which banks have accepted their responsibilities and started working with their stakeholders.

The 1992 United Nations Environment Programme (UNEP) *Statement by Banks on the Environment and Sustainable Development* was a significant step on the part of managers in recognising the pivotal position that banks occupy. It set out several commitments by leading international banks on their responsibilities towards environmental management including public awareness and was signed by over 40 banks. This UNEP initiative continued to gather momentum and by June 1999 over 150 banks had signed.

Yet, several years after the initial *Statement*, the progress that banks have made in engaging with stakeholders on environmental issues has been uneven. Indeed, few banks have taken a lead in implementing the types of measure contained in the UNEP *Statement*. The Green Alliance's report on UNEP signatory banks, *Banking on the Future* (Hill *et al.* 1997), found that less than half of the respondents had reviewed progress against the commitments of the *Statement* since signing it. By contrast, a survey of UK banking by Lachowicz (1998) reported that all respondents had incorporated risk assessment of environmental liability into their lending procedures. The difference in priorities is perhaps explained by the financial incentive in reducing potential liability.

When one considers how important the environment is in terms of lender liability on environmentally damaging activities or long-term economic development, it is curious that every bank does not address environmental issues with more urgency. However, the tide is turning and there are increasing instances of banks accepting their responsibilities and adopting various sustainable development programmes. Helping the tide turn are NGOs who provide an additional means by which poor environmental and social performance can be translated into financial risks (see Chapter 17).

John Bray explained in Chapter 3 how information now spreads much faster than before—as a result of video, Internet and satellite links—and that there is no hiding place for poor performance on social and environmental issues. In Chapter 2 Cheryl Rodgers explained how the effects of global process on states described by Peter Newell in Chapter 1 mean that large corporations can no longer assume their own legitimacy and must *earn* public respect through transparent communication and dialogue. In this chapter I argue that constructive relations with NGOs are both possible and profitable for the banking community.

◢ Negative equity: conflicts between banks and NGOs

One of the oldest and long-lived examples of NGO pressure on banks was the campaign against apartheid in South Africa that started in the 1970s. It continued until 1986 when Barclays Bank sold its interest in Barclays National (RSA), which controlled almost a quarter of South Africa's banking market and made massive loans to its government and businesses. International pressure combined with large-scale consumer boycotts made Barclays' continuing involvement in South Africa untenable as it began to impede expansion into US and European markets, and its staff were subjected to hostility from campaigners. Barclays lost 50% of student accounts during the boycott while the 'End Loans to South Africa' campaign group estimated its loss of turnover during the boycott to be around £6 billion (Vidal 1999).

During the 1980s, campaigners began to focus on the role of banks, in particular the World Bank, in supporting major infrastructure projects such as the construction of dams, power stations and roads in developing countries. NGOs believed that many of these projects cause irreparable damage to the environment and to the social fabric of the indigenous communities. In many cases, inadequate or non-existent impact assessments are made—the main beneficiaries seemingly being the contracting companies from the West and officials of the host government receiving political kudos and bribes. Even in strictly financial terms, researchers found that the returns had often been between one-third and one-sixth of those predicted (Pearce 1991).

The growth of local opposition groups allied with environmental NGOs in the West erupted at the annual meeting of the World Bank in Berlin in 1988 when tens of thousands of demonstrators lobbied the bankers and government representatives to real effect. A year later, the World Bank was proclaiming its conversion to the goal of 'greening the Bank'. While this did not convince many campaigners, it was a signal that the World Bank was beginning to take notice of criticism about its lending programmes and a starting point for reform and improved dialogue with more of its stakeholders. Since then, the Bank has continued to reassess its role with regard to the social and environmental impact of its activities, surviving an attempt in 1994–95 to have it wound up. Its president in the late 1990s, James Wolfensohn, was a driving force behind the plan to cancel the debt of the poorest countries supported by the church and aid movement coalition, Jubilee 2000, and has conducted a public campaign against corruption by politicians and businesses (Brummer 1999).

Commercial banks are now being targeted by NGOs campaigning for changes in the international financial system so that it does not undermine policies for sustainable development. The Carnival against Capital in June 1999, in the City of London, probably marks the beginning of a protest movement against banks that appear unresponsive to people's concerns for issues such as debt relief or the financing of environmentally damaging projects.

While this campaign for banks to show greater responsibility on the international stage is relatively recent, local community action continues to be a factor in shaping commercial bank policy. For example, a customer campaign supported by disability groups forced Lloyds TSB to abandon the trial of an automated bank in Reading, UK, in the first half of 1999 and reinstate cashiers. Many customers preferred face-to-face contact with staff, while customers with disabilities, with no means for assisted service, felt ignored and unserved. A good example of the sensitivity that banks still have to learn was that of the Bank of Scotland's involvement with controversial US evangelist Pat Robertson (see Box 7.1), where the bank had to beat a hasty retreat in the face of determined opposition from a powerful coalition of groups angered at the evangelist's rhetoric about certain social groups.

◢ Profiting from a clear conscience

There is another side to the relations between banks and NGOs. One can point to a wide and growing range of initiatives and products being developed by banks to improve their environmental performance and to appeal to an increasingly aware public. The following examples are from the United Kingdom:

☐ The Co-operative Bank engaged in extensive consultation with its customers and leading NGOs before adopting a proactive stance on ethical lending. As a result it has strict criteria on which companies it will do business with—this excludes arms manufacturers and companies harmful to animal welfare. It has extended this by adopting 'The Natural Step', a management philosophy based on ecological principles, and applying it to its lending policy—recognising that the bank's indirect impacts are much greater than the direct impacts of its operations. However, the Co-op Bank recognises that there are potential contradictions between its policies and those of its parent body, the Co-operative Wholesale Society, which has, for example, allowed GM crop trials on its land (Tickell 1999b).

☐ In March 1999, the Bank of Scotland (BoS) announced it had begun talks with Robertson Financial Services (controlled by controversial evangelist Pat Robertson) aimed at creating a telephone banking operation in the US.

☐ As soon as talks are announced, many BoS customers express opposition to the proposed partnership with Robertson because of his extreme views on many issues including religion, feminism and homosexuality. BoS responds by letter to angry customers that 'Those views, as with the personal views held by all the people we do business with, do not determine the basis of their business relationship with the bank.'

☐ Pressure mounts with hundreds of private customers and many large corporate account holders threatening to close their accounts—churches and AIDS groups are among the leading campaigners. The TUC considers cancelling its affinity credit card. BoS's share market value is reduced by £402 million (5%).

☐ Robertson publicly criticises Europe's tolerance stating that 'in Scotland you can't believe how strong the homosexuals are' and warns that Scotland 'could fall right back to the darkness very easily'.

☐ At the end of May 1999, BoS informs Robertson that the deal is off and pays over £10 million in compensation. The pressure group, Equality Network, warns the bank that it must rebuild its reputation for equal opportunities (Bell and Fraser 1999).

Box 7.1 **Case Study 1: Bank of Scotland**

Source: Pallast and Laurance 1999

☐ NatWest Bank was the first high-street bank to actively embrace environmental issues by setting up its Environmental Management Unit in 1990. In addition to auditing its own activities and services, one of its most innovative partnerships has been that formed with the World Wide Fund for Nature (WWF) to promote environmental management to small businesses. This collaboration produced the 'Better Business Package' in the form of a video, training pack and CD-ROM, which are available at low cost to its business account holders.

☐ Woolwich plc established its Green Issues Management Unit in 1994. Since then it has initiated a sustainability programme throughout the bank covering all operations, including suppliers and customers. Its first environmental financial services product, the Energy Saver Mortgage, was launched in 1998: this gave borrowers a home energy rating report on their new property together with a package of energy efficient appliances.

☐ For its clients in the UK, the Dutch Triodos Bank, an independent bank with social and environmental objectives as its founding principles, offers an innovative package of savings and investment products closely linked to social and environmental NGO campaigns. These include its Organic Saver, Just Housing, and Energy Saver savings accounts; and the North–South investment plan. All the bank's investments are made to projects and enterprises that create social and environmental value: for example, micro-credit banks and fair trade associations in developing countries.

Conclusions

These examples show that the banking sector has moved a long way towards improved relations with NGOs throughout the 1990s. International initiatives such as the UNEP *Statement* as well as continuing campaigns on issues such as debt relief for developing countries have ensured that progress by banks on sustainable development and environmental performance has continued to be made. Nonetheless, a number of outstanding issues will require the close attention of banks over the next few years:

☐ Banks, and the financial services in general, should exercise corporate citizenship in a manner that reflects the improved understanding of their social and environmental responsibilities.

☐ For stakeholder dialogue to be credible, communication of environmental performance must be clear, timely and efficient. The Business in the Environment's 1997 *Index of Corporate Environmental Engagement* reported that 'the financial sector is demonstrably the sector with the most ground to make up'. The banks say that it is unfair to compare their environmental performance with other industries as their impacts are largely indirect and harder to measure. Nonetheless, it indicates the problems posed by the lack of clear benchmarking standards and reporting protocols for the financial services in communicating their progress (see Chapter 17).

☐ Financial services need comparable and auditable standards—existing EMS standards are seen as irrelevant as most of industry's impacts are indirect. Few banks or insurers have ISO 14001 or EMAS registration, though there are continuing discussions with the EC to produce a revised version of EMAS for the financial services.

☐ Banks have a cultural difficulty in reconciling the demand for greater transparency of their policies and procedures with commercial confidentiality. Unless this is overcome, this will remain a major obstacle in their relations with NGOs and effective stakeholder consultation.

☐ There is a potential danger of banks being targeted over emotive issues such as genetically modified organisms (GMOs) and animal rights where some campaigning groups may see lenders and investors as targets for applied pressure. Such campaigns may be just the tip of an iceberg of the social movement for accountability from the financial sector (see Chapter 17).

No bank can afford to ignore their environmental and social responsibilities without seriously risking its long-term commercial viability. Successful management of NGO relations can help to anticipate and avoid many potential problems. It can even help to improve profitability, as in the case of some of the smaller, niche banks such as the Co-operative Bank and Triodos Bank. The challenge for the major banks now is to translate this success onto a larger stage.

☐ The EBRD was established in 1991 following the collapse of communism in Central and Eastern Europe. Its aim was to assist the transition of the region's 27 countries towards market economies. The bank's 60 shareholders include representatives from the client nations and the rest of the world, especially the EC and G7 countries. Uniquely for a major international bank, its environmental policy is a cornerstone of its founding document.

☐ The bank promotes development of the private sector through its investment operations and channelling of foreign and domestic capital. By acting as the lead partner, it shares risks and enables many projects to attract investment that would not otherwise be able to do so. Its Municipal and Environmental Infrastructure programme fosters private-sector investment in urban infrastructure projects such as water treatment and waste management facilities. One example is St Petersburg's water treatment plant—the city is the largest single point of source pollution in the Baltic Sea.

☐ The EBRD has attracted controversy over its investment in nuclear power plants, which have been subject to considerable pressure from governments and campaigners. The bank has to balance the environmental consequences of bad management against the economic dependency of countries where up to 90% of electricity is generated from nuclear energy (*Economist* 1997).

☐ Despite criticisms, the EBRD has proved that it is possible for a major international investment bank to be a positive force for sustainable development. Assisted by extensive stakeholder negotiations and thorough project assessment procedures, it has achieved an enviable return on its investments—well above the average for the region. Though not directly comparable with commercial banks, the EBRD has clearly shown that it is possible to combine principles of environmental responsibility and financial success.

Box 7.2 **Case Study 2: the European Bank for Reconstruction and Development (EBRD)**

PART 3

Organisations' Experiences

MEETING SOCIAL AND ENVIRONMENTAL OBJECTIVES THROUGH PARTNERSHIP

The experience of Unilever

Anne Weir

Unilever, UK

Unilever, which makes branded food, laundry and personal care products worldwide, is committed to contributing to sustainable development. We base our actions on the life-cycle management of our products. This means we acknowledge the idea of extended responsibility—that we share with other stakeholders in our supply chains an interest in ensuring we have a sound economic base, a healthy environment and flourishing communities.

We at Unilever are far from having all the answers on how to fulfil the obligations of sustainable development, but we are determined to find solutions because we recognise that the prospects for our business are intimately linked with society's ability to build a more sustainable future.

We see the idea of partnership, working with others—including critics—in pursuit of a common goal, as one of the ways to drive change. We use the term 'partnership' in the widest sense to describe engagement and co-operation with those directly involved in the supply chain, and with others in society who can help us find new and sustainable ways to meet common objectives.

We see three core principles of successful partnership:

☐ A need to engage stakeholders along the supply chain

☐ Recognition that progress can only be made through consensus

☐ A willingness to establish a non-competitive framework

◢ Unilever's experience

Most of the potential environmental impact of Unilever's activities lies outside the company's direct control. This is shown clearly by life-cycle assessment (LCA), a management tool that helps to gauge the overall environmental impact of a product, from design through use, to disposal. LCAs show that the potential impacts of Unilever's activities occur primarily when our raw materials are produced—especially in farming and fishing—and when consumers use and dispose of our products.

We recognise that, if we are to reduce these impacts—as part of our extended responsibilities—we have to work with others as partners to get results. Partnerships now represent an important part or our resources for the sustainable development of our business. Indeed, as suggested by Fowler and Heap in Chapter 10, we see partnerships helping us to achieve our long-term strategic business objectives.

How then have we used partnerships in support of our environmental and social objectives, and what lessons can be drawn from our experience? Here are three examples of partnerships that each seek to address the need to foster more sustainable patterns of production and consumption.

The Marine Stewardship Council

By the early 1990s conclusive evidence existed that over-fishing had put global stocks of fish for human consumption at serious risk. Events, such as the closure of the Canadian Grand Banks fishery in 1992, sent a loud signal that the marine environment was in danger; that jobs and the future of fishing and coastal communities were in jeopardy; and that an important nutritional resource could be threatened.

At the same time public awareness and concern about the potential crisis in world fisheries was being raised by international environmental organisations. Unilever, one of the world's leading buyers of frozen fish, recognised that, unless major fisheries took stronger steps to become sustainable, the company would no longer have access to its valued raw materials.

For Unilever it became clear that the way forward was not just a question of looking after a few important fisheries. Because of the complex relationship between the many different fish species and wild stocks in the marine ecosystem, the solution had to involve ways to help make fisheries right around the world sustainable.

This was a huge challenge and one we could not take on alone. While Unilever has some influence in the world's fish markets, it is by no means dominant—we process less than 1% of the world's fish catch. Progress, we knew, could only come about by working with others who shared our goal, both inside the industry and outside. The solution started to take shape in 1995 in discussions with the World Wide Fund for Nature (WWF). The two organisations had come together for different motives but a common purpose: the need to assure the long-term sustainability of global fish stocks and the integrity of the marine ecosystem.

Drawing on WWF's experience in forestry conservation, they agreed to work together with Unilever to set up a Marine Stewardship Council to run a fisheries certification scheme that could endorse sustainable fisheries management and operational practice. Fish in shops sourced from certified fisheries would be able to carry a logo on the pack; in this way consumers could choose fish products from well-managed fisheries. We believe that this is what consumers will do, and in this way the market will reward responsible fishing.

The partners each brought wide-ranging skills, knowledge and networks to support the formation of the MSC. Unilever also made a commitment at the inception to source all its fish from sustainable fisheries by 2005. Together they undertook an inclusive, global consultation process, including discussions with environmental and marine experts, scientists, fishing industry and trade representatives, government officials and regulators, and many others connected with the marine environment.

The output of the consultation, which ran over eight workshops and two expert drafting sessions, was a set of broad principles and criteria that provide a framework for promoting environmentally and economically viable fishing. The Unilever–WWF partnership achieved a key milestone in July 1998 when the MSC became an independent non-profit organisation.

Early in 1999 the independent Marine Stewardship Council announced details of its certification scheme and it has since started the process of accrediting professional assessment bodies to carry out assessment and certification of fisheries around the world. The first certified fish products are due to reach the market in early 2000.

Although the MSC now operates independently from the partners, both Unilever and WWF clearly have a large stake in the successful introduction of the certification scheme among fisheries around the world. An important factor in this will be the scope provided for local and regional fisheries management to determine, within the framework laid down in the MSC's principles and criteria, the priorities for achieving sustainable fishing practice under local conditions.

Changing fishing practice is one side of the solution. The other is to help consumers understand sustainable fishing. This involves building awareness of the MSC logo and then promoting an appreciation that fish products bearing the logo have been caught in a sustainable way, which not only conserves stocks but also supports those communities who depend on fishing for their livelihoods.

The MSC consultation process achieved much more than simply setting the framework for a certification scheme. It provided a platform on which the complex issues influencing the development of world fisheries could be mapped out on behalf of the many different stakeholders in the industry. A future concern for the MSC will certainly be to ensure that the certification scheme is accessible to fishers and fisheries in countries with developing economies. The MSC could play a role in ensuring an equitable distribution of marine resources to all who have a stake in such fisheries by fostering continued access for them to world markets.

Unilever's partnership with WWF in the MSC initiative ran to a clearly defined agenda— to set up the MSC and to launch a certification scheme. These goals have been achieved and the emphasis is now on extending the network of organisations engaged with and working alongside the MSC. This is particularly important in order to maintain and build momentum behind a widespread move towards certification standards in fisheries around the world.

Living Lakes

For Unilever, a longer-running partnership dealing with clean water conservation—started in Germany in 1990—has now been given an international perspective under the umbrella title 'Living Lakes'.

The model for Living Lakes is a nine-year co-operation between Unilever and Deutsche Umwelthilfe on the regeneration of Lake Constance. This is Europe's largest drinking water reservoir lying between Germany, Switzerland and Austria. Established on what we now understand as Agenda 21 guidelines, the Lake Constance initiative brought local environmental NGOs, businesses and public authorities together to eliminate pollution from the lake and to build a thriving and sustainable economy in the vicinity (Jacoby 1998).

Unilever's involvement arose from its interest in understanding how the use of its products might impact on lakes and wetlands. A range of environmental measures were studied to understand how to control and eliminate pollution from the lake. The research revealed that one of the most significant contributors to lake pollution came from fertiliser running off from farmland surrounding the lake and along the rivers that feed into it (International Lake Constance Conference 1999).

The solution developed through the partnership extended from wildlife conservation and regeneration, to changes in agricultural practice—the region now has a thriving organic farming industry—and the development of new business and employment opportunities. Tourism has provided the basis of regeneration and this depends on the lake remaining a thriving natural resource. For the Lake Constance partners the project has shown that success in building long-term sustainable development and the conservation of natural resources comes through building local ownership of the resource. By helping to create stakeholders in the economic, social and environmental sustainability of the lake and its surroundings, the project has provided the conditions needed for enduring sustainability.

The Living Lakes partnership between Unilever and the newly formed Global Nature Fund, seeks to take this principle of common stewardship of lakes and wetlands, and replicate it at key sites around the world (see Table 8.1). The partnership's aim is to create a network of Living Lakes that will be available as regional models for conservation and sustainable development.

The areas listed are already the focus for conservation, education and local development programmes. They have contributed scientific knowledge and project management expertise to the shared knowledge and best practice resource, which is at the heart of the overall Living Lakes organisation.

For Unilever, Living Lakes is also a platform on which to work with organisations locally. It is a useful partnership that can help us understand how the company's products may impact on the local environment, and in what way Unilever can better contribute

CONTINENT	COUNTRY	LAKE
Africa	South Africa	Lake St Lucia
North America	USA	Mono Lake, California
Europe	Greece	Nestos Lakes
Asia	Russia	Lake Baikal, Siberia
Asia	Japan	Lake Biwa
Europe	Germany	Lake Constance
Europe	Spain	La Nava
Europe	UK	Norfolk Broads

Table 8.1 **The Living Lakes projects**

to sustainable development. At the present time, the majority of Living Lakes projects are in OECD countries. A priority for Unilever now is more local engagement in lake and wetland projects in countries with developing economies.

Sourcing tea

Our principles of partnership also underpin the mission of the Tea Sourcing Partnership (TSP), of which the Brooke Bond Tea Co., a subsidiary of Unilever, is one of the founder members. Formed in April 1997, the TSP is open to tea packers of branded and private-label tea, currently in the UK only. Membership of the TSP includes 13 tea-packing companies, comprising 40 UK tea brands, including supermarket own labels—accounting for about 60% of all the packed tea sold in the UK. The partnership's core belief is that partners share responsibility for the social and ethical conditions involved in producing the tea they buy.

The TSP is working to improve conditions on tea estates and factories by promoting compliance with national legislation. This is because knowledge of labour law and its enforcement is often weak in many tea-growing countries. Also, respect for cultural and legislative differences in tea-growing countries is regarded as necessary to gain the level of support and co-operation needed from local tea growers and manufacturers.

TSP started by documenting all the relevant national legal requirements (laws and union agreements). It then developed questionnaires for its suppliers tailored to each country's legislation. These cover terms and conditions of employment, health and safety, maternity provisions, education and housing. The TSP is seeking to work with the tea associations in each producer country. In Kenya, for example, the Tea Board distributes questionnaires on behalf of TSP to suppliers.

Responses to the questionnaires are audited and validated by BVQI (Bureau Veritas Quality International), an internationally recognised certification company with experience of auditing in over 70 countries. The audits are carried out on-site at tea estates/factories by auditors who are familiar with the local culture and language. The auditors talk to several members of the workforce at a variety of levels and use a combination of auditing skills, interview techniques and powers of observation.

Suppliers who do not comply with relevant legal requirements will be given reasonable notice to raise standards. If they continue to fail to demonstrate compliance, TSP members will cease to trade with the estate or factory.

Tea is imported into the UK from around 30 producing nations. The scheme is focused on the countries of production that are some of the most important exporters to the British market. The long-term aim is to cover over 1,500 estates in seven countries: Kenya, India, Indonesia, Sri Lanka, Malawi, Zimbabwe and Tanzania, which account for just under 80% of UK imports.

In order to contribute to the development of best practice in the field of ethical trading, the TSP joined the Ethical Trading Initiative (ETI) in June 1999. This is a government-backed alliance between the commercial sector, trade unions and NGOs, and provides the TSP with a useful forum in which to share experiences with and learn from other stakeholders. It is currently working with the ETI on the use of best practice monitoring and independent verification methods.

◢ Lessons learned

Building an effective framework for environmentally and socially responsible business practice along complex international supply chains requires long-term commitment from all stakeholders and partners. This can best be achieved through a measured, sensitive approach to raising standards that continuously engages all the key interests.

The conditions needed for a successful partnership are:

☐ A high level of public awareness to motivate stakeholders

☐ Recognition by traditional adversaries that they have common interests which will help them achieve shared objectives

☐ Agreed ground rules, to include:
- Common working principles
- Transparent goals
- Agreed boundaries—deal with non-related issues outside the partnership
- An inclusive, participatory approach—essential where wider stakeholder buy-in is critical
- Co-ordinated roll-out of solutions—discourage partners and stakeholders from seeking short-term advantage outside the partnership, such as in PR and marketing
- Acting as ambassadors to stakeholders immediately outside the partnership.

◢ Conclusions

We believe that partnerships can help to change the rules of the game—for example, the relationship between production and consumption in specific markets. They can also create new momentum to find and then generate innovative solutions that are owned by all stakeholders as well as fostering a sustained raising of social and environmental standards on a win–win basis.

There are, however, potential risks for partners. It is always possible that at any time a key player in the partnership, or another important stakeholder, may cease to see their best interests being served by such a partnership and decide to withdraw. As a result, the vital link such partnerships can provide between consumers and producers may also start to break down. Retaining the commitment of all partners, and sustaining their confidence that the success of the partnership will serve their best long-term interests, is not easy to do. Indeed it can be very demanding on often scarce resources.

So it is vital to carry into a partnership the view that sustainable development calls for lasting changes in business operations and in consumer behaviour. By focusing on a long-term process of change and improvement rather than on setting and meeting absolute standards in the short term, partnerships can play a vital role in driving responsible business practice.

As a company committed to operating in a socially responsible manner—contributing to economic progress, environmental care and social development—Unilever wishes to engage in ongoing dialogue with its stakeholders. Partnerships are a valuable part of this process, helping us to ensure that the standards and values applied in our business are appropriate for the societies in which we operate. Such standards need to be globally coherent yet responsive to local social norms and priorities.

But the process of engagement through partnership provides the greatest value where it helps to unlock the inertia of debate. Above all, it can act as a powerful medium for promoting real, practical progress on the ground towards sustainable development.

This chapter © 2000 Unilever

WORKING NON-'STOP' FOR SUSTAINABLE DEVELOPMENT

Case study of a Canadian environmental NGO's relationship with businesses since 1970

Marie-France Turcotte

Concordia University, Canada

This chapter presents a case analysis of the relationships of a Canadian NGO, called 'STOP', with various businesses since its inception in 1970. STOP is a Montreal-based, grass-roots environmental group which is active at the regional level and at the Canadian and North American levels. It has been involved in many issues such as air quality, water quality, waste management, acid rain and energy. The chapter draws on more than 70 hours of participant observation, document analysis and information exchanges with past presidents and members concerning STOP's activities and relationships with the business community (see Box 9.1). From an inductive analysis of this data, a typology of STOP's relationship with businesses is developed, which includes lobbying for environmental regulations, opposing business projects, participating in multi-stakeholder initiatives, consulting contracts for business organisations and 'natural alliances' with some industries. By considering all types of relationship that exist between STOP and various businesses, this chapter adds to a growing body of literature describing the relationships between NGOs and businesses as complex sets of conflict and collaboration (Pasquero 1991; Westley and Vredenburg 1991; Kelman 1992; Clair *et al.* 1995; Turcotte 1995, 1997; Bendell 1998; Hartman and Stafford 1997, 1998; Roome 1998). The analysis adds support to the argument that the environmental NGO sector influences corporate activity in a number of key ways, and demonstrates that one NGO can adopt various tactics in its attempt to influence corporate activity.

THIS CHAPTER IS BASED ON A CASE STUDY OF AN ENVIRONMENTAL GROUP. THE researcher was a participant observer at STOP between 1993 and 1996, representing more than 70 hours of observations, during which extensive notes were taken concerning STOP members' activities and decision-making processes. Documentary analysis was also undertaken, and for this a short history of STOP published in 1996 for the 25th anniversary of the group (STOP 1996) was particularly instrumental. The researcher was involved in the production of that special issue of *STOP Press* by researching archival documents (press clippings and internal documents) on STOP's activities. These documents were obtained from past presidents' and current members' hand-written documents regarding their perceptions of STOP's achievements under their direction or since their involvement.

Data was analysed through an inductive process (Strauss and Corbin 1990). The units of analysis were those of STOP's activities that might have an influence on business or industries. A typology of STOP's relationships with businesses was then developed. Significant examples are presented in the section below to illustrate each category. The discussion on the contribution of environmental NGOs to sustainable development is based on this typology.

Box 9.1 **Methodology**

◢ Lobbying for environmental regulations

Turcotte (1995) observed that, for the majority of environmental groups, one of the most important initiatives was to lobby governments to promote legislative modifications and law enforcement, which eventually resulted in additional constraints on industry. With this approach, governments become intermediary agents in NGO–business relationships. The history of STOP provides numerous examples of lobbying concerning, among other issues, air quality, water quality, non-smokers' rights and waste management. STOP's involvement in the issue of air quality is hereby described as a case in point.

Lobbying at regional level

Since its establishment in 1970, STOP has been a key watchdog of all aspects of the Montreal Urban Community (MUC)'s air pollution control programme (emission limits, ambient air monitoring, response to citizens' complaints, enforcement, access to information and budgets). STOP has helped to provide public support for stronger MUC air quality rules (MUC by-law in 1970, replaced by by-law 44 in 1978, replaced by by-law 90 in 1986). Since 1975, STOP has helped citizens with local air pollution problems involving several industrial sources, assisting local residents in documenting their cases. Moreover, it has succeeded in obtaining public access to emission data and pushed for tougher emission standards. In 1989, under pressure from STOP, the MUC adopted laws increasing fines for non-observance of air and water quality regulations. Also, in 1994, STOP helped to convince the MUC to postpone a request by Montreal's oil refineries to burn dirtier fuels.

Lobbying at provincial level

Since the early 1980s, STOP has been urging the government of Quebec and the MUC to implement a mandatory motor vehicle emission inspection and maintenance programme (similar to the programme in place in Greater Vancouver since 1992) on the basis that the air quality benefits of stringent emission standards applicable to new vehicles are not realised unless all vehicles are properly maintained. In 1982, STOP testified before a committee of the Quebec National Assembly covering the Montreal Urban Community Act. STOP's principal recommendation was incorporated into the new legislation and the MUC was given jurisdiction over motor vehicle emissions for the first time.

Lobbying at federal level

Since its inception, STOP has been urging the government of Canada to adopt stricter motor vehicle emission standards. In 1981, a House of Commons subcommittee formally endorsed STOP's recommendation that Canada's new passenger car exhaust pipe standards needed to be as stringent as those in the United States. In 1986 and 1987, STOP published the 'Thirteen Million Source Cleanup', a guide to motor vehicle emission standards and pollution control equipment. Following this, the federal government imposed strict emission standards on all new cars. Since then, STOP has supported the implementation of reformulated petrol and low-sulphur diesel fuel for all on-road vehicles in Canada. It has argued that air quality benefits from so-called 'alternative fuels' vary widely and that leaner motor vehicle fuels can help to improve air quality. From 1992 to 1994, STOP was an active participant on Environment Canada's advisory committee, which helped to develop the National Pollutant Release Inventory (NPRI). The NPRI requires larger factories in Canada to report annually on their releases to the environment of more than 100 chemicals.

Lobbying at international level

Throughout the 1980s, STOP was an active member of the Canadian Coalition on Acid Rain. STOP argued that Canada would have to put its own house in order before it could hope to influence US action on sulphur dioxide (SO_2) emission reductions from over 200 coal-fired power plants. In 1981, STOP submitted a brief to the House of Commons subcommittee on acid rain and testified at the hearings. The brief focused on the inadequacies of the federal and provincial control programmes, particularly on uncontrolled SO_2 emissions from the Noranda copper smelter in north-western Quebec, and on weak federal nitrogen oxides (NO_x) exhaust emission standards for new cars. Several STOP recommendations were incorporated in the first report of the subcommittee, entitled 'Still Waters'. In 1983, STOP's research director, Bruce Walker, spent two weeks in Washington, DC, as a guest of the US Information Agency to pursue Canada–US clean air issues, in particular acid rain. In 1985, STOP's efforts began to bear fruit when Quebec required Noranda to reduce its SO_2 emissions by 50% by 1990. In 1987, Canada imposed tighter NO_x emission rules for new cars. In March 1991, Canada and the United States signed an Air Quality Accord dealing with acid rain and STOP was invited to witness the signing ceremony in Ottawa. Also, in 1986, STOP presented a brief and made a presentation to the United Nations Brundtland Commission on Environment and Development hearings in Ottawa. A STOP member served on the National Task Force on Environment and Economy that was set to recommend Canada's response.

◢ Opposing specific business projects

In 1993, STOP and many other environmental groups were involved in Montreal's waste management plan. At stake was a contract with the multinational corporation, Foster Wheeler, for the construction and maintenance of an incinerator. A coalition of groups objected to the contract since they believed that its nature and the scope of the equipment employed would discourage efforts to decrease the quantity of waste produced in the first place. In other words, even though the ability of technology (the projected incinerator) to reduce atmospheric emissions was recognised (compared to older incinerators), the incineration option was discredited because it only provided a second-best solution. In addition, this option was applied at the end of the consumption management process, rather than at the beginning. The project was thus considered by opponents to be an unacceptable choice for environmental reasons as well as for economic reasons. Indeed, on that issue, 'tax dollars' were central to their arguments. At the end of a public hearing on the issue, the commissaries recommended the cancellation of the project for environmental, social and economic reasons. However, the commissaries had only a recommendation power and, at the time, the local authorities decided to go on with the project. Two years later, Foster Wheeler's contract with the regional waste management agency was finally cancelled because, as a result of the lobbying efforts of opponents such as STOP, an increasing number of local authorities changed their view on the value of the incinerator project.

◢ Multi-stakeholder collaboration processes

A multi-stakeholder collaborative process (MCP) is defined as an interaction mechanism at the 'domain' level based on a consensual decision-making process that brings together various stakeholders (Gray 1989; Wood and Gray 1991) in order to accomplish a 'metamission' or to solve a 'metaproblem'. A domain is defined as a diverse group of stakeholders who are linked by a shared problem or a mutual interest. In other words, a MCP refers to collaborative initiatives among the representatives of firms, industry, governmental organisations, and non-governmental organisations. MCPs have often been presented as new mechanisms of co-ordination between various stakeholders and economic organisations in order to solve metaproblems, which neither the market alone nor the regulatory approaches could solve (Kelman 1992).

In Canada, the report from the National Workforce on the Environment and the Economy (1987) recommended the creation of the National Round Tables on the Environment and the Economy, in order to gather together the stakeholders concerned with environmental issues (governments, businesses, environmental organisations, unions, universities and indigenous people). This approach has rapidly been adopted at various levels of government (federal, provincial, regional, municipal) and, in 1995, more than 200 MCPs were accounted for across Canada (Babin 1995). Since 1989, STOP has been involved in more than 20 multi-stakeholder committees and collaboration processes, such as the Nitrogen Oxides (NO_x) and Volatile Organic Compounds (VOC) Management Plan Advisory Committee organised under the auspices of the Canadian Council of Environmental Ministers (CCME), the National Packaging Protocol Task Force, the Federal-Provincial Acid Rain Task Group, the National Pollutant Release Inventory Working Group and the *Table de collaboration 3R*.

Turcotte (1997a, 1997b) has thoroughly studied the case of the *Table de collaboration 3R*. In this specific case, the MCP provided a space for interaction among the participants, giving them opportunity to listen to each other and express their views on ways to influence current practices by intervention on the markets, by regulation or by way of cultural change. In short, the MCP offered the opportunity to develop consensus on general statements, to learn about the domain and to incrementally innovate (double-loop learning). This, in turn, contributed to giving a direction to the domain, to augmenting a problem's tractability, and finally to solving the environmental meta-problems addressed by the MCP. (See Turcotte 1997a, 1997b for more information on the outcomes and limits of this MCP.) Studies of more cases will be needed to fully assess the value of MCPs toward sustainable development.

◢ Consultation contracts

In the 1990s, STOP received a fee from Hydro-Quebec, a major utility company in Quebec, in exchange for consultation services. In the autumn of 1993, the strategic planning department of Hydro-Quebec initiated a consultation, which was supposed to be concluded in 1995 with the publication of the development plan for 1995. The rules for public participation within this business consultation process were established by Hydro-Quebec: the company was consulting on issues over which it had control; the company was ready to be influenced through the consultation but was to remain responsible for its decisions. The purpose of the consultation was to obtain input from organisations representative of various stakeholders in society (Hydro-Quebec 1994). A financial compensation (between $18,000 and $25,000) was made available by Hydro-Quebec to support the participation of NGOs.

For the first year and a half, meetings were regularly organised where representatives from business, professional, social and environmental groups expressed their views on Hydro-Quebec options. The views of the various participants for the most part conflicted.

Unfortunately, it is not possible to assess the outcomes of this business consultation because it was postponed and eventually cancelled when a ministerial public hearing on energy was announced. Nevertheless, in 1996 and 1997, STOP received other consulting contracts from Hydro-Quebec to provide written reports on STOP's perspective on energy and environment-related issues.

◢ 'Natural alliances'

Turcotte (1995) has described the 'natural alliances' between environmental groups and those industries or companies that gave rise to alternatives that were less harmful to the environment. The naming of this category was inspired by the fact that natural alliances alternatively or simultaneously refer to: (1) alliances that develop 'naturally' because the actors have common interests; and (2) the common interests are related to respect for the natural environment. In this case the use of the term 'alliance' does not imply a formal relationship, but a situation where the NGO works toward the same objectives as a company, albeit often for different motives. Four types of alliance are identified: suggesting improvements; lobbying to obtain environmental services; industry development; and public relations initiatives.

Suggesting improvements

The relationships of many environmental groups with the public transport industry provide a prime example for natural alliances. STOP has often supported public transportation as a way of protecting the environment and thus could be seen as a promoter of that industry. However, STOP's initiative toward public transportation was not limited to the promotion of its use but also included critical comments for service improvements. Over the years, STOP has taken many opportunities to offer critical comments and suggestions for improving the services of the *Société de Transport de la Communauté Urbaine de Montréal* (STCUM). For instance, STOP was critical of the design of the new buses introduced by the STCUM in 1996 because they were uncomfortable for passengers. The rationale behind this critical approach was that, in order to increase the use of public transportation, the quality of the service should not only be maintained (despite an often difficult financial situation for public transportation firms) but it should also be improved.

Lobbying to obtain environmental services

Since 1970, STOP has been notifying the public that the sewage on the Island of Montreal was not treated in any manner before being discharged into the St Lawrence River. STOP aimed to sensitise municipal, regional and provincial authorities on the issue and filed legal suits to stop the pollution of the river. In 1975, the regional agency responsible for environment services, the *Communauté Urbaine de Montréal* (CUM), started the construction of a collection system to transfer the sewage water to a purification plant. The purification plant construction started in 1980 and it became operational in 1988, but only a small amount of the Island sewage water was then treated. Therefore STOP continued its campaign and succeeded in convincing the authorities to add, in addition to the physical treatment initially planned, chemical treatments that would extract phosphates and most of the heavy metals. Since 1996, all of the Island sewage water is now being purified with a physico-chemical treatment. STOP activities have thus contributed not only to obtaining a better environment, but also to creating opportunities for the environmental service-related industries.

Industry development

Since 1970, STOP has been involved with the selective collection of domestic waste, not only by lobbying governments to promote this industry and in public education, but also at the operational level (see Table 9.1). Indeed, along with other NGOs, STOP has been instrumental in the experimentation of the selective collection operations and in the further development of that industry in Quebec.

Public relations initiatives

Another example of a natural alliance was when the NGO acted as a public relations agent for selective waste collection companies. In 1993, STOP was informed that the public agency responsible for waste management in the Montreal suburbs was about to reject bids for selective waste collection and recycling on the basis that these bids were too costly. STOP members were concerned that this would lead to a total abandonment of selective collection and recycling and so began discussing the issue with managers of the various companies involved. They discovered operational and financial problems in the formulation of tenders and wrote a report, pointing out to the agency and to the public that the problems were related to the specifics of the tenders and not to selective collection *per se*. Following this initiative, the initial vote was cancelled and the door-to-door selective collection of waste was resumed. By 1995, the collection of waste proved to be a profitable activity, generating revenue for the municipality.

◢ Discussion and conclusion

This chapter has shown that one NGO can have a complex set of conflictual and collaborative relations with corporations. What are the influences of these relationships on the role of business in sustainable development? Lobbying for more environmental regulations and stricter enforcement, as well as opposing specific business development projects, are most often perceived to be in conflict with business interests and economic development. This view, however, should be nuanced by two considerations.

| Year | EVENTS | OPERATIONS | | |
		OPERATIONS	PUBLIC EDUCATION	INFORMING GOVERNMENTS
1970	STOP's volunteers organised the selective collection of newspapers and glass.	✓	(✓)	
1974	STOP organised the selective collection of 78,000 telephone books (the equivalent of 2,500 trees).	✓	(✓)	
1979	STOP organised a competition, 'Renaissance', to promote the re-use of products and materials.		✓	
1979	STOP presented the Quebec government with a petition to introduce a deposit system for wine bottles.		(✓)	✓
1981	A STOP brief recommended the Quebec government to orient its grants and policies in order to promote the installation of de-inking plant and the development of stable markets for recycled material.	(✓)		✓
1989	Since 1989, STOP has closely monitored the activities of the *Régie intermunicipale de gestion des déchets sur l'île de Montréal* (RIGDIM, regional agency responsible for waste management).	(✓)		✓
1993	Following many unsuccessful calls for services, the RIGDIM voted to cancel the door-to-door selective collection of waste programme. STOP took the initiative to consult the entrepreneurs and showed to the RIGDIM that the higher costs of the bids were pertaining to the specifics of the calls for tenders. Following this initiative, the calls for tenders were revised with more efficient specifications, the initial vote was cancelled and the door-to-door selective collection of waste was resumed.	(✓)		✓
1993	STOP informed the public that domestic waste selective collection proved to be a profitable activity. By analysing the case of one municipality, STOP showed that door-to-door selective collection was not more expensive than traditional waste collection. Following this, another municipality became the first in Quebec to be paid by the company providing the selective collection services.	(✓)		✓

✓ Category of activity to which the event corresponds
(✓) The event has an influence on this category of activity

Table 9.1 **Involvement of the environment group STOP in the development of the selective collection of waste industry in Quebec**

The first consideration pertains to the fragmentation of business and industrial communities. Competition and conflict of interest exist among industries. For instance, the gas industry is in competition with the hydroelectric industry to sell energy. There are also conflicts of interest regarding environmental regulations within an industry. For instance, environmental leaders within an industry (or 'best of sector') might consider more stringent regulations favourably as it would 'level the playing field'. These leaders would then profit from a competitive advantage over their rival: while the leaders will have already gained the 'know-how' by managing these environmental constraints, the other competitors will suffer from significant operational burdens.

The second consideration pertains to an argument put forward by Porter and van der Linde (1995). According to these management strategists, properly designed environmental standards can trigger innovations that lower the total cost of a product (resource productivity), improve its value, and thus improve competitiveness. This view is contrary to the prevailing view that environmental regulations erode competitiveness. The improvement in resource productivity is often the key to enhancing competitiveness. Epstein and Roy (1997) claimed that managing environmental issues effectively contributes to competitive advantage, especially when environmentally related cost data are identified with the support of managerial accountants. In this sense, lobbying for more environmental regulations and opposing specific business projects would not only contribute to protecting the environment, but also would contribute to achieving a better (or at least different) economic development, benefiting certain companies.

Participation in multi-stakeholder initiatives and consultation contracts reflects the building of bridges (Westley and Vredenburg 1991) between business organisations and environmental NGOs. They provide a ground for dialogue, which can prove to be beneficial for corporations. Theoretical development by Hofstede (1980) and Pestoff (1990) can be helpful in attempting to assess the value for a company and for society of consulting critical NGOs, such as STOP. Indeed, in order to ward off the tendency to listen only to those who share an organisation's own values, Hofstede (1980) suggested that firms should be open to the insights provided by civic action groups. In fact, these groups are essential to the spread of social and political innovations that the institutional and political establishments could never generate on their own. Pestoff (1990) described how the Swedish government had institutionalised a role of 'counter-power' for non-profit consumer organisations by giving them official mandates within regulatory agencies. According to Pestoff (1990), the institutionalisation of dialogue between civic action groups and businesses could be more efficient at the company level, as well as at the collective level, since social demands would thereby be acknowledged more readily.

The 'natural alliances' described above do not preclude the environmental NGO from criticising its business ally, and the outcomes of the critical dialogue that then arise can be understood in a positive sense, given Hofstede (1980) and Pestoff's (1990) analyses. Such dialogue could accelerate the company's capability of integrating new demands from the clientele rather than having to wait for a buy/no buy response from the market. Furthermore, the increased demands and constraints could stimulate innovation and enhance the competitiveness of the business organisation.

In conclusion, the case study showed that the environmental NGO, STOP, through its various types of relationship with business organisations, helped shape aspects of the economy in order to make it less environmentally damaging. Lobbying for more environmental regulations, opposing specific business development projects, and participating in multi-stakeholder initiatives, consultation contracts and 'natural alliances', all contributed to the ecological, social and economic dimensions of sustainable development.

BRIDGING TROUBLED WATERS
The Marine Stewardship Council

Penny Fowler and Simon Heap

INTRAC: The International NGO Training and Research Centre, UK

The Marine Stewardship Council (MSC) is the product of a partnership between the international NGO, World Wide Fund for Nature (WWF), and the multinational company, Unilever plc. Established in February 1997, the MSC's mission is to work for sustainable marine fisheries by promoting responsible, environmentally appropriate, socially beneficial and economically viable fisheries practices, while maintaining the biodiversity, productivity and ecological processes of the marine environment.

The MSC has established a broad set of principles and criteria for certification of sustainable fisheries. Only fisheries meeting these standards will be eligible for certification by independent accredited certifying firms. Ultimately, products from fisheries certified to MSC standards will be marked with an on-pack logo, allowing consumers to select seafood products they know come from sustainable, well-managed fisheries.

This article analyses the motivations, organisational issues, key benefits and challenges for WWF and Unilever arising from the partnership and explores the lessons of this process for future business–NGO partnerships.

◢ The WWF–Unilever partnership

The WWF–Unilever partnership was established on the basis of a shared objective to ensure the long-term viability of global fish stocks. However, the motivations for each partner in pursuing a common objective are considerably different and relate to their respective organisational missions.

WWF is the world's largest independent conservation organisation with more than five million supporters. WWF's mission is to protect the diversity of life on earth. It is a science-based, practical organisation that practises, and raises funds for, the conservation of wildlife and habitats in the UK and around the world (WWF 1997, 1998). WWF's motivation to establish the MSC is driven by its mission to protect marine biodiversity and the environment. WWF's Endangered Seas Campaign aims specifically to address the issue of declining global fish stocks and WWF considers the MSC to offer a fundamentally new approach for achieving that goal.

Unilever's corporate purpose is:

> to meet the everyday needs of people everywhere—to anticipate the aspira-
> tions of . . . consumers and customers and to respond creatively and competi-
> tively with branded products and services which raise the quality of life
> (Unilever 1998).

Unilever's motivations to establish the MSC coincide with its business objectives of ensuring long-term financial returns to its investors. Unilever is one of the world's largest buyers of fish, controlling about 25% of the frozen fish market in Europe and the US, and declining fish stocks present a clear risk to Unilever's fish business.

◢ The global fisheries crisis

Fish provides 20% of the world's animal protein supply, with the consumption of industrialised countries being about three times that of southern countries. Fishing is one of the world's most important economic activities: there are an estimated 12.5 million fish workers globally. With their families, those directly dependent on fishing for their livelihood amount to 50 million people (Murphy and Bendell 1997a).

The backdrop to the MSC initiative is a crisis in global fisheries. According to the United Nations Food and Agriculture Organisation (FAO)'s report, *The State of World Fisheries and Aquaculture 1996*, 60% of the world's 200 most valuable commercial fish stocks are overfished or fished to the limit (MSC 1998). In some areas, excessive fishing has driven staple species such as northern cod and Atlantic halibut to commercial extinction. Worldwide, governments pay tens of billions of dollars annually in fisheries subsidies to an industry that catches only $70 billion-worth of fish. Contemporary fishing practices waste 18–40 million metric tons of undersized and unwanted fish and kill untold numbers of seabirds, turtles, marine mammals and other ocean life annually (MSC 1996). Consequently, when WWF-International launched its Living Planet Campaign in 1995, it identified 'Endangered Seas' as one of its main campaigning issues for the coming years.

◢ The partnering process

Like many global environmental problems, the fisheries crisis appeared to have its roots in the action of unrestrained market forces and a paralysed intergovernmental process. Whereas WWF had targeted national and intergovernmental bodies for a number of years, with limited success, the market had been largely overlooked. Consequently, WWF's Marine Advisory Group decided that they should consider a new approach and target the demand side of the fishing industry: consumers and business. On sabbatical from WWF-US, Michael Sutton was hired by WWF-International to work on fisheries as part of the Living Planet Campaign. One of the stated objectives for the Endangered Seas Campaign was to create social and economic incentives for sustainable fisheries, not as a replacement for legislation but as a potential catalyst to spur governments to take the necessary steps.

Previously, WWF's Forest Programme had initiated the Forest Stewardship Council (FSC) in 1993, in collaboration with DIY retailers, particularly B&Q (see Chapter 12). The FSC sets standards for, and promotes certification of, forests and forest products on the basis of environmental and social principles. It evaluates, accredits and monitors independent certification organisations that inspect forests around the world and certify them if they meet the FSC Principles of Forest Management. The similarity of the MSC's name is no coincidence. Murphy and Bendell (1997a) describe the influence the FSC experience had in the original conception of the MSC, with the open-plan office at WWF's headquarters in Surrey enabling WWF Endangered Seas Campaign staff to learn informally about the FSC and consider its applicability to fisheries. Subsequently, a member of the WWF's Forest team at the time, Jem Bendell, was contracted to investigate the potential of developing a 'Marine' Stewardship Council. This suggests that the skills acquired and developed by NGO staff in the general area of market-oriented campaigns can be transferred from one industrial sector to another, and from one sustainability issue to another.

Unilever has an organisational commitment to sustainability which is set out in various publications, including an annual *Environment Report*, the first of which appeared in 1996. The 'Chairmen's [Sir Michael Perry and Morris Tabaksblat] Message' stated that:

> . . . environmental performance is a central issue for the Company and one which has a direct bearing on long-term business success . . . Unilever's environment policy confirms our intention to continue to lead the Company towards carrying out its business in an environmentally sustainable way . . . and our continuing determination to contribute to the well-being of the communities which we serve (Unilever 1996).

In 1997, Unilever produced a statement on sustainability outlining Unilever's three-level approach to the subject:

1. Producing safe products from clean processes as efficiently as possible; in short: eco-efficiency

2. Encouraging more sustainable consumption patterns

3. Engaging with others to build effective partnerships to deliver real solutions to the challenge of sustainability (Unilever 1997)

As part of the second level of its commitment to sustainability, Unilever has developed a tool to help it understand the overall impact of its business activities on the environment: the *Unilever Imprint*. This enables Unilever to develop a shared understanding of its environmental impact and to agree priorities for action.

Although fish was not at the top of Unilever's sustainability agenda according to the *Unilever Imprint* analysis, concerns about the long-term availability of fish supplies existed and Unilever was in touch with scientists undertaking research into the state of future global fish stocks. In 1995, Jackie McGlade, a researcher at Warwick University, informed Unilever and WWF of their mutual interest in this issue. Soon after, Simon Bryceson of Burson-Marsteller, the world's largest PR firm that specialises in 'perception management', became involved in facilitating dialogue between Unilever and WWF. Unilever is a long-standing client of Burson-Marsteller and it had already sought advice from Bryceson about its existing dialogue on sustainable fisheries with Greenpeace (Germany). Bryceson advised Unilever that WWF was a more suitable partner than Greenpeace on the grounds that WWF is a more 'conservative' NGO with previous experience of working with business through the FSC.[1]

For WWF and Unilever to come together to work in partnership towards a mutual objective requires a shared perception of the added value of the partnership, over and above what each organisation could achieve on its own. Through partnership, WWF recognised that it could offer Unilever the possibility of an enhanced environmentally friendly image in return for Unilever supporting the development of the MSC and making certain concrete changes in its fish-buying practices. For Unilever, the choice of an NGO partner resulted from a recognition that a solution was required to address the problem of declining world fish stocks that was broader than a purely industrial response. This was because a variety of different stakeholders would need to be brought on board, including competitors, customers, suppliers and fishing fleets, if the whole market was to begin to demand more sustainable fishing practices. Unilever saw WWF as a likely partner because it had already established a history of engaging in partnerships to solve conservation problems: for example, through its involvement in the development of the FSC. Additionally, WWF has an international network equivalent to Unilever which the partnership could utilise to promote the initiative and a public profile likely to appeal to Unilever's customers. In addition, the International Projects Manager at Unilever, Amanda Long, suggests that the company's culture of partnership, dating back to Unilever's formation as a merger between the Dutch company Unie and the UK Lever Bros, facilitated the company's willingness to work closely with WWF.[2]

There was considerable internal resistance within both WWF and Unilever to working with the other. WWF fisheries staff were concerned about how the partnership might affect their relations with intergovernmental agencies and coalitions of other NGOs and fishworker unions. Others, not working on the fisheries issue, were worried that a partner-

1   Interview with S. Bryceson and N. Bent, Public Affairs Department, Burson-Marsteller, London, 7 September 1998.
2   Interview with A. Long, International Projects Manager, Unilever, Walton-on-Thames, UK, 5 November 1998.

ship between one part of WWF and one part of Unilever might give a green hue to all of Unilever's operations, including chemicals and agricultural commodities, where WWF might be in conflict with the company. More fundamentally, some environmental activists have a fixed oppositional stance against working with business resulting from their analysis that there is no place for multinational companies in a sustainable future. WWF employees sharing this view felt uncomfortable with the Unilever partnership and made their concerns known, occasionally in public. WWF presents itself as a solutions-focused NGO that offers alternatives as well as criticism, however, and the Unilever partnership was supported by the WWF management as the logical application of this philosophy.

The internal reward system within a multinational company such as Unilever is not conducive to the development of creative market mechanisms for environmental sustainability. With a fairly rapid turnover in staff between different posts and depart-ments, incentives revolve around short-term profitability, and employees are unlikely to change their practices if it potentially jeopardises their chance of meeting a target and getting a bonus. Therefore, the NGO partnership was approved within Unilever largely because it won the backing of Antony Burgmans (now vice-chairman of Unilever). Burgmans recognised the MSC's potential contribution towards Unilever's long-term strategic business objectives and his support was crucial to the partnership in the face of substantial resistance from some Unilever employees, particularly operational staff, who have a less strategic and more short-term, profit-driven perspective.

Getting this commitment from the top, which resulted in early 1996 in a joint statement of intent to establish the MSC being signed by directors of WWF and Unilever, required a certain degree of pressure and persuasion from below. Key actors from each organisation played a crucial role in overcoming internal political obstacles and gaining a critical mass of support for the partnership. According to Sutton of WWF, it is no coincidence that two North Americans, himself and Caroline Whitfield (ex-Unilever), drove the idea of the MSC. There is far greater experience and acceptance of NGOs working with business in North America than in Europe. As a Canadian, Whitfield had seen the devastating impact of the collapse of fish stocks in Newfoundland and this further explains her interest and commitment in securing the partnership with WWF.

◢ The MSC standards, structure and governance

The objective of this business–NGO partnership was to build a new institution to generate market incentives for sustainable, responsible fishing. To do this, the new institution would have to manage three key processes relating to standards: their development and review, their implementation and their promotion. An accreditation council model was seen as the most appropriate way of managing these processes, where standards would be developed and reviewed by interested stakeholders, implemented by accredited certification bodies, and promoted by the secretariat of the accreditation council.

The MSC Principles and Criteria for sustainable fisheries determine the basis for assessment and, if successful, certification of fisheries throughout the world (see Box 10.1). From September 1996, a series of international workshops in the UK, Australia, New Zealand, Germany, USA, Canada, South Africa and Scandinavia discussed a draft MSC standard. Further consultations have since been conducted in developing countries, in Africa, Latin America and Asia, and a consulting firm has been hired to oversee this process (MSC 1998).

The consultations sought to cover a wide range of stakeholders involved in world fisheries. From 1997, the MSC started to establish National Working Groups in different countries, which are intended to provide a direct line of communication between fisheries representatives and the MSC Advisory Board. To date, there are National Working Groups in the UK, Germany, the Netherlands and a process has begun to set up formal dialogue in Argentina, Chile, Ecuador, Mexico and Peru in Latin America. The MSC has also initiated a series of certification and feasibility studies to contribute to the further development of the Principles and Criteria and to provide insights into the practical issues involved in fisheries certification. The MSC has drafted a manual to guide its accreditation of independent certifiers wishing to undertake certification of fisheries. The first certification began in spring 1999: the Thames–Blackwater Herring Drift Net Fishery, a small-scale enterprise of trawlermen supplying Sainsbury's Essex stores; Australia's Western rock-lobster fishery; and the similarly large and valuable business of the Alaskan salmon fishery, made up of thousands of operators catching 200 million wild salmon a year (Tickell 1999a).

The MSC was initially established under an Interim Board chaired, in his personal capacity, by Roger Cooke, Senior Partner at Coopers & Lybrand (now Pricewaterhouse-

Box 10.1 **MSC principles and criteria**

THE THREE MSC PRINCIPLES REFLECT THE MSC'S DEFINITION OF SUSTAINABLE marine fisheries (see p. 142) and form the basis for detailed criteria that will be used to evaluate each fishery seeking certification under the MSC programme:

1. A fishery must be conducted in a manner that does not lead to over-fishing or depletion of the exploited populations and, for those populations that are depleted, the fishery must be conducted in a manner that demonstrably leads to their recovery.

2. Fishing operations should allow for the maintenance of the structure, productivity, function and diversity of the ecosystem (including habitat and associated dependent and ecologically related species) on which the fishery depends.

3. The fishery is subject to an effective management system that respects local, national and international laws and standards and incorporates institutional and operational frameworks that require use of the resource to be responsible and sustainable.

The MSC Principles and Criteria relate only to marine fishes and invertebrates and to marine fisheries activities up to but not beyond the point at which the fish are landed.

Coopers) and comprising members from WWF and Unilever. This was disbanded in February 1998, and in June 1998 the seed funding from the founding partners ended and the MSC became independent, with funding from a number of charitable trusts. The perceived, and actual, independence of the MSC is crucial to its credibility as a neutral body because its business is to set global, industry-wide standards in a multi-stakeholder industry, and a lot of time and money has been expended in pursuit of this goal.

Since the MSC's full independence, Unilever is no longer involved in either the day-to-day running of the MSC or its promotion. Unilever's competitors tolerated the company's involvement in the early stages of the MSC's evolution but now want Unilever out in order to have confidence in the capacity of the MSC to operate as an independent standard-setting and accreditation body.

The intention to create an inclusive, stakeholder-driven body has meant a somewhat complex governance structure. The MSC has a Board of Trustees with a maximum of ten members, appointed in their personal capacities, which meets formally once a year. The Rt Hon. John Gummer MP (a former UK government minister with responsibility for the environment) has been recruited as chair of the Board of Trustees and board members are currently being recruited. Board members are appointed by the chair after consultation with other board members and are required to have an international background. The intention is to recruit a balanced board membership to ensure that no one nationality or stakeholder interest predominates. Board members are nominated for a three-year term, are automatically trustees of the charity, and represent the MSC in public.

An MSC Advisory Board comprises stakeholders who advise the Board of Trustees and Standards Council and put forward the views and considerations of the National Working Groups. The Advisory Board meets every two years and is intended to provide a vehicle for open and transparent discussion of issues. Between meetings, the board communicates frequently via the Internet, which facilitates low-cost international dialogue (Tickell 1999a). The Advisory Board is comprised of three chambers from the following three key stakeholder groups:

1. Those that make an economic living from the seas

2. Those that have an environmental conservation perspective on the use of marine resources

3. Those with an educational, social or consumer perspective on the use of marine resources

Chairs of National Working Groups automatically become members of the Advisory Board. National Working Groups are intended to provide guidance on all aspects of the MSC's activities and to promote the use of the MSC certification and logo scheme. Their members are stakeholders who ensure that national and regional considerations are represented and taken into account by the MSC. In addition to the National Working Groups, the MSC website[3] enables anyone with access to the Internet to participate in discussions about the MSC.

3   www.msc.org

A range of committees and working parties will increasingly oversee the functioning of the MSC's work. For example, each chamber that comprises part of the Advisory Board elects nine representatives to sit on the MSC Standards Council which will have the responsibility and authority to further develop the MSC principles, criteria and certification standards. These committees and working groups are accountable to the Board of Trustees.

The MSC Secretariat is based in London and is responsible for day-to-day activities, including fundraising, accreditation, developing and licensing the MSC logo, education, promotion and publicity for the MSC's work. The board appoints a chief executive who heads the Secretariat. Profits from the trading company, MSC International, are covenanted back to the MSC.

The MSC Development Director is responsible for raising funds for the core operating costs of the MSC on the basis of a business plan. This plan sets out the likely time-frame within which sufficient income will be generated through the accreditation of certifiers for the MSC to become financially independent. Clearly this time-frame will be affected by many factors outside of the MSC's direct control such as the pace of fisheries certification, retailers getting certified products on the shelves and consumer take-up of products bearing the MSC logo. Board members are involved in fundraising efforts through their international contacts. The majority of the MSC's funding is presently derived from US and, to a lesser extent UK, foundations. Possible future sources of funds for the MSC include businesses and national governments.

The MSC Principles and Criteria form the basis for the assessment of fisheries by independent certification bodies accredited to the MSC. Fisheries that are deemed to comply with the MSC criteria and principles through this assessment will be awarded MSC certification. The MSC Principles and Criteria provide globally applicable standards by which sustainable fishing can be measured for any commercial fishery throughout the world. One benefit of this is that it appears to comply with World Trade Organisation (WTO) rules requiring that no WTO member country discriminates between like products imported from other WTO member countries.

The MSC's broad definition of sustainable marine fisheries are those that:

> ensure that the catch of marine resources is at a level compatible with long term sustainable yield, while maintaining the marine environment's bio-diversity, productivity and ecological processes, taking into account:

- relevant laws
- ecological sustainability and ecosystem integrity
- responsible and effective management systems
- benefits from the fishery
- social considerations.[4]

Unilever is currently undertaking test cases with key suppliers as part of a strategy to fulfil its pledge of sourcing all its fishery products from sustainable sources by 2005. The setting

---

4   MSC website, www.msc.org

of this target lends credibility to the MSC and demonstrates Unilever's commitment to taking concrete action towards achieving the goal of sustainable marine fisheries.

As a means of promoting the MSC, stakeholders are offered the opportunity to publicly endorse the MSC's mission by signing a Letter of Support to become MSC signatories. To date, the MSC has attracted almost 100 signatories, the majority being either food retailers, fish buyers or fish processors, around a dozen conservation organisations and a handful of fish-workers' organisations.

◢ A model stewardship council?

The MSC is the second stewardship council established with the involvement of WWF and private-sector companies. Is there an emerging model for business–NGO partnerships based on these two experiences? A comparison of the separate processes to establish the FSC and MSC highlights key differences and questions about the potential replicability of the stewardship council model in other sectors such as agricultural commodities, oil or mining.

The MSC and the FSC are the same in that they are both joint exercises by NGOs and industry to promote a market-led solution to an environmental problem. Both the FSC and the MSC involve the development by an independent council of principles and criteria for certification and eco-labelling. The certification is undertaken by independent certification bodies and paid for by companies. From the point of view of WWF, both initiatives are intended to influence industries reliant on natural resources.

Where the MSC fundamentally differs from the FSC is in terms of the process of consultation to establish the Council and to determine its governance structure. In the case of the FSC, stakeholders were directly involved in determining key principles and organisational concepts for the FSC. In contrast, although the governance structure of the MSC stresses the importance of inclusivity, the origin of the MSC was the partnership between WWF and Unilever and the structure and governance of the MSC was proposed by the partners (after taking advice from Coopers & Lybrand) who then carried out initial consultations. This was partly in response to the experience of the process to establish the FSC which was expensive and time-consuming. There was a perceived trade-off by WWF and Unilever between undertaking lengthy consultations with all stakeholders and making a more substantial and timely impact on the industry. WWF agreed to forgo a 'traditional' NGO consultation process in order to streamline the development of the MSC and secure the maximum industry support possible. This contrast in levels and processes of stakeholder participation is not restricted to the consultation process but also applies to the governance structure of the different councils.

Whereas the FSC is a membership organisation that helps to engender a sense of belonging and ownership for those involved, Coopers & Lybrand advised against this structure for the MSC on the grounds that it would impose rigidity and result in overly complex and time-consuming decision-making procedures. They could not have regarded the principle of democratic stakeholder participation as essential for achieving the aims of the partners, and advised that the MSC could always become a membership organisation in the future but could never revert to become a non-membership organisation if it was initially established with a membership. This advice was accepted and, although a series of stakeholder consultations has been undertaken to discuss the MSC's Principles and Criteria, the ultimate decision on issues of structure and governance rests with the MSC board in what could be described as a top-down model of institution-building.

One of the key factors for the success of the FSC is that it embraced a wide range of people and organisations in a democratic governance model in order to make them feel they have a stake in the organisation (Murphy and Bendell 1997a). This has enabled FSC stakeholders to overcome seemingly insoluble problems and disputes. The MSC does not attempt to be democratic in its governance and this accounts for some of the challenges to the MSC's credibility, particularly within the international development NGO community which regards inclusive consultation and democratic decision-making processes as crucial for legitimacy and effectiveness.

There has already been a vigorous debate about the MSC among its stakeholders. All stakeholders expressed initial anxieties about how the MSC will work in practice, although many welcomed the initiative as a step forward. The fishing industry has presented the greatest resistance to the MSC. It is suspicious about the central role of Unilever (its main customer) and WWF-International (its perceived rival) in establishing the MSC. Some Northern governments, fearful of independent scrutiny of their fisheries management regimes, have also opposed the MSC.[5]

In July 1996, an editorial in *Samudra*, the newsletter of the International Collective in Support of Fishworkers (ICSF) declared that:

> The MSC initiative has not won the total confidence of fishing communities, either in the North or the South because of their great distrust of Unilever. The idea would have been taken far more seriously by fishworkers' organisations had WWF consulted them before plunging in.

The MSC is clearly aware of the need for a sense of ownership of the initiative by stakeholders, but this remains an issue of contention for some stakeholders. Julia Novy, Developing Countries Consultant for the MSC, states that:

> Any initiative which aims to bring about changes in fisheries practices is most likely to succeed if those who are changing their behaviour feel that they 'own' the initiative . . . Facilitating ownership of the initiative among stakeholders requires recognition of the interdisciplinary nature of fisheries (MSC 1998).

However, some commentators regard democratic participation as central to the effectiveness of civil institutions such as the MSC, so that attempts at developing a 'feeling' of ownership among stakeholders fall short of real participation through joint ownership (Bendell 1998). Other commentators are inherently suspicious of Unilever's agenda in establishing the MSC, given the company's contribution to the depletion of global fish

5   Interview with M. Sutton, Director, WWF-International Endangered Seas Campaign, Godalming, UK, 27 August 1998.

stocks over the years and the fundamentally unequal power relationship between a multinational company such as Unilever and poor fishing communities in the South. Unilever's approach to sustainability does not match the views of some NGOs; they consider that Unilever's interests simply do not coincide with the interests of their key constituents, such as the conservation of the world's natural resources and the improvement of the lives of the poor and marginalised in developing countries. Some Northern development NGOs have expressed strong reservations about the ability of eco-labels to promote truly sustainable consumption patterns in Europe and the United States which they regard as being essential to the achievement of sustainable livelihoods for poor fishing communities in developing countries.

A lack of confidence in the ability of the MSC to include sustainable fisheries criteria that fully reflect the social, cultural and livelihood interests of the majority in fishing communities appears key among the concerns of some development NGOs and fishworkers' groups. Some NGOs oppose the fundamental concept of certification systems such as the MSC on the grounds that eco-labels will never address the root causes of global poverty and may exacerbate already unequal power relations:

> The MSC is based on a Northern driven neoliberal agenda . . . The MSC's interest in the South would seem to be mainly as a source of fish products which could be accredited. Fish sporting the MSC label will only be marketed in the North . . . It will be easier for the MSC to certify fisheries on scientific evidence, rather than on more socially based traditional knowledge systems (O'Riordan 1996).

Sutton of WWF considers the criticism from development NGOs to be misdirected because the biggest problems facing global fisheries are in the North. Southern fisheries tend to be more sustainable simply because they are smaller-scale. He argues that some small-scale fishers in the South have been excited about the prospect of certification through the MSC because they see it as an opportunity to open up new export markets and gain advantage over their offshore competitors.

Murphy and Bendell (1997a) defend the MSC from claims that it will threaten unemployment in the fishing industry by arguing that, if certification is structured so as to discriminate against capitalised, industrial and large-scale fishing (the major cause of fishery decline), the reduction of catch and the stimulation of employment can be mutually achievable objectives. They believe that the MSC could help to switch market demand to less technologically advanced, more labour-intensive fishing practices, resulting in a win–win scenario for global fishing communities.

Although the key actors involved in the MSC take a pragmatic view, recognising that they will never get all parties in the global fishing industry on board, they are also deeply aware of the potential threat to the MSC's credibility posed by strongly opposed stakeholders. Complex stakeholder relations demand sensitive management. The ability of the MSC to get—and keep—all of its stakeholders on board with the processes of setting standards and certification will be a key determinant of the success of the MSC.

◢ Summary and conclusions

On the basis of this analysis, it is possible to identify some key lessons of the WWF–Unilever partnership for companies and NGOs considering embarking on a joint initiative.

Both parties need to agree a well-defined but flexible plan at the outset which defines common ground and forms the basis of the partnership. Partnerships need adequate resources to be devoted to them to ensure effective management. It is essential that NGOs have professional staff to relate to businesses and that companies have the internal capacity necessary to deal with NGOs. Partnerships are about human relationships and it was a great help in the process to establish the MSC that the key individuals involved got on well at a personal level.

For business–NGO partnerships to work, NGOs must take the time to understand a business, what it does and its constraints in order to be able to propose realistic solutions. Likewise, companies must take the time to understand what NGOs do and their value. Successful partnerships are rooted in very practical considerations. Anything that an NGO can do to reduce a company's business risk—whether in terms of public relations or the financial bottom line—is useful and a potential basis for collaboration.

Partners can sometimes have different perceptions of each others' motivations. For example, WWF identifies the pressure on Unilever from Greenpeace (Germany) as a significant factor in bringing Unilever to the MSC partnership. However, Unilever claims that the role of environmental NGOs was not a fundamental driver for them: their main motivation was to address their supply problem. Since the power of external ideas is dissipated before it reaches the centre of a multinational company such as Unilever, it is important that NGOs correctly identify and reach core people with influence. For multinational companies, significant internal pressure is required to achieve policy change.

Similarly, if NGOs want to change an industry by working with one or a few companies, they must gain the support of the lead companies in the industry. Many companies in the fishing industry are not yet convinced of the importance of the MSC, but Unilever believes that those that are on board include the key driving companies. Incremental change in a key company can result in more substantial change throughout an industry.

Stakeholders can have very different perceptions of indicators that demonstrate a successful partnership. Although the broad objective may be the same, the indicators of success, particularly intermediary milestones, are likely to be different. WWF has set itself a target of having at least ten fisheries certified to MSC standards by 2001. For Unilever, the real success of the MSC depends not only on the MSC logo becoming internationally recognised and on Unilever achieving its target of sourcing all its fish from MSC-endorsed sources by 2005, but on improving the global fishery situation and therefore securing the long-term health of their business. This is why they partnered WWF rather than embarking on an industry-only scheme. In the short term, the partnership with WWF has already been beneficial to Unilever in other ways: in changing the culture in Unilever to make it more open to working with other groups in society in pursuit of common goals. Unilever staff have benefited from learning about the wider environmental impact of its activities and they are evidently proud of working with WWF.

To some observers—including the Control Risks Group (1997), McIntosh *et al.* (1998) and the World Business Council on Sustainable Development (WBCSD 1997)—the MSC is already considered a success, although the first fish products have yet to be certified. These people contrast the success of the MSC with the failure of governments and the United Nations to make progress in taking steps to protect global marine resources and suggest that a market-led initiative is required to solve a problem that has been caused by the market. McIntosh *et al.* are extremely encouraged by the MSC partnership. Their assessment is that 'this form of partnership between business and key stakeholder . . . could be the future for the solution of many of the world's problems' (1998: 226). They also note the consensus-building approach by WWF, although the market-led approach of the MSC might not find approval from other environmental NGOs.

Nevertheless, other NGOs can play a crucial indirect role in the partnering process. It was the funded research and media publicity of environmental NGOs such as Friends of the Earth, Greenpeace, the Royal Society for the Protection of Birds and the Sierra Club, as well as WWF, that brought the global fisheries crisis to the world's attention (McIntosh *et al.* 1998). NGOs that practise a policy of direct action can drive private-sector companies into the arms of more business-friendly NGOs. Regardless of joint initiatives such as the MSC, it is important that NGOs keep up their adversarial, uncompromising advocacy and action roles in order to maintain the pressure and incentives for companies to change. Referring to Elkington and Fennell's typology of NGOs (see Chapter 11), NGO 'sharks' can help NGO 'dolphins' in flushing out potential private-sector partners. But could contrasting NGO approaches be undertaken in a more co-ordinated fashion or will capricious NGO campaigns and the mere threat to a company of becoming an NGO target prove their continued worth?

The perceived success of a business–NGO partnership ultimately depends on the perspective of the judge. The newness of the MSC makes it difficult for stakeholders, and observers, to assess its impact on global fisheries and the fishing industry as yet, and it will be interesting to revisit stakeholder opinions of the MSC as the initiative develops.

How far are the lessons of the MSC applicable to business–NGO partnerships in other sectors? The MSC experience suggests that it is currently easier to translate environmental issues into a business/financial case for corporate change than it is to translate the social aspects of sustainable development. The motivation to establish the MSC from Unilever's side was a clear strategy to offset the significant business risk posed by depleted fish stocks. Development NGO concerns that the MSC will pay inadequate attention to social issues are partly driven by a recognition that the threat to fish supplies is the primary motivation for companies such as Unilever to seek collaboration with WWF and other stakeholders. Development NGOs are developing more market-oriented initiatives, such as Christian Aid's 'Change the Rules' campaign and the Ethical Trading Initiative to persuade UK retail companies to address social issues in their supply chain. As a result, Unilever may find that its relations with NGOs, on issues associated with its fish business, are not adequately dealt with through its participation in the MSC. Equally, as an organisation committed to promote 'socially beneficial' fisheries, the MSC secretariat may face increasing pressure from development NGOs and unions to provide greater access to standards development. Only time will tell whether this leads to new forms of business–NGO collaboration or confrontation.

The process of engagement between WWF and Unilever stemmed from the convergence of a number of crucial factors, including the identification of a common objective, the facilitation of intermediaries, the creativity of staff in both organisations and the pre-existence of the FSC. Key among these factors appears to be the vision, goodwill and personal commitment of certain individuals. The MSC clearly has more work to do to bring its stakeholders, particularly fish-workers and development NGOs, on board. The complex stakeholder relations of the MSC require skilled and sensitive management and the success or failure of that process is likely to prove the ultimate test of the MSC in the long term.

PART 4
Seeking and Managing Collaboration

PARTNERS FOR SUSTAINABILITY

John Elkington and Shelly Fennell

SustainAbility Ltd, UK

Sadly, the inevitable has started to happen. Some of the early relationships between major companies and organisations best known for their championing of environmental or social agendas have started to break up. Pakistan's Grameen Bank, which has done so much to advance the cause of micro-credit, formed a link with the US company Monsanto—and then was forced to break it off because of intense pressure from international non-governmental organisations (NGOs). And several other companies, notably in the oil sector, have found their innovative stakeholder relationships being tested almost to the limit.

It is hardly surprising that partnerships such as these sometimes fail. What is more surprising is how often they succeed. This article explores some of the ways in which such relationships and partnerships are being constructed, and some of the emerging corporate strategies not only for making them happen but for making them *work*.

Over the past decade, relationships between environmental groups and business have warmed considerably. So what triggered this thaw? There are a number of answers. For one thing, once environmental performance began to be seen as a competitive and strategic business issue, a number of companies started to court the environmental lobby—inviting groups to discuss key issues related to the company's environmental impact. The more proactive among them entered into formal dialogue, and a few even went so far as to enter into partnerships.

Some—though certainly not all—environmental groups welcomed the opening of corporate doors: many NGOs had become hugely frustrated with the collective lack of progress in securing environmental improvement through legislation. With increasing numbers of companies at least attempting to display environmental credentials, direct work with business seemed to offer a fresh opportunity. Perhaps most importantly, the broadening of the environmental agenda to incorporate sustainable development highlighted the key role that business can—and must—play. Quite simply, NGOs realised that business participation was essential to the development of any long-lasting solutions.

In 1996, BP asked SustainAbility to investigate this changing world of business–NGO relations. BP had a long track record of working with NGOs, and wanted to take a more strategic approach to these relationships. In particular, the company's board wanted to know whether it should be thinking in terms of developing a strategic alliance with one or more of these groups. And, if so, with whom and to do what?

In this article, we summarise some of the key findings of that project, and extend the analysis to incorporate recent trends in NGO–business relationships. We propose a typology of NGO 'species'—developed to help BP evaluate potential partners—which is based on the way different NGOs relate to companies. Conversely, we offer a typology of companies, based on the differing ways they relate to stakeholder groups. This, we hope, will aid both environmental NGOs and companies as they sift through the ever-increasing number of offers to engage in partnerships.

◢ The shifting nature of NGO–business relationships

We first set out to gain an overview of the changing nature of business–NGO relationships from the perspective of companies and NGOs across North America and Europe. We conducted the research in two stages. We surveyed over 60 NGOs and companies worldwide, asking them to assess the sincerity of corporate environmentalism, the most important influences on environmental performance, and the elements that make for successful partnerships.

We also sought to gain a better understanding of the dynamics that make or break any individual alliance. To this end, we went on to interview some 20 companies and NGOs with direct experience with this sort of partnership. Among their number are companies as diverse as The Body Shop, General Motors, McDonald's and Monsanto,[1] and NGOs such as the National Wildlife Federation, the World Wide Fund for Nature (WWF) and Greenpeace.

We found the results surprising. Rather than illustrating the gulf to be bridged, the survey showed a high degree of convergence between companies and NGOs. The NGOs were watching environmentally proactive companies with great interest, and welcomed the upsurge in corporate environmentalism. Interestingly, though, the NGOs polled believed that the gap between leaders and laggards in a given industry were more significant than did companies.

Significantly, both groups expected further improvement in relations: over 85% of our respondents believed that partnerships will increase over the next five years, and argued that NGOs should get involved in *more* company partnerships. Table 11.1 summarises the key drivers motivating each group to engage with the other.

---

1   See footnote on p. 14.

DRIVERS FOR BUSINESS ENGAGEMENT WITH NGOs	DRIVERS FOR NGO ENGAGEMENT WITH BUSINESS
☐ Markets	☐ Growing interest in markets
☐ NGO credibility with public on issues and priorities	☐ Disenchantment with government as provider of solutions
☐ Need for external challenge	☐ Need for more resources, e.g. funding, technical and management expertise
☐ Cross-fertilisation of thinking	
☐ Greater efficiency in resource allocation	☐ Credibility of business with government
☐ Desire to head off negative public confrontations	☐ Cross-fertilisation of thinking
☐ Desire to engage stakeholders	☐ Access to supply chains
	☐ Greater leverage

Table 11.1 **Drivers toward partnerships**

Despite the general optimism about partnerships, however, neither NGOs nor companies expected an end to confrontation. Indeed, several factors were thought to be looming which could reverse the trend toward collaboration. In the USA, for example, a number of NGOs expressed dismay over companies' willingness to work with them while at the same time attempting to undermine existing environmental regulations. For their part, companies pointed to violations of confidentiality—and trust—as show-stoppers. Table 11.2 lists a number of factors that could slow the spread of partnerships.

Table 11.2 **Potential brakes on partnerships**

BRAKES ON BUSINESS-LED INITIATIVES	BRAKES ON NGO-LED INITIATIVES
☐ Concerns over confidentiality of information shared with NGO	☐ Belief that company is only seeking public relations benefits, rather than real environmental improvement
☐ Difficulties of addressing broadening agenda of sustainability-focused groups	
☐ Inability to deal with schizophrenic tendencies of NGOs	☐ Perceptions of inconsistency in company environmental behaviour (inability to deal with schizophrenic tendencies of companies)
☐ Desire to protect 'weakest link in chain'	
☐ Short-term financial concerns	☐ Conflicts with membership and fundraising base
☐ Concerns over splintering of NGO movement, and corresponding reduction in business value of alliances	☐ Decisions to devote energies to protecting environmental regulatory structure

Among the key conclusions, several have proven to be particularly relevant as we have watched the development of partnerships over the past several years. For example, we pointed out at the time that partnerships require both companies and NGOs to grapple with the internal 'schizophrenia' within their own organisations.

Often, the decision to enter into a partnership comes down to individuals: typically, those who believe that more progress can be made by working together than by fighting each other. This view is not always universally shared across an organisation, and those promoting partnerships often find themselves in direct conflict with their more sceptical colleagues.

The tensions within—and across—NGOs can be particularly acute. To try to deal with this tension, a group of US-based environmental NGOs (and SustainAbility) joined together in a formal network to debate the advantages and disadvantages of relationships with business. The aim is to share experiences and brainstorm about strategies—to help ensure that time spent working with companies results in demonstrable environmental progress.

Another issue we identified had to do with diminishing NGO resources. Once, many business people thought there were too many NGOs for comfort. If current trends continue, we argued, we would probably see a shortage of credible NGOs willing and able to work alongside business. Thus, we concluded, companies that lead their competitors in forging strategic alliances with key NGOs could enjoy a strong 'first-mover' benefit (see Elkington 1997a).

This has played out in a number of ways. First, the number of companies interested in forming stakeholder dialogue has expanded considerably; NGO resources have remained constant. As a result, the individuals within NGOs that are most amenable to dialogue with companies are increasingly besieged with invitations. Sheer time constraints dictate that only a few invitations can be accepted.

Perhaps more important in the long run, however, is a creeping disaffection with company–NGO dialogue. While some NGOs continue to welcome the opportunity to express their opinions directly to a company, others have come to view stakeholder dialogue as a substitute for—rather than a precursor to—real action to reduce impacts.

To date, calls for boycotting dialogue appear to be directed primarily toward individual companies, which are thought to be particularly insincere. These cases threaten to taint the efforts of companies in general: particularly if the benefits of dialogue are not evident.

◢ Assessing potential partnerships

In addition to establishing the state of play in business–NGO relations, we also sought to help BP make sense of what these trends might mean for its own future actions. This required a way of assessing potential partnerships—and partners.

With respect to partnerships, we developed a spectrum of possible types of relationship between an NGO and a company—from the traditional adversarial position to a fully collaborative strategic alliance (see Table 11.3).

TYPE	ACTIVITIES	COMPANY PARTICIPATION LEVEL	TARGET AUDIENCE
Challenge	Media campaigns; boycotts	Reactive response	Customers; shareholders
Sparring partner	Periodic exchanges; 'healthy conflict'	Reactive or proactive response; formal or informal communication mechanism	NGOs; regulators
Support	Charitable giving; sponsorship; gifts in kind; secondments	Primarily financial contribution to support project	Customers; public
Product endorsement	Endorsement by NGO; eco-labelling	Initial audit/assessment of operations/practices; ongoing information exchange/verification	Customers; NGOs
Company endorsement	Ratings; certification	Initial audit of operations, practices, reporting; ongoing information exchange/verification	Shareholders; NGOs
Site or project dialogue	Environmental mediation; EIAs	Formal communication process; joint agenda-development	Communities; NGOs
Strategy dialogue	Discussions over business issues	Joint agenda-development; research; formal communication process and results dissemination	NGOs; regulators
Project joint venture	Formal partnership for duration of project	Project planning and development; financial support	Communities; NGOs
Strategic joint venture	Formal partnership or public alliance	Full business participation; jointly developed principles or strategy	NGOs; public

Table 11.3 **Types of company–NGO relationship**

Over the past few years, Monsanto has taken the concept of sparring partners to new heights. Seeking to overcome European resistance to genetically modified organisms (GMOs), the company has taken to the streets and airways to put its case forward—and, ostensibly, to listen to the opposition. Over summer 1998, a series of advertisements in the UK invited the public to contact the company to debate the issues; some of the adverts went so far as to present opposing NGO viewpoints. Unfortunately for Monsanto, the external view is that the company consulted but then did little or nothing to change the way it behaved in the marketplace.

The 'endorsement' style of partnership, whether of products or companies, shows signs of flourishing. With respect to company endorsement partnerships, the Council on Economic Priorities (CEP) has introduced SA 8000, a social accountability certification scheme that companies can apply for to demonstrate ethical labour practices. To earn the standard, companies must undergo a series of site inspections—both company-operated and major suppliers—by third-party verifiers, to ensure adherence to the SA 8000 principles. To date, a number of large multinational companies have submitted their operations to the test, including Toys'R'Us and Avon.

Product endorsement partnerships are also on the increase, with timber (see Chapter 12), fish (see Chapter 10) and bananas among the products that can carry, or will soon be able to carry, an NGO-approved label. Although supported by the most progressive companies, who welcome the opportunity to lock in a niche customer base, government support for these certification schemes may be undermined by zealous application of free trade laws. Last spring, for example, the US ran foul of the World Trade Organisation (WTO) when it tried to block the import of shrimp caught without special nets designed to protect sea turtles: the WTO ruled that the US must allow the imports.

A newer type of product endorsement partnership is found in emerging 'climate-neutral' certification schemes. In the UK, the Carbon Storage Trust is promoting a scheme whereby companies can offset their own greenhouse gas emissions with tree planting. The gas retailer Amerada Hess is among the companies that have joined up with the Trust: it is now marketing a 'premium' branded gas product on this basis. SustainAbility is also instituting such a scheme. As a service company, we will estimate the indirect greenhouse gas emissions associated with activities conducted for each major project (e.g. air travel).

Shell—a company that had not expressed much interest in NGO partnerships at the time of the BP study—has since launched one of the most ambitious strategy dialogue partnerships yet seen. As part of its multi-year effort to implement triple-bottom-line accountability (see Elkington 1997b),[2] the company is involved in detailed discussions with a wide range of NGOs to develop a set of indicators for measuring and reporting annual contributions toward sustainability.

In 1996, examples of the most collaborative type of relationship—which we termed 'strategic joint venture'—were thin on the ground. Since that time, however, this type of alliance shows signs of taking off.

One unfolding strategic joint venture is the multi-party Global Reporting Initiative (GRI). Initiated and led by the US NGO CERES (the Coalition for Environmentally Responsible Economies), GRI brings together a number of NGOs and companies to carve out a framework for sustainability reporting. The outcome will hopefully be a jointly endorsed proposal for standardised reporting on corporate environmental and social impacts, applicable across sectors.

---

2 The triple bottom line embraces economic, social and environmental value added (or destroyed).

Strategy dialogue partnerships are not limited to NGO–company relationships, of course, but can also be found in company-to-company interactions. In the world of ethical investment, we see increasing willingness on the part of ethical funds to engage directly with companies to try to change behaviour. One of the UK's longest-standing ethical funding organisations, Friends Provident, recently expanded its activities from passive screening of companies for inclusions in its portfolios to include proactive dialogue.

Looking across the emerging set of partnerships, two key trends seem to be taking hold:

☐ Increasing corporate boldness. Some companies are interested in moving up the ladder of NGO relationships—taking on progressively more collaborative (and challenging) partnerships.

☐ Safety in numbers. Many companies have opted to interact with a range of NGOs, rather than cast their lot in with one particular organisation. One notable exception is BP, which is working with the US-based Environmental Defense Fund to implement an internal greenhouse gas trading programme. Similarly, NGOs are wary of being out on a limb with an individual company, preferring to work in coalitions with other like-minded organisations—or, at the very least, to share experiences.

◢ NGO typology

Once a company decides what level of alliance it is comfortable with, the next step is to assess the suitability of particular NGO partners. To facilitate this task, we constructed a typology of NGOs.

It is difficult to generalise about environmental NGOs, given that they are so diverse. NGOs concentrate on a wide array of environmental (and often social) issues; span local, regional, national and international 'jurisdictions'; represent numerous forms of decision-making structure and management; and are driven by widely different political philoso-phies. Some NGOs are staffed by only a handful of people, relying largely on volunteer efforts, while other NGOs are large, international, highly professionalised organisations.

These inherent differences in form, approach and style extend to views on developing relationships with business, whether in true partnerships or in dialogues. Before entering into an alliance with an NGO, a company would want to know where the organisation fits into the overall environmental movement.

To make the diversity easier to grasp, we distinguish between four main types of NGO, based on two separate sets of characteristics. First, consider the following trait: the extent to which the NGO seeks to integrate the role of businesses and 'public interest' groups in achieving environmental goals. At one end of the spectrum, there is the integrator: this is a group that places a high priority on developing productive relationships with busi-ness, and strives to identify non-confrontational, 'win–win' strategies. At the other end of this spectrum, one can imagine the polariser: this group has made a strategic decision not to develop close working relationships with business, preferring to concentrate its energies as a watchdog.

Second, consider another dimension, based on the whether the NGO discriminates between companies within an industry with respect to their real or perceived environmental commitment and performance. At one end of this spectrum, we have the discriminators. For them, the challenge is to understand the issues facing a particular industry and to track the progress made by individual companies compared to industry benchmarks. At the other end of the spectrum, there are the non-discriminators. For them, companies' relative environmental performances are not of particular interest. Rather, the focus of attention is typically the environmental burden of the industry in general.

With these two dimensions in mind, we propose a four-celled box of NGO types, using species of marine animal to illustrate behavioural characteristics (Table 11.4). Let us now use the model to evaluate how NGOs might go about relating with companies.

The NGO 'shark'

Typically, this is not a highly evolved challenger, and creativity and intelligence are not its strengths. To compensate for these deficiencies, a shark generally pursues a single-minded attack strategy, based on the smell of blood. With its narrow vision, a shark cannot spend much of its time searching for ideal bait or distinguishing between what comes its way: any creature that can be attacked is a potential meal.

Given its limitations, an NGO shark tends to focus its rhetoric on easy targets, such as the overall pollution contribution of a particular industry (or, in the most extreme form, industry in general). Its preference for attack leads a shark to focus on companies as the environmental problem, not part of the solution. A company interested in forging a partnership with a shark would be putting itself at considerable risk. One would be hard-pressed to expect loyalty, much less an attitude of collaboration in pursuit of a shared goal.

In a crisis, you can count on the NGO shark joining in on the attack.

The NGO 'orca' (killer whale)

Orcas are interesting—and often misunderstood. With their fierce appearance, orcas tend to inspire a similar fear to that created by sharks. In reality, orca attacks are likely to be more selective. Most cases of attacks on humans appear to have resulted from orcas mistaking people (particularly in wetsuits) for seals or sea lions.

A relationship with an orca could prove extremely difficult for a company. The few cases, such as Ecover's relationship with Greenpeace in the area of environmental auditing, involve companies with a very strong environmental reputation and enjoying high levels of stakeholder trust. As discriminators, orcas know and understand who they are working with: they know the issues within the industry and how to assess a particular company's progress against the industry's best practices.

NGO CHARACTERISTICS	*Polariser* Business-unfriendly: avoids alliances with companies; prefers confrontation to collaboration	*Integrator* Business-friendly: seeks productive relationships with companies, prefers collaboration to confrontation
Discriminator Scrutinises company performance: takes relative environmental progress into account in target and partner selection	**Orca** ☐ Highly intelligent, strategic ☐ Can adapt behaviour and strategy to situation, but prefers to use fear to accomplish goal ☐ Fierce in appearance ☐ Uncertain in behaviour ☐ Likes deep waters; can travel great distances ☐ Associates with—and supports—own kind ☐ Eats sea lions	**Dolphin** ☐ Intelligent, creative ☐ Adapts behaviour and strategies to context, but strategic in approach ☐ Popular spectacle ☐ Can fend off sharks ☐ Equally comfortable in deep or shallow water; can travel great distances ☐ Can be a loner—or intensely social
Non-discriminator Ignores company performance: tends to view all companies as fair game	**Shark** ☐ Relatively low intelligence ☐ Tactical ☐ Acutely responsive to distress signals ☐ Blood in water triggers feeding frenzy ☐ Poor eyesight and peripheral vision ☐ Undiscriminating in terms of targets ☐ Associates with own kind; no mutual support ☐ Swims and often attacks in packs	**Sea lion** ☐ Moderate intelligence ☐ Tactical ☐ Popular spectacle ☐ Friendly ☐ Menu item for both sharks and orcas ☐ Tends to stay close to shore in safe waters ☐ Believes in safety in numbers—uneasy if too far from the group

Table 11.4 **Typology of NGOs**

In a crisis, you can count on the NGO orca to do the unexpected. Benefits to the company are likely to be incidental to the project, rather than a pre-planned outcome of the association.

The NGO 'sea lion'

Nature conservation organisations often fall into this category. Sea lions are typically seen as cute and friendly, and are usually found in groups not too far from shore. While a sea lion may be initially a bit shy about contact with other creatures, throwing it a fish can make an instant friend. Although moderately intelligent, sea lions are not known for particularly bold or creative behaviour.

A sea lion is in many ways the opposite of a shark, at least in terms of being a potential partner for a company. The relationship—as far as it goes—will be extremely safe and cordial (particularly if the sea lion expects more fish to arrive). This type of partnership would work best for 'easy' types of partnerships, such as marketing or public relations exercises, i.e. those that do not directly concern the viability of a company's core operations.

However, there are a number of drawbacks to partnering with a sea lion for more difficult, company-specific projects. The gravest risk may be that of the sea lion attracting direct attacks from sharks or orcas. Because they are not particularly discriminating, sea lions will work with most companies, regardless of environmental record or commitment. This can leave them vulnerable to attacks on the basis that they are not 'sufficiently green', are 'compromised by fundraising needs', or are 'more interested in cosying up with a particular company than in ensuring that it makes real environmental progress'. If these attacks are sufficiently fierce, the value of the partnership for the company may be considerably reduced.

In a crisis, you can count on most NGO sea lions to scatter, making a great deal of noise. This may confuse predators, but is very unlikely to directly protect a partner company's flanks. To every rule, however, there is an exception. Some of these NGOs may stand their ground and fight. But don't count on it.

The NGO 'dolphin'

This is one of the hardest strategies for an NGO to develop and sustain, but it is also the strategy and positioning to which growing numbers of NGOs surveyed aspire. The dolphin's intelligence and creativity is legendary, as is its apparent 'friendliness' to other species.

The business-friendly, intelligent approach of a dolphin makes it an ideal partner for a company serious about reducing its environmental performance and serious about engaging stakeholders. As integrators, they bring the necessary 'partnership skills' identified in the survey: trust, openness, and willingness to understand the other's perspective. As discriminators, they bring credibility to the project: unlike sea lions, dolphins are not interested solely in fish; rather, they seek interesting projects requiring a sophisticated and intelligent approach.

In a crisis, you can count on most NGO dolphins to stick around. Their role will very much depend on the extent to which they have built up a respect for a company through close joint working. If they know of problems, they are quite likely to raise them. But there are stories from around the world of dolphins saving swimmers or pilots in distress by circling them and warding off incoming sharks.

◢ Typology of companies

After completing the BP study, we continued to use the model as we helped companies and NGOs to assess potential alliances. The interest it generated prompted us to think about how companies might be categorised along similar lines.

One dimension—willingness to engage with NGOs and civil society more generally—can be captured by whether the company has essentially a closed or an open strategy with respect to the outside world. The 'open' company—and there are more and more of them these days—is one that actively seeks to engage with most or all of its stakeholders, even those opposed to its activities or practices. The hope is that understanding the perspectives and views will help its own decision-making—and ultimately the financial bottom line.

The open company often hosts formal or informal dialogue sessions, where members of the public are invited in to learn more about the company and express any concerns. External communication is not relegated wholly to the public relations department, but is shared by the company's top management.

Whether a company is open or closed says nothing about its actual triple-bottom-line performance, however. For this, we need another dimension. As a rough dividing line, we use the extent to which a company is positioning itself to be part of the sustainability solution—or is resigned to remain part of the problem. These two strategies are summarised in Table 11.5. Let us look briefly at each of these four company types.

Table 11.5 **Styles of corporate engagement**

	CLOSED	OPEN
SOLUTIONS	**Bachelor lions** (e.g. also-rans)	**Golden geese** (e.g. market-makers)
PROBLEMS	**Vampire bats** (e.g. stealth corporations)	**Tireless spiders** (e.g. turn-around prospects)

Golden geese

Most people want to buy from, work for and invest in these businesses. These companies have the solutions and successfully communicate the fact. Their eggs are golden. They market sustainability, creating the markets of the future. Stakeholder engagement is second-nature—and effectively conducted as an integral part of business strategy.

Strategy options

Build on success. Explore the potential for bringing in bachelor lions and even some tireless spiders as sources of tomorrow's solutions. Screen out vampire bats from the value chain.

Bachelor lions

These companies may have potential solutions, but they fail to effectively communicate the fact. Stakeholder engagement is either non-existent, or directed at the wrong target audiences. As a result, these individuals remain on the outskirts of the pride, their genetic potential lost to the future. A sudden turn of fate may favour their chances, but the statistics suggest that most will fall by the wayside.

Strategy options

Study the golden geese and understand their sources of competitive advantage. Make more of what you have. Play the long game. Focus on the best potential opportunities and persevere. Avoid the company of vampire bats: they can drain your strength.

Vampire bats

These companies may fill a useful niche in a particular business ecosystem, but they do so—consciously or not—by adopting stealth tactics. Because they fail to appear on society's radar screens, they can sometimes get away with the environmental or social equivalent of murder. And, like rabid bats, they can cause huge damage. Some accumulate liabilities, of which shareholders and customers are unaware until it is too late. Even golden geese may find that their value chains include a growing proportion of vampire bats as Internet purchasing spreads. Prices may come down, but risks can soar. There is money to be made in vampiring, but the transparency revolution will make this style of operation increasingly hazardous to publicly owned companies.

Strategy options

Consider the potential benefits of coming clean, owning up to—and addressing—key problems before the world discovers them and it is too late. Consider what it would take to mutate from a vampire bat into a golden goose. The key is to become a partner of choice not because of low prices but because of sound triple-bottom-line performance. But, if you intend to stick with your old habits, avoid high-profile, multinational customers: sooner or later, they will begin screening their supply chains.

Tireless spiders

These companies may well be outsiders, but there could be a pay-off here. Robert the Bruce watched a spider trying and trying again in a Scottish cave and took heart from its eventual success. These companies have their problems, but they are open about them. As a result of effective stakeholder engagement, the flow of new ideas is boosted and there can be real sympathy for managements attempting the apparently impossible. Sometimes, a tireless spider succeeds in making a series of jumps and connections, providing a platform for future growth. Keep an eye out for tireless spiders in high-risk–high-return markets.

Strategy options

Do not expect to succeed simply by virtue of endlessly repeating a failed strategy. Innovate. Engage key stakeholders and explore with them novel ways of meeting their unmet needs. And keep enough energy in reserve so that you can redouble your efforts when conditions change for the better. Sometimes, a following wind can make all the difference.

◢ Summary

This chapter is the result of research undertaken as a response to increasing interest from corporations in their relations with environmental NGOs and civil society. We have found that there is a new enthusiasm for business–NGO partnerships, while at the same time not all are proving to be successful either for the partners or for promoting sustainability. This is because there are many complex processes to be managed when considering, developing or implementing a business–NGO partnership, and these processes differ depending on the strategies of both the companies and the NGOs involved. We have proposed a typology of NGOs which has already aided a major corporation in managing their relations with NGOs. This categorisation of NGOs may also prove to be productive in helping campaigners reflect on their own business-related strategies. In a similar vein, we have ventured a new typology of companies based on their strategy towards stakeholder engagement and the sustainability agenda. Together, we hope this analysis will help both NGOs and companies to consider, and where appropriate enter into, partnerships for sustainability.

CULTURE CLASH AND MEDIATION

Exploring the cultural dynamics of business–NGO collaboration

Andrew Crane

Cardiff Business School, UK

The 1990s have witnessed an unprecedented surge in interest and activity in collaborations between firms and non-governmental organisations (NGOs), with an impressive number of initiatives currently in operation across the globe (see Lober 1997; Murphy and Bendell 1997a). While research into these developments has, to date, been relatively limited, it has become clear that quite specific questions, issues and problems arise in the context of business–NGO collaboration compared to the rather more researched phenomenon of business–business collaboration (e.g. Varadarajan and Rajaratnam 1989; Hamel *et al.* 1989; Oliver 1990). Indeed, given that the goal sets of the organisations involved are almost by definition going to be weighted very differently in terms of commercial and social objectives, differences, even clashes, in organisational cultures and values might be expected to be an intrinsic part of such ventures (Hartman and Stafford 1996; Milne *et al.* 1996). To date, this issue has received scant attention in the literature, and therefore the time for more considerable reflection and analysis of these posited clashes, and their role in influencing the success or otherwise of programmes designed to promote sustainable development, is considerably overdue.

This chapter seeks to explore business–NGO collaboration from an organisational culture perspective. It does so principally in order to develop a more rigorous examination of the possibilities and problems of 'culture clash' between such diverse partner organisations, and thereby to explore the likely implications for how these collaborative arrangements might be managed. Martin's (1992) typology of perspectives on organisational culture is used as the central organising theme for understanding different interpretations of culture in this context. The main focus of the chapter is a case study conducted by the author of a current collaboration, the WWF 1995 Plus Group. Evidence from this case is examined according to Martin's categorisation and this is used to explore the cultural dynamics underlying the introduction of the scheme in participating organisations.

The chapter proceeds by offering a brief review of the literature pertaining to business–NGO collaboration, followed by a short introduction to the organisational culture literature, and in particular to Martin's (1992) typology. The case study methodology adopted by the study is then explained before setting out the details of the Plus Group. The main part of the chapter deals with analysis of the case from an organisational culture perspective, showing how cultural differences between business–NGO collaborators might be understood and accommodated, as well as highlighting some of the limitations associated with particular ways of conceptualising those differences. In the concluding part of the chapter, the contribution of the organisational culture perspective to our understanding of business–NGO collaboration is evaluated, and some recommendations proposed.

◢ Business–NGO collaboration

Although examples of collaboration between businesses and NGOs have occurred at least since the 1970s, relationships between them have commonly been characterised as highly aggressive and confrontational (Westley and Vredenburg 1991; Stafford and Hartman 1996; Murphy and Bendell 1997a). During the 1990s, however, while considerable conflict still remains between these groups, there can be little doubt that both the extent and degree of collaboration between them has been growing steadily. While reliable figures on the scale of such business–NGO alliances are not readily available, there is considerable case study and anecdotal evidence to suggest that the number of formal alliances has indeed grown significantly over the past decade, with Lober (1997) and Murphy and Bendell (1997a) both providing details of numerous recent examples, and suggesting reasons for the growth in such activity. Moreover, a 1996 SustainAbility survey suggested that this growth was likely to be maintained into the new millennium with over 85% of its respondents believing that partnerships would increase over the next five years (Elkington 1997a). Similarly, the degree of interaction between commercial and civil organisations appears to have intensified. Both Stafford and Hartman (1996; Hartman and Stafford 1997) and Murphy and Bendell (1997a), for example, set out examples where NGOs have not merely been the passive recipients of the philanthropic gestures of PR-smart companies, or the 'brand-for-hire' endorsers of existing company products, but have played a critical role in developing corporate policy and effecting the strategic development of their commercial partners.

With collaboration then taking on increasingly complex and more interconnected forms, there is clearly a need for partner organisations to be able to work closely and effectively together over the medium to long term. Westley and Vredenburg (1991), however, suggest that this might be problematic, given the divergence of goal and value systems underlying commercial and not-for-profit organisations; hence there is likely to be some form of 'strategic bridging' across culturally heterogeneous organisations. Milne *et al.* (1996) also attempt to set out the types of cultural difference that might occur and lead to culture clash, emphasising, in addition to goal incongruity, the prevalence of perceived differences in beliefs, attitudes, problem-solving approaches and ways of working. Hartman and Stafford (1996: 415) take up this theme, emphasising how 'bridging relationships are inherently precarious' but, they argue, 'not necessarily doomed'. They suggest that the stability of the alliance is likely to be inversely related to the degree of conflict evident in the partners' cultural values and to the level of goal incongruity. However, they contend that this can be mitigated if partners succeed in recognising and managing these differences, and manage to foster a degree of trust, openness and commitment.

As yet, however, despite allusions to these cultural differences and their potential importance, there has been little formal empirical examination of how they might be manifested and experienced in practice, how they might be dealt with or managed by alliance members, and whether indeed they are a significant element of the collaborative process. The most compelling evidence so far is that provided in recent empirical papers by Milne *et al.* (1997) and Crane (1998), both of which suggest that culture clash does occur in business–NGO collaboration, but neither of which explore the issue in any real depth. It is evident also that the application of the organisation culture concept to business–NGO collaboration has as yet been only very partially applied, and there is an impressive collection of work in the organisation studies literature—much of it critical of the types of assumption and approach characteristic of the use of culture in the business–NGO collaboration literature[1]—which might be fruitfully brought to bear. Hence, this study has sought to explore specifically the cultural dimension of business–NGO collaboration in more detail.

◢ The concept of organisational culture

While organisational culture is clearly an important concept in understanding business–NGO relations, it would be a mistake to assume that its use is not in itself problematic. The organisational culture literature has grown rapidly and in many diverse ways since it was first established in the mainstream organisational studies literature around the early 1980s.[2] Such developments, though, have created a field with enormous ambiguity

---

1   For further discussion of the use and misuse of organisation culture in relation to green business, see Crane 1995 and Newton and Harte 1997.

2   There are a number of excellent reviews of the organisation culture literature, the most comprehensive probably being Brown 1995. Alvesson and Berg (1992) also provide a good account of the considerable growth in this literature during the 1980s.

surrounding its key concepts and their definitions, as well as critical differences in the kinds of perspective commonly applied by culture researchers. Indeed, one of the foremost organisation culture theorists, Joanne Martin (1992), talks of the 'state of conceptual chaos' that surrounds the subject, and this can provide serious obstacles to any attempts at modelling and understanding business–NGO relations through the culture perspective. Nonetheless, with culture clearly a key issue in the understanding and management of such relations, it is less appropriate to dismiss culture altogether than to recognise the range of possibilities, the potential criticisms, and the limitations, of any given perspective.

Basically, culture is regarded here as being concerned with a broad range of phenomena: various artefacts such as behaviours, stories, myths, symbols, language, etc.; cognitive beliefs, values, attitudes, and codes; and basic, taken-for-granted assumptions (Schein 1992). These are the basic contents of the culture concept, and might be regarded as three different, though interrelated, cultural levels. Martin (1992), however, makes a critical distinction between the ways in which culture can (and has been) understood and modelled, and these three perspectives—integration, differentiation and fragmentation—form the analytical core of the paper.[3]

The **integration** perspective assumes that there is a single unitary culture that is widely and relatively unambiguously shared throughout the organisation. Hence, the organisation here has one identifiable set of behaviours, values and assumptions which are accepted and internalised by organisation members and which set it apart from other organisations. The **differentiation** perspective identifies unity mainly at the level of subcultural groupings and focuses on the conflict and inconsistency experienced between these groups. Hence, the organisation can be seen as a collection of distinct subcultural groups, organised, for example, around hierarchical levels, organisational functions, gender, race, or any number of other features. Finally, the **fragmentation** perspective assumes little cultural consensus within the organisation and concentrates attention on the ambiguity and complexity of the cultural terrain. Here, the assumption that individual values, beliefs and world-views are shared to any meaningful extent within the organisation is essentially rejected.

This chapter attempts to show the possibilities and limitations associated with each of these three perspectives as they apply to the experiences of those actually involved in the everyday reality of business–NGO collaboration. They are used to interpret the responses provided by collaboration participants in respect to cultural distinctions. In this way it is intended to provide a more informed understanding of the role of culture in business–NGO collaboration. The three perspectives are also used to examine the possibilities for how culture clash might be mediated during the collaboration process.

3 There are a number of other important categorisations that have been introduced into the culture literature, but it is beyond the scope of this chapter to consider them in sufficient depth to do the arguments justice. See, however, Brown 1995 for a discussion of *espoused culture* versus *culture-in-practice* and Smircich 1983 for a discussion of *culture as metaphor* versus *culture as variable*. See Crane 1995 for an examination of these in the context of organisational greening.

◢ Case study approach

The research method used to develop these insights has been the single case study. This was considered to be the most appropriate method, given that the study was essentially exploratory and required qualitative depth in order to capture the full cultural complexity of the alliance phenomenon (see Bonoma 1985; Smith 1991). The case selected was the WWF 1995 Plus Group, an ongoing UK green alliance between (at the time of fieldwork) 75 companies and an environmental NGO, the World Wide Fund for Nature (WWF). Formally in operation since January 1996 (but effectively formed in 1991[4]), the Plus Group is focused on the environmental management of forest sources for wood and wood-based products (i.e. those with wood, paper and/or pulp components). It is a particularly high-profile collaboration in the UK, and, as one of the first examples of an NGO having direct impact on the internal operations of the business partner, could be seen as a model, or a test bed, for the type of highly interactive business–NGO relationships that are said to be emerging (Aspinwall and Smith 1996). For the study of cultural clash and mediation, the Plus Group is an especially instructive case study, since the membership includes a very diverse range of corporate partners from large PLCs to green niche operators and co-operatives.

A grounded, inductive, research methodology has been used whereby the concern has been to draw out data relating to culture in general rather than to investigate any particular propositions or hypotheses. Data collection consisted principally of a series of 17 semi-structured interviews conducted with individual representatives[5] from 13 member organisations during 1996, i.e. after the initial development of the group and the formalisation of its systems and membership criteria, but before many of its proposed benefits had been realised. Interviews covered a range of issues relating to the management of the group, and some of the more general findings are discussed in Crane 1998. Considerable additional data in the form of informal discussions, in-house documentation, marketing artefacts and archival material was also collected. An additional group of 27 interviews were carried out with three corporate members of the group as part of a wider study of environmental management and marketing; this data has also been incorporated into the analysis presented here. Organisations were sampled theoretically, such that they were considered to provide insight into the emergent theory rather than reflecting any kind of systematic statistical sampling (Glaser and Strauss 1967). Pragmatic considerations, though, also played a important role here, for there were only a limited number of firms that agreed to be part of the study and which could be practically included. Most interviews were recorded on audiotape and then transcribed; all other data was recorded in field notes and then written up before being subjected to analysis.

---

4 The Plus Group can be regarded as an prolongation of an earlier, virtually identical alliance, the WWF 1995 Group. This had been in operation since December 1991, but, having reached its original date of termination, was renamed and relaunched as the Plus Group (due to terminate in 1999). For the purpose of this study, they are regarded as a single alliance.

5 The individuals consulted were the main representatives of corporate partners plus two members of the WWF project team.

The form of grounded analysis used was highly iterative in nature, with data being successively broken down, or 'coded' such that themes, patterns and relationships could be identified and established (Strauss and Corbin 1990). These were then developed further into theoretical constructs and stories while constantly comparing back with the original data to 'check' their validity, and to determine what new data had to be sought. Corroboration of analysis was sought by content analysis of interview transcripts, and by cross-referencing across organisations and with published data. Successive iterations of coding and analysis were thus conducted until logical, plausible and internally consistent findings emerged. It should be recognised, however, that this is only one interpretation that could have been placed on the data, albeit one that has been arrived at after an exhaustive process of analysis and re-analysis. The approach used is to some extent inherently subjective, but its value lies in its potential for uncovering the richness of the area under study and developing considerable depth of insight.

◢ The WWF 1995 Plus Group

The avowed aim of the Plus Group alliance has been to ensure an appropriate level of environmental management at the forest sources used to produce the components of products marketed and sold by member companies (Bendell and Sullivan 1996). These members have included, among others, major UK companies such as B&Q, The Body Shop, Boots the Chemist, Railtrack, Sainsbury, Tesco, as well as numerous smaller and less-known organisations, including many of the above's suppliers. The project has involved the establishment of an effective means for assessing and certifying forest management procedures based on widely accepted criteria, and the development of an eco-label and market for products meeting these standards. This centred on the formation of the Forest Stewardship Council (FSC), an independent membership NGO made up of representatives from environmental and social groups, the timber trade and the forestry profession. It was formally established in 1993 to evaluate, accredit and monitor certifiers of forest management practice, and is now central to a number of national collaborations across the globe between buyer groups and NGOs. The formation of a green alliance to tackle these problems has represented a significant departure from the usual conflict between businesses and environmental groups in relation to timber-based products, particularly since NGO demonstrations were clearly an important catalyst in the initial creation of the group (Murphy 1996a, 1996b).

Under the criteria for membership of the alliance, member companies have been required to pledge themselves to a number of commitments relating to their sourcing of relevant products, the ultimate aim of which has been to phase out by 1999 all forest sources not meeting standards adjudged to be 'well managed' as defined by the FSC (based on a range of social, environmental and economic sustainability indicators). The principal environmental management system introduced through the alliance has been supplier questionnaires, circulated through the supply chains of member companies, and in turn feeding into company databases of forest sources and management systems. Questionnaires track the chain of custody of timber-based product components, with a view to encouraging source forests to develop certified management systems. FSC endorsement can be attached to products in the form of an eco-label, although, at the time of fieldwork, few certifiable products had reached retailers' shelves. The role of the WWF in the collaboration has been to manage and co-ordinate the alliance, to set targets (in view of the arguments and needs of current and prospective business members), to assess companies' progress towards them, and to act as a gatekeeper for membership.

◢ Cultural differences and similarities

Respondents indicated a range of cultural differences and similarities within the domain of the alliance, and these can be usefully examined from each of Martin's (1992) three perspectives, as the following sections illustrate.

Integration perspective

The integration perspective has dominated the (albeit limited) literature to date that has considered cultural issues in relation to business–NGO collaboration. Here the assumption is that the partnering organisations each have a single, unified culture which is shared by its own members, but which is distinct from that of the other organisation(s). It is this difference between the organisational-level cultures of environmental groups and businesses that is seen by Hartman and Stafford (1996) among others as creating inherent tension in collaborative arrangements. In the current study, such differences between the WWF and the business partners were indeed referred to by many respondents, with some corporate respondents in particular focusing on the different ways in which problems tended to be approached, apparent variations in time-scales for reaching decisions and implementing policy, and the vastly different context in which decision-making had to take place. Essentially, for some corporate executives there were considerable doubts as to the WWF's understanding of businesses priorities, prompting suggestions from some quarters that they were 'too short-sighted business-wise', 'blindly changing parameters' and, hence, 'unable to appreciate commercial pressures'. As one company representative put it: 'There's a real culture clash between those two styles . . . from my personal experience, I don't think you can bring the two together.'

However, not all respondents were as dismissive; and, overall, cultural differences were in the main seen as acceptable, given the inevitability of some kind of difference between business and NGO partners. In fact, it was the relative similarity and congruence of the WWF to business organisations, compared to other 'fanatical' pressure groups (as they were often labelled), that most respondents saw as contributing both to their company's enthusiasm for the initiative, and to the relative smooth running of the alliance process:

> The WWF is considered to be for the socially acceptable green person isn't it? Whereas, if you want to be a little more awkward and argumentative you go

and join Greenpeace or Friends of the Earth or something like that . . . I suppose [my company] can be said to be conservative with a small 'c', and we would go along with a pressure group that is socially acceptable. Everybody accepts WWF because it's nice people isn't it? They don't take the aggressive attitude (planning manager, corporate partner).

Fineman and Clarke's (1996) study of firms' responses to green stakeholders makes a similar point, arguing that companies have been generally unwilling or unable to accept the legitimacy of concerns raised by the more confrontational green pressure groups. For companies, a willingness on the part of NGOs to adopt their preferred mode of raising and resolving issues—setting up meetings and working groups, having 'civilised' office-bound discussions, etc.—rather than traditional pressure group tactics of direct action, confrontation and boycott appears to be the only way that collaboration will be contemplated. If cultural differences exist, then it seems that it is the pressure groups that must adapt, not businesses. The following company respondent, for example, states unambiguously where they see the burden for achieving cultural harmony lying:

> The WWF might become a bit more business-like, but I don't think the businesses are going to become more WWF-like—other than the fact that they will try and introduce an ethical policy . . . But the way of working? I hope not. I may resign if [respondent's company] becomes more like the WWF! (environment manager, corporate partner).

Just as all pressure groups were not seen as the same, so too were member companies rarely regarded as culturally homogenous, and it was common for respondents to describe them as falling into broad cultural groups. First, the retailers in the group represented a significant presence, and, in terms of size and turnover, conducted a significant majority of the business activity relevant to the initiative. Having organised themselves into a discrete sub-group within the overall group, the retailers tended to be seen by some as a different kind of entity to the other corporate members, with their own goal systems and ways of working. The green niche companies were also to some extent seen as forming a particular cultural group, operating with distinctly different priorities to those companies with broader strategic positions. Indeed, they were seen in some quarters to be closer culturally to the NGO partner than the other commercial organisations. But, again, the differences between organisations should not be overemphasised, and the experiences of one green niche firm that had developed out of a charity project funded by the WWF was instructive on this point. As the chief executive explained, the workings of a charity and a commercial organisation (albeit an environmentally attuned one) were increasingly becoming more homogenous:

> Certainly, a lot of the phrases and a lot of the systems are being introduced into the voluntary sector from the commercial sector (chief executive, corporate partner).

So, from the unitary perspective, the overall impression suggested by respondents was that cultural differences between organisations did exist, and did matter, and certainly could be the cause of certain conflicts, but it was clear that these tended to be viewed in a relative way. Hence, some charities were seen as more similar to commercial organisations than others, some companies were seen as more similar to particular companies than others, and some companies were seen as more similar to charities than others.

Differentiation perspective

Despite being the most common view of organisational culture, the integration perspective is not, however, the only one that can be applied to business–NGO collaboration. Indeed, this particular lens provides a picture that tends to miss many of the essential dynamics that underlie the collaboration process, and could even fail to recognise some of the more critical elements in the effective management of business–NGO relations. By focusing more on the subcultural level, then, a different, and to some extent more important understanding can be developed. The differentiation perspective does not then assume that any of the collaborating organisations can be seen in terms of a single unified culture that distinguishes it from the other organisation(s). Rather, it focuses attention on the cultural groups and micro-communities that might coalesce around particular functions and social groups within the organisation. Cultural heterogeneity between these groups, then—and any attendant clash, conflict or mediation—becomes the key issue, not whether organisations as a whole are similar or different.

Certainly, respondents from the Plus Group quite frequently described situations and issues in terms of subcultures. As with the descriptions of unified cultures, subcultures tended to be outlined in terms of degrees of environmental awareness/concern and commercial awareness/concern. Hence, there was a widely held belief that the project team within WWF actually responsible for the running of the Plus Group was in many ways more in tune with business interests than was much of the rest of the organisation. As this WWF respondent suggests, the members of the project team needed to be 'business-friendly', and this inevitably imposed a certain cultural distance with other parts of the organisation:

> If you are in corporate partnerships [within the WWF] you have to work with business continually: so you're more of a business person than you are an environmentalist. If you are a forests officer then you are somewhere in between. Inevitably, there are different cultures of people in an organisation (project manager, NGO partner).

So, for the NGO partner, subcultural differences were seen as inevitable, and in fact as essential for the success of the collaboration: the need to maintain both commercial and environmental credibility meant that only by seeing the organisation as culturally differentiated could all constituencies be satisfied.

Subcultural differences also extended, though, into the corporate members, reflecting the different roles played by certain employees and/or functions in the operation of the initiative. Company representatives in the alliance were frequently drawn from general management (in the smaller companies) or technical, quality or environment sections (in the larger companies), but crucially only rarely from the marketing or procurement division. As a result, the role of company representatives in their host institutions was principally to influence existing purchasing arrangements habitually conducted by other staff, rather than to oversee the procurement process or to initiate new arrangements themselves.

In general, these differences in role were reflected in distinct subcultural identities, such that many company representatives presented themselves as being more environmentally aware and concerned than their procurement colleagues. Hence, the representatives tended either to be specialist environmental staff, or at least 'enthusiastic amateurs', whereas salespeople and buyers were predominantly described by interviewees as 'not environmentally conditioned' but very much more 'hard-nosed', driven mainly by concerns for cost reductions, sales margins and, more colourfully, 'screwing down the current supplier another 5%'. Clearly, within these subcultures, individuals might in many respects display a healthy diversity, but substantial unity was certainly evident in terms of differences in terms of cultural knowledge and frames of reference, particularly since individual roles, goals and systems of assessment tended to reflect these divisions. What this means is that company representatives often felt more culturally aligned and bonded to their environmental counterparts in *other* companies than they did to their immediate colleagues in the procurement division of their *own* companies. Hence, subcultural affiliations could not only form within organisations, but even across them.[6]

Fragmentation perspective

Such views of culture are not, however, without their critics, and Martin's final perspective on organisation culture, fragmentation, suggests that the emphasis placed on the sharing of culture is too static and reductionist. In the fragmentation view, culture is seen as much more ambiguous, and the cultural affiliations and interpretations of the individual are seen as constantly shifting, and frequently contradictory. Hence, those involved in the business–NGO alliance might be indeterminate in their beliefs and values, and thus

> sporadically and loosely connected by their changing positions on a variety of issues. Their involvement, their subcultural identities, and their individual self-definitions fluctuate depending on which issues are activated at a given moment (Martin 1992: 153).

Through this perspective, then, culture clash would be seen as issue-based and highly contextual rather than based on overall group differences, and would occur both across and within individual organisations. Moreover, clash might even be manifested *within* the individual, since their transitory membership of shifting coalitions could potentially lead to personal ideological tension.

Among the Plus Group members, the fragmentation perspective helped to shed light on the apparently contradictory positions held by some respondents, and how they

---

6   This clearly has strong parallels with the development of cultural identification among particular professions where professional training and socialisation engenders particular values and frames of reference that are widely shared by practitioners regardless of their institution of employment.

seemingly operated with multiple role identities. This was most evident in the case of those company representatives who felt themselves to be very much with a foot in both camps with respect to the initiative. They wanted the project to work well, and this meant collaborating horizontally with immediate competitors in order to develop buying power; at the same time, however, given that most firms had rationalised their membership in terms of developing some kind of differential edge over competitors, they also wanted to prevent these firms from becoming members:

> From a business perspective . . . anything that gives me competitive advantage is going to be welcome . . . so from that perspective I'd be happy if everybody stays away and gives us a free run. On a broader scale, ultimately it's got to become better if more people become involved and committed to it (marketing manager, corporate partner).

As such, managers in member companies might be seen as drifting between apparently conflicting subcultures, thus challenging both the integration and the differentiation perspectives. More deeply, some managers clearly lived with some form of value ambiguity regarding their environmental beliefs, since they found themselves frequently emphasising different justifications for their organisation's involvement in the project according to the situation and the audience. Hence, company buyers would be confronted with a clear no-nonsense business argument for the initiative, while meetings with other environmentally committed representatives might bring forth more moral and emotional rationales. Thus, respondents would sometimes offer apparently contradictory assertions of their own environmental beliefs—again, what position they took depended on the particular role they were asked to play. However, this did not seem to be a cause of a great deal of stress on the part of respondents, and seemed very much to be regarded as an intrinsic part of the ambivalence and theatre of corporate life.

So what we have, then, is three varied accounts of the cultural dynamics of business–NGO collaboration as seen through the distinctive lenses of integration, differentiation and fragmentation. Martin's (1992) suggestion is that neither perspective is more right, or more 'real', than the others, but that any cultural context can be better understood by using all three. Hence, it is not the concern here to assess each perspective's relative contribution to our understanding of business–NGO collaboration, but to use them to develop a more rounded picture of this phenomenon, and to aid in identifying the means of managing it more effectively. It is to this, and in particular the role of cultural mediators, that the discussion now turns.

◢ Cultural mediators

Given the rather different representations of business–NGO collaboration offered by the three perspectives on culture, and the clear evidence of perceived culture clash of various forms suggested by them, two key questions need to be resolved. First, how can, or should, the different representations be reconciled? And, second, how can this perceived clash be dealt with, if at all, in the alliance process? Case evidence from the Plus Group initiative revealed that the key issue in addressing these issues was the role played by what are referred to here as 'cultural mediators'. Essentially, these are certain individuals and groups within the alliance who were found to act as bridges between some of the various constituencies involved, principally by establishing common meanings and understandings across cultural boundaries. Effectively, they were translators of cultural knowledge between cultural and subcultural groups, providing shared vocabularies and frames of reference, such that cultural clash did not impose impossible obstacles for effective communication to take place and for mutual respect and understanding to be fostered.

The Plus Group project managers in the WWF were cultural mediators in that they had to translate the environmental goals of their organisation and its concomitant values of conservation, dialogue, participation, etc. into a form acceptable, and even desirable, for business interests. Hence they had to prove how the WWF, and the Plus Group project, were not antithetical to business goals and beliefs. This took the form of setting up appropriate formal systems ('they've been able to set up practical goals') articulating benefits in terms readily appreciated by business ('[the WWF] are actually addressing [commercial] issues and saying to us: in a business sense we understand that, unless there is a business payback to you, you're probably not going to be interested') as well as adopting the appropriate symbolic trappings of corporate convention—an outwardly 'professional' approach conducted by 'short-haired, suit-wearing' managers providing the requisite diet of glossy brochures and corporate launches. Hence:

> [The WWF] are aware that they can't afford to have a stereotyped environ-
> mentalist approach. They can't be woolly and indeterminate on things. They
> can't have high moral principles and ideas but not have actually any degree of
> a sense of reality with it, because there's no way they'll get to tie business in
> (environment manager, corporate partner).

So the project team operated as mediators between the unitary cultures of the WWF and the business partners. Environmentally committed company representatives also adopted similar roles, mediating between the commercially oriented culture of their firms and what was still perceived as a relatively idealistic approach on the part of the WWF. To this end, they too sought to distance themselves from the stereotypical 'environ-mentalist' image of the 'beads and braids brigade', which might have weakened their credibility within the organisation. Again, there was a strong emphasis here on ensuring that they communicated the correct level of pragmatism and professionalism in order to achieve corporate approbation. In this way, the cultural mediators could be regarded as helping both sides to see the position of the other in what might otherwise be a relationship between incompatibles:

> Pressure groups are in the business of campaigning and they are not in the
> business of making other people's lives easy. I'm not in the business of being
> good to pressure groups. And the businesses are selling what they sell . . . so
> its a constant tension between everybody's needs. And we try to smooth the
> waters—I'm not sure successfully, but we try (environment manager, corpo-
> rate partner).

Critically, there was a general consensus that the perceptions of cultural difference between the two partners tended to be increasingly allayed, or at least accepted, over time. Mutual adaptation and learning smoothed the waters of cultural heterogeneity. Thus, the corporate partner might grow more comfortable with green issues, and, as the following company representative indicates, the NGO partner might become more attuned with the commercial approach:

> [The WWF] have very idealistic objectives . . . but my immediate director . . . encourages me to take the line of: 'try to teach them how to be commercially minded!' [laughs]. And they are, they are! They are beginning to understand. And I think deep down they understand where we are coming from. But of course they can't be seen to be changing camps—they've got to be idealistic to drive it forward (planning manager, corporate partner).

So, while cultural change of some kind might have been beneficial to the running of the initiative, it was also accepted that too much adaptation could erode the particular strength that each partner brought to the partnership in the first place—the systematic procedures and commercial 'clout' of the businesses, and the credibility and motivation of the NGO. Hence, the degree of balance in this respect appears to be a critical one, particularly, it seems, for the NGO partner, since it is they who, in the search for market-based environmental solutions, appear to shoulder the greatest burden for change.

As a means of bridging and buffering heterogeneous cultural beliefs, behaviours and attitudes, cultural mediators were also strongly associated with the subcultural view of organisations. Clearly, where there is a group of such individuals, they might be seen as occupying a distinct subculture within their own organisation, e.g. the project team in the WWF, or particular environment teams in the corporate partners. This might even, as it was argued earlier, be manifested as a cross-organisational subcultural affiliation. Indeed, for the corporate partners, respondents emphasised how mediation was necessary not just *between* themselves and their NGO partners, but *within* their organisation. As it has been argued, the representatives saw themselves as subculturally distinct from company buyers and therefore it was seen as necessary again to adapt their own cultural frames of reference in order to communicate with and motivate these key constituencies in the initiative. Hence, buyers were perceived as needing 'hard-nosed' commercial arguments with clear directives and performance incentives, rather than 'emotive' or 'ethical' arguments, in order to act on the policy on a day-to-day level:

> How I go about [motivating the buyers]—all I can do is try and make the case . . . show how it relates to customers and how . . . there's a danger of losing business ultimately if we don't actually come up with . . . the [certified product] that those people are going to want to buy (environment manager, corporate partner).

Obviously, one of the problems with this is that, although mediation may be essential to lubricate the wheels of collaboration, it can dilute, even corrupt, the cultural meanings that any particular constituency may have wished to preserve intact. Much like 'Chinese whispers', the message intended may not be the one received after being filtered through different cultural layers. This might be seen as a particular concern for NGOs establishing collaborations aimed at environmental or other social goals, since some of the key objectives in this case may well be associated with consciousness-raising, education, and surfacing and challenging of entrenched assumptions and values.

There must also be concerns regarding the particular individuals charged with the role of cultural mediation and its concomitant needs for boundary-spanning and cultural reinterpretation. Clearly, this requires a certain understanding of cultural differences and the different bonds and affiliations that might exist within the domain of the alliance. Without the requisite dexterity in the skills of cultural transition and translation, these individuals might easily falter in their responsibilities, particularly if they do not even recognise that this is an essential part of their role. Moreover, the fragmentation perspective on culture would suggest that identifying cultural ties and affiliations might be highly problematic given such complexity and dynamism in any cultural context. More worryingly, perhaps, the individual mediator might experience considerable stress on account of the need to engage and express different, even contradictory, values and beliefs. Hence, unless collaborators recognise the role of the cultural mediator, and prepare for it accordingly, then fractures in the alliance might well develop from these points of stress, creating adverse outcomes at both the personal and organisational levels.

◢ Conclusion

The evidence presented here shows quite strongly how different conceptions of organisation culture can lead to different understandings of business–NGO collaboration, and even to variations in prescriptions for how they can be effectively managed. Crucially, some of the limitations of the integration perspective, so commonly applied to this phenomenon, have been revealed, suggesting that a more considered interpretation of culture should be applied in the future. This seems to be particularly the case for academic researchers, since it is clear from the results here that practitioners, as a matter of course, already tend to see culture in multiple ways. As has already been noted (Crane 1995; Newton and Harte 1997), the green business literature has a propensity to import concepts such as organisational culture from other fields without attending to their full implications and without considering more critical perspectives. It is hoped that this chapter will provide at least some impetus for researchers into business–NGO collaboration to refrain from taking this particular route.

Finally, it should be clear from the analysis that some dexterity with cultural analysis can be extremely useful in understanding business–NGO collaboration, particularly given the potential for various forms of clash illustrated by the respondents in this study. Confronting the need to address cultural disharmony within, as much as across, collaborating organisations is essential, and would certainly be a fruitful avenue for future research. The role of cultural mediators in this respect appears to be a key one, and their skills in acting as cultural bridges may well be crucial to the success of the collaborative effort, and to the types of value typically communicated and institution-alised as part of this effort. Collaborating organisations would therefore be well advised to acknowledge both the necessity and dangers of such a role—or certainly at least to accommodate for them, since it would appear that some form of mediation may well emerge naturally as part of the alliance process. The mediating role, however, is unlikely to be adopted with ease, and it is certain to be complicated by arrangements such as those in the Plus Group, where much of the key work of the initiative is conducted among groups culturally removed from those deciding and implementing policy. In this light, careful selection of personnel and some degree of appropriate training might well be highly advantageous in order to improve the odds of collaborative success. This would be especially relevant where the possibilities for stress on the part of mediators might be significant given the fragmentary nature of their cultural context and the need to juggle, even reconcile, what might be perceived to be highly incongruous values.

THE ART OF COLLABORATION

Lessons from emerging environmental business–NGO partnerships in Asia

Christopher S. Plante

The Asia Foundation, USA

Jem Bendell

New Academy of Business, UK

This is precisely the logic of the ancient Art of War: Know your enemy, know yourself, know where you are, know what is going on.

◢ Four essentials of the 'art of war'

The great military strategies of China and the Ottoman Empire are often used by modern-day businesses to gain strategic advantage in marketplace 'warfare'. Using knowledge gained through hundreds of years of armies deploying these tactics to capture territories and win over citizens, many businesses focus on the enemy or 'competition' and the territory or 'market', as they analyse their strategies.

Consequently, there are four elements to a competitive business strategy: know your enemy, know yourself, know where you are and know what is going on. To know your enemy is to know your competition for buying supplies, employing staff and selling products. To know yourself is to understand your key competences and advantages—and to know your weaknesses also—in relation to your own objectives and to the competition. To know where you are is to understand the social, economic, environmental, cultural and political context of your business operations: for example, the legislation for regulating your company. To know what is going on is to use that knowledge of yourself, your enemy and your operating environment to understand the 'bigger picture', and forecast changes in your markets, supplies and competition—and plan accordingly.

Many of today's successful companies are effective in their application of these four elements of business strategy. However, if one focuses exclusively on the *ends*—winning the battle in the marketplace—then the *means* of achieving those ends can be overlooked. The problem is that the *means* of achieving business ends can have side-effects on 'your enemy', 'where you are', 'what is going on' and therefore 'yourself'. Ignoring the impact of the means can impact negatively on the business ends. It is useful to remember that ancient war tacticians warned against dismissing the relationship warring parties held with the people on whose territory they fought. Consequently, management needs to consider the impact of their business operations on the citizenry or general public, who are ultimately influenced and affected by their operations.

We believe that inadequate attention to the means of winning the business battle is a mistake. Public opinion and the impact of private-sector operations on the local environment make for strategic assets, or liabilities. It depends on how businesses understand the non-governmental organisations (NGOs) that represent and catalyse community opinion. In this chapter we describe examples of positive and negative relations between businesses and NGOs in a number of Asian countries. From the 'Art of War' metaphor, we argue that there are distinct advantages for business through partnership with NGOs, and extend the metaphor to the 'Art of Collaboration', which includes a fifth element: *know your allies*.

◢ Communities fighting corporations

> Monsanto's [cotton] field trials in Karnataka [India] will be reduced to ashes in a few days. These actions will start a movement of direct action by farmers against biotechnology, which will not stop until all the corporate killers like Monsanto, Novartis, Pioneer etc. leave the country. [If] we play our cards right at the global level and co-ordinate our work, these actions can also pose a major challenge to the survival of these corporations in the stock markets. Who wants to invest in a mountain of ashes, in offices that are constantly being squatted (and if necessary even destroyed) by activists? (Professor Nanjundaswamy, Karnataka State Farmers' Association, November 1998).

The rhetoric is strong, the argument clear and the future bleak for corporations who try to compete for control rather than partner for prosperity. Protest against companies who do not appear to embrace the sustainable development agenda, with the concurrent respect for human rights and the ability of communities to control their own resources, is widespread in Asia. The issue of genetic engineering provides one example.

On 28 November 1998, and again on 2 December, contingents of Indian farmers in the Karnataka region, chanting 'Cremate Monsanto' and 'Stop genetic engineering', uprooted and burned genetically engineered cotton fields in front of a bank of TV cameras and news reporters (Cummins 1998: 1). NGOs, including the Karnataka State Farmers'

---

1   See footnote on p. 14.

Association, have called on Monsanto[1] to 'get out of India', and for the government to ban field tests and imports of genetically engineered seeds and crops. This form of conflict appears to be having an affect, with the Andhra Pradesh provincial government requesting Monsanto to halt all field trials of Bt 'Bollgard' cotton in the state, and government officials in New Delhi reiterating that the so-called 'terminator technology' seeds—patented by Monsanto—will not be allowed into the country (Cummins 1998).

Conflict between NGOs and agri-businesses is not restricted to India. On 8 December 1998 in Manila, under the slogans of 'Stop the Terminator Seeds' and 'Put a Face on the Enemy', the South-East Asia Regional Institute for Community Education and 12 other environmental NGOs organised a militant mass demonstration outside Monsanto's corporate offices (Cummins 1998). In mid-November, the Pesticide Action Network (PAN) of Asia and the Pacific launched a Safe Food Campaign at the Asia Pacific People's Assembly in Kuala Lumpur, Malaysia. Dr Vandana Shiva, speaking in Kuala Lumpur, described Monsanto as a 'global terrorist', forcing 'hazardous food' on countries, using 'tremendous pressure and misleading promotional campaigns' to prevent people from choosing 'the food they want', and refusing to segregate and label genetically engineered foods and crops (quoted in Cummins 1998: 1).

Such antagonistic relations are not a new phenomenon in Asia. For example, in 1993, after Dr Romy Quijano (a toxicologist from the General Philippine Hospital and pesticides adviser to the Philippines Department of Agriculture) presented a paper at an NGO-run conference on the 'Effects of Pesticides against Women', the German-based company Hoechst filed a $813,000 lawsuit against him. Although Hoechst's case against the academic was thrown out of court, many believe it has undermined freedom of speech and NGO campaigning in Malaysia (Rowell 1996).

Repression can sometimes be violent. For example, in 1995, NGO activists campaigned against chemical company DuPont's plan to build Asia's largest nylon factory in Goa, India. The activists alleged that the $200-million plant would pollute rivers, deplete drinking water supplies and desecrate sacred Hindu land. At one demonstration in January 1995, police fired on protesters, killing one. Reportedly enraged at the death, the protesters went on the rampage and burned down DuPont's project office. Later that year, amid continuing protest, DuPont announced that it was moving its plant to the neighbouring state of Tamil Nadu (Rowell 1996).

The activities of logging companies have also led to violent confrontation across Asia. One example is the struggle of the Penan forest-dwelling peoples of Malaysia, who have campaigned against loggers for years by blocking roads in the rainforests. Mining companies have also come into confrontation with forest communities and their NGO representatives. The Indonesian environmental NGO, Walhi, has campaigned for a number of years against the world's single-largest mining operation: Freeport copper mine in Irian Jaya (or West Papua). The mine is jointly owned by the New Orleans-based Freeport McMoRan Copper and Gold Corporation and the British company Rio Tinto Zinc (RTZ). Walhi claims that the mine is 'massively damaging the rich biodiversity of the area and harming the health of and sustenance of local indigenous communities' (Roberts 1995: 13). Such criticism has been met with attempts to undermine the opposition, such as Freeport's unsuccessful attempt to stop US government funding for

Walhi, and direct repression by government forces on the ground (Roberts 1995: 13). For example, in May 1995, the local catholic Bishop, Mgr H.F.M. Munninghoff, reported that troops were torturing the locals inside Freeport's containers, in the company's security positions. Northern NGOs have amplified the struggle of local groups, with the London-based human rights organisation TAPOL claiming that 'there is a major operation under way to crush all resistance to the company and to physically "cleanse" the territory of local people who are regarded as a threat to the activities of the company' (TAPOL 1995: 1-3). One Western commentator on the environmental movement across Asia, Andrew Rowell, concludes that:

> Dissent in some [Asian] countries is barely tolerated and the backlash against an organisation for speaking out on an issue—whether political, economic, ecological or religious—could be severe. In some countries the simple expression of free speech is not tolerated, let alone political discussion or dissent. It can be classified as a subversive activity, punishable by harassment, imprisonment, torture and death (1996: 260).

This raises the issue of whether the processes of partnership between businesses and NGOs in the West can occur across Asia when civil liberties are not always protected. While the battle to build democratic civil societies continues, already there are signs that, for some issues of interest to local communities and NGOs, and for some businesses, there is a move from war to peace. Much of this emerging collaboration is being supported by grants from abroad, including those made by The Asia Foundation (Box 13.1).

◢ The dividends of truce and collaboration

The paradox of business–NGO relations is that out of conflict often springs collaboration. Partnership between warring businesses and NGOs may seem a long way off in sectors such as genetic engineering and mining. However, in the case of logging companies and deforestation, protest in the North and South was a key catalyst in the establishment of a multi-stakeholder certification system run by the Forest Stewardship Council (FSC). Because of the history of confrontation on the deforestation issue, it was believed that any successful standard-setting body would have to involve businesses and NGOs from around the world. Members of Southern NGOs have a voice through the FSC, with representatives of NGOs such as the Foundation of the Peoples of the South Pacific (Papua New Guinea) and SKEPHI (Indonesia) either sitting on the board or participating in specialist working groups. While this is a global initiative, within Asia there is an increasing number of business–NGO partnerships; they might not attract the banks of TV cameras that burning cotton fields do but they are nonetheless important in the sustainable development of the continent.

If we return to the farmers' movement in India, there is also a partnership story to tell. The Peddireddy Thimma Reddy Farm Foundation in Hyderabad, India, is dedicated to the protection and strengthening of farming and farm communities. Inspired by Gandhian concepts, the NGO promotes a vigorous agricultural industry that embraces

THE GOAL OF THE ASIA FOUNDATION'S NGO–BUSINESS ENVIRONMENTAL Partnership is to encourage NGOs to move beyond their traditionally adversarial role with the private sector, and work in collaboration with businesses to address industrial pollution in Asia. Through these unique partnerships, NGOs contribute fresh ideas on how to correct pollution problems through clean production while gaining a better understanding of the difficulties faced by industry operations in their efforts to be competitive.

The NGO–Business Environmental Partnership, administered by The Asia Foundation through a co-operative agreement with the United States Agency for International Development and the United States–Asia Environmental Partnership (US–AEP), awards incentive grants to NGOs to support these efforts. The programme's goals are to:

☐ Provide incentives to Asian NGOs to engage industries in developing environmental management strategies

☐ Enhance CP training to integrate process improvements with profitable business practices

☐ Encourage companies to prevent, reduce, and recycle wastes

☐ Create replicable and sustainable models in the private and public sectors

☐ Increase public awareness of NGO–business collaboration as a win–win option for economic growth and environmental protection

Since 1995, 53 NGO–Business Environmental Partnership grants ranging from US$10,000–30,000 have been awarded to NGOs in nine Asian countries. Workshops introducing the concept with case studies of cross-sector collaboration were conducted in all of the countries with thousands of participants in all. The evidence that these partnerships are good for both NGOs and industry is substantial. Continuing success will depend on how well the benefits of NGO–business partnerships are shared and encouraged. US–AEP and The Foundation are supporting nine best-in-practice NGO–business models through a working group and workshops designed to increase the viability and use of partnership opportunities.

Box 13.1 **NGO–business environmental partnership**

rural development and international markets. The director, P. Chengal Reddy, is both an advocate of the farmer and a facilitator for agri-business.

In 1996, Peddireddy received an NGO–Business Environmental Partnership incentive grant to work with Suvera Processed Foods Private Limited, a local agri-processing company, to address pollution in the mango-processing industry. Each of Suvera's 27 mango pulp-processing factories in India's Chittoor District dump 2,000 tons of waste every harvest season. To reduce Suvera's processing wastes and convert remaining wastes into new products, Peddireddy focused on clean production research, training, consultation and technical analysis.

The project began with site visits and measurement of resources, including raw materials, facilities, tools, water, land, human capital and waste-streams. Suvera benefited from Peddireddy's familiarity with local environmental conditions and its research capabilities, training and social expertise. Initial training in clean production was given to selected workers and managers, and small experiments were conducted.

In the next phase, the NGO identified opportunities to reduce pollution and extend the company's season of employment into the off-season by converting mango waste into new products such as fuel, cocoa-extender,[2] cattle feed and fertiliser. In addition, machinery manufacturers were involved in discussions to reduce large energy losses in the processing plant.

Suvera Foods tapped into the NGO's strengths through its partnership and achieved a 95% reduction in waste, leading to minimised waste hauling costs. New by-products resulted in new sales for Suvera. Reduced chlorine use improved local sanitation and the water supply. Investigation of a new pesticide treatment accounted for a 40% increase in pest-free, processable mangoes. New raw material processing (off-season fruits and vegetables) is leading towards a longer season of employment, increasing company profits and employee income. Working conditions for skilled and unskilled labour, mostly women and children, have improved. Most importantly for the long-term sustainability of cross-sector partnerships, interest in clean production has expanded among NGOs and industries in other parts of India.

Peddireddy's successful partnership with Suvera resulted in a new partnership project with VBC Ferro Alloys Limited and a second NGO, Centre for Resource Education. Begun in 1997, this second project focuses on introducing environmental management systems to decrease silicon fine waste, coal and coke dust, and chrome slag in the ferro-alloy sector. New by-products have been developed and tested which have the capacity to completely eliminate these materials from the waste-stream. With a replication strategy and a public awareness media campaign in place, the initiative has a strong chance of success. The Federation of Andhra Pradesh Chambers of Commerce and Industry in Hyderabad is supportive of the project. Accordingly, local politicians have become aware of and enthusiastic about the possibilities of business–NGO partnerships.

Peddireddy's activities exemplify a business–NGO partnership model of a traditional grass-roots organisation working with a business on issues of mutual self-interest. Their success is measured by the growth of their efforts from improving the production and environmental and health impacts of mango/fruit-processing factories to tackling the waste problems of the local ferro-alloy plants. Findings of the project have been circulated to a number of government institutions such as A.P. State Scheduled Caste, Scheduled Tribe, and Backward Class Finance Corporations, the A.P. Khadi & Village Board, and the Directorate of Industries. Peddireddy's latest proposal envisages funding by financial institutions such as local and state banks.

Partnerships such as Peddireddy and Suvera or VBC harness the advocacy and environmental expertise of the NGO membership with the manufacturing and efficiency goals and environmental management issues of the business communities.

---

2 Cocoa can be extracted from the seed knell of mango nut. The extracted ingredients can be used in manufacturing soft drinks.

◢ War and peace

It would be misleading to suggest that there is a broad trend for more collaborative projects between business and civil society in Asia, as has been suggested is the case in the West (Murphy and Bendell 1997b). Conflict between corporations not embracing the sustainable development agenda, with the concurrent respect for human rights and the ability of communities to control their own resources, is still rife. However, against a backdrop of antagonistic relations, there are increasing numbers of partnership initiatives, such as the Peddireddy–Suvera case. When the political climate does not squash free speech, community action and constructive dialogue, and where corporates embrace their stakeholders, much can be achieved. The following examples show what traditional 'enemies' are achieving by working together.

First, there is the example of the Wisnu Foundation working with hotels in Bali, Indonesia. On the island of Bali in Indonesia, the Wisnu Foundation began as a confrontational, environmental advocacy group. Wisnu concentrated on exposing the illegal dumping of the largest hotels' wastes. They photographed garbage identified by hotel logos that had been dumped in the river, on the beach, and along the road, sending the photographs to the local media to pressurise the hotels to clean up. Consequently, 13 hotels agreed to be part of an effort to reduce their waste and, according to Wisnu, improve their materials management and profitability. Nine of the hotel partners backed out of the project in the beginning, but asked to be re-included after observing the results of the project with the four hotels that stuck with the initial partnership agreement and showed bottom-line improvements. The local authorities are backing the project and service workers will be trained in environmental management and proper housekeeping techniques.

Second, and also in Indonesia, there is the example of the Pelangi Foundation working with hospitals in Jakarta. This medical waste partnership culminated in the issuing of a threefold set of guidelines for environmental management in Indonesian hospitals. The *Guideline for Hospital Environmental Management Systems* utilises a long-term environmental management approach that involves everyone in the hospital and is an operationalisation of the ISO/DIS 14001 and ISO/DIS 14004 for hospitals. The *Guideline for Hospital Pollution Prevention* activates pollution prevention practices and eco-efficiency in hospitals. It contains profiles of Indonesia hospitals; profiles of hospital wastes; pollution prevention perspectives; and implementation of pollution prevention programmes in the US. The *Guideline for Hospital Environmental Audits* provides an instrument for the assessment and evaluation of environmental management in hospitals.

The outcome of this effort shows the resources that are brought to bear by the combined work of the partners and the linkages that are established. Pelangi's research and the hospitals' willingness to co-operate and expose their operations to an outside organisation for constructive engagement and problem-solving is remarkable. Pelangi used its governmental and business connections to work on waste solutions that can be institutionalised for the hospital sector in Indonesia.

Third, there is the example of the Green Consumers' Foundation and its work with Unilever. The Green Consumers' Foundation is an NGO established to protect consumers and fight for environmental improvements in Taiwan. It helped a major household products producer, Unilever, reduce the packaging and associated costs of its most popular detergent. Together, at the conclusion of their project, the partners demonstrated their accomplishments using life-cycle assessment software, researched and used by the NGO, to more than 30 businesses.

A fourth example is the work of the Industrial Environmental Management Office at the Federation of Thai Industries (IEM/FTI). The brainchild of Dr Pitsamai Eamsakulrat, the Multiple Business NGOs Training on Clean Technology (CT) initiative trained both grass-roots environmental advocacy NGOs and FTI members in 1998. As a result of the co-ordinated training and discussion of mutual interests, a group formed from the training, identifying themselves as the 'IN Group' (i.e. industry and NGOs) and announced their intention to practise and spread the clean production concepts into Thai society. They have since held more workshops and membership of the IN Group has expanded from 30 to more than 80 members.

The FTI partnership would never have come about without the lessons learned from other partnerships and the flexibility of the NGOs and businesses to respond to the invitation in their own way. Two other examples, from Bangladesh, are provided in Boxes 13.2 and 13.3.

However, not all NGOs have been in conflict with industry and government over the environment, human rights and economic development. Despite evidence to the contrary, both the existence and efficacy of anti-corporate protest is disputed by some members of the NGOs and businesses involved in the partnerships funded through The Asia Foundation. For example, the former director of the Green Consumers' Foundation, Mr Jay Fang, argues that, while there was public antagonism with Unilever, behind the scenes there were efforts all along to find ways of working together. In addition, during a gathering of the first 28 NGO partners and four of their business partners in Jakarta in 1997, it was pointed out to the American facilitator that many of their partnerships were not born out of adversarial relations. It was argued that confrontation does not have the same priority in the East as in the West and that the partnerships came from respect and a desire for harmony over discord.

While the question of whether The Asia Foundation's work is helping to reduce social protest or not is unanswered, it is evident that the partnerships undertaken by non-adversaries are also delivering significant environmental benefits. One example is the joint project of the NGO Gono Unnayan Prochesta (GUP) and Madaripur Chamber of Commerce and Industry in Bangladesh. GUP, which had never been confrontational with industry, worked with the Chamber to organise a national workshop which discussed their survey of industrial effluent from 18 textile facilities and ways of optimising chemical and water use while reducing pollution and costs.

The fact that there exists a complex variety of NGO stances and tactics can be regarded as an opportunity for the proactive business. It means that there are more scenarios for applying a new 'Art of Collaboration'.

IN DHAKA, BANGLADESH, THE SOCIETY FOR ENVIRONMENT AND HUMAN Development (SEHD) is collaborating with the Nur Bhai Tannery. This partnership evolved over more than a year of negotiations with various tanneries and followed the rejection of the first proposal. The society met with individual tanneries numerous times to persuade the tanneries to work on a joint environmental improvement project and were unsuccessful. Tanneries held that they had nothing to gain and a lot to lose by subjecting themselves to untested ideas and innovations from the environmental NGO. Continued persistence finally paid off when Nur Bhai Tannery agreed in April 1997 to participate in a project to reduce its effluent through a combination of pollution prevention and waste treatment activities.

The project, Mitigating Environmental Pollution in Tannery Industry, is being implemented by SEHD and Nur Bhai, with leather technologists and leather technology students. The partnership has made significant progress in addressing the specifics of tannery waste-streams and the options for waste reduction and materials substitution.

SEHD and the semi-mechanised tannery of Nur Bhai began with an inventory and background research. A full assessment of the operation of Nur Bhai and neighbouring tanneries, including the fully mechanised Paramount Tannery, with an emphasis on pollution and mitigation of pollution was completed. After the assessments, chemical analysis of BOD (biological oxygen demand) and COD (chemical oxygen demand) levels were determined for soak, lime, de-limed, bated, chrome, dye, and fat liquors as well as accumulated wastes. Literature and background information was gathered and these items were analysed and drafted into a detailed report that was intended to be syndicated to the press. Because of the sensitivity of the industry, no report has yet been issued. The goal of industrial reporting will be difficult to achieve, but eventually may happen.

In one test, buffalo hides were processed using experimental processes up to the wet blue stage with fewer tannery chemicals, water, and in less time. The finished leather is of superior quality and traders have been informed of this positive new development. This one experiment will lead to recommendations for less-polluting leather processes.

As a secondary result of the project, workers were provided with gloves, masks and boots to protect their health. The workers have been trained and are more aware and more cautious about handling hazardous materials produced in the tannery factories.

☐ A complete report, in English or Bangla, with comparative analysis and recommendations, is available from SEHD for US$5.

Box 13.2 **SEHD and the Nur Bhai Tannery**

BANGLADESH ENVIRONMENTAL LAWYERS' ASSOCIATION (BELA) USES THE LEGAL system to achieve its environmental advocacy objectives. In its partnership with Quasem Textile Mills Limited for Promoting an Active Regulatory Regime in Textile Industries, BELA has demonstrated its ability to employ its research and regulatory strengths to work with, instead of against, the textile industry.

Samples from Quasem and surrounding mills were collected and analysed and a status paper was prepared so that the industry could enumerate important issues to be addressed in light of existing legal provisions. The mills felt both threatened by what the samples would reveal and yet relieved that the discovery process was being conducted in close co-ordination with authorities and BELA, which was becoming an increasingly important intermediary for all sides. Industrial and environmental regulations are murky issues, and BELA walked both the regulators and the regulated community through an awareness process. In a gesture of goodwill and trust, the mill authority committed itself before the authorities and BELA to adopt an effluent treatment plant. This action demonstrates the importance of making an effort to correct industrial and environmental problems, as stakeholders know the high costs for an effluent treatment plant are too prohibitive and the focus then shifts to lower-cost clean production technologies instead. The mill authority drafted a Balancing, Modernisation, Reconstruction, and Expansion project. It undertook temporary measures to avoid discharging waste-water into the adjacent river, thus minimising hazards both to the general public and to other resources, notably fisheries. Wastes were captured in a reservoir within the mill site. On visiting the site, a Department of Environment official expressed concern that such measures still needed further safeguards. Economic constraints were discussed and the official subsequently proposed suggestions for improving the temporary measures, which again were accepted by the mill authority.

Despite regular interaction among all relevant agencies, BELA felt that more agencies could be involved in the process in order to ensure the long-term impact of the initiatives. The NGO therefore conducted a search to identify the highest-polluting textile industries. An extensive field investigation involved both videos of company operations and interviews with industrial personnel, members of the public, and health and fishery officials. Legal notices were served against industries that were visibly polluting the surrounding environment and ignoring repeated warnings from the Department of Environment. Quasem, being an early partner of BELA, enjoys first-mover advantage.

Box 13.3 **BELA and Quasem Textile Mills**

◢ Towards an art of collaboration

We make specific recommendations for the management of partnerships in Box 13.4. However, as commercial enterprises, governments and NGOs have unique organisational cultures, the processes of cross-sector collaboration are particular to each situation. Therefore, it is sensible not to over-generalise: business–NGO partnerships are an art not a science. Thus, in our concluding discussion, we return to the points relating to the 'Art of War'.

Know your enemy

Companies often think of NGOs as enemies. For such companies, who like to keep their stakeholders at arm's length, NGOs often do turn out to be enemies. In many cases, repression of, and violence against, NGOs is the result. Whether companies are directly involved in such warring or not, if they refuse to recognise their responsibilities as major market players and ignore their stakeholders, then they are complicit in it.

In the longer term, business needs NGOs. Political, environmental and economic security are the themes underlying most NGO campaigns. These themes relate to the essential, stable background against which business can compete and thrive. With governments under increasing pressure to provide attractive investment opportunities, so their ability and desire to provide political, environmental and economic security for their citizens is reduced. In such a situation, where regulation is minimal, business can externalise as many social and environmental costs as possible. As other companies *can* do this, so logic suggests that every company *must* do so in order to remain competitive. To put it simply: without good regulation, business must become nastier. The tragedy is that, if all companies do this, then the people will become so poor, sick and alienated that production, consumption and profits will not be sustained. NGOs and the rest of civil society are helping to plug this regulatory gap. Their protests can reduce profitability while their partnerships can enhance profitability: hence they provide a business reason for acting in a less unprincipled and more sustainable, responsible, manner.

Consequently, managers have a choice of enemy. They can choose NGOs and be complicit in the kind of repression we outlined at the start of the chapter: they can choose the no-win scenario. Alternatively, they can choose new enemies in undemocratic government, irresponsible business, and weak or unenforced regulation and become part of a sustainable future: they can choose the win–win scenario.

Know yourself

Strong NGOs know their identity, their purpose, means and position in civil society. They continually assess how they rank and how they relate with other members of their own sector and across sectors as well. Most businesses, however, have only a superficial understanding of who they are as community citizens and what their values are related to where they operate. The emergence of corporate social auditing is a recognition that

FROM THE EXPERIENCE OF PROJECTS SPONSORED BY THE ASIA FOUNDATION AND US–AEP, some general principles can be identified and recommendations made for managers. The best principle to remember is that good partnering establishes trust and reduces misunderstanding. We identify six key recommendations:

Make contact. The numerous NGO–business partnership examples mentioned should convey some sense of the productivity of partnerships. Draft a plan to meet them, even if this is only a one-time opportunity to introduce yourselves. The exchange of information itself builds goodwill and trust. Furthermore, the other sector often has valuable contacts. They can have numerous reasons to want to co-operate with you. Environmental groups can help level the playing field and work with businesses and associations to design effective industrial systems that integrate mutual concerns. Think beyond the plant fence and outside the management 'box'. Brainstorm and consider every option. Chart scenarios with potential partners.

Proceed cautiously. Of course, there are risks. Partnerships may open a facility and business to detailed scrutiny. It presents NGOs with knowledge about your operations and facility that you may not want to reveal. There is the possibility of partnership failure, ending with bad relations or more. Survey and measure the risks before and as you go. The best strategy for avoiding problems is (1) clear and frequent communication and (2) performing partnership activities in phases, understanding that all partners have the right to slow or stop implementation of plans if serious issues emerge.

Design a realistic strategy. Choose a scenario and approach that combines positive, bottom-line results with improved understanding of the other partner(s). A phased approach towards continued partnership allows both partners to engage at their own pace. Use mileposts.

Evaluate the results. This action is the fundamental consideration of any organisation contemplating a collaborative effort. You will be thinking of the possible results from the beginning of your strategy. Measurement of results in effectiveness and impact are key in any well-run operation, whether profit or non-profit. Like environmental management systems, the process of partnership is continuous and adaptable.

Recognise limitations. Partnerships cannot deal with all sustainability issues. Once a programme of work has been agreed, it is often difficult to introduce new issues until some time has past and the partners have built up mutual trust. In addition, some issues will lie beyond the expertise or financial capabilities of the partners. A partnership should not preclude the role of governmental regulation, or be used as a shield against criticism on issues not addressed in the partnership.

Be open to change. A strategy based on current and projected social, political, environmental and economic conditions should not be adhered to religiously when that terrain changes. For example, the Asian economic crisis adds a largely unforeseen factor for companies operating in the region. Millions of people, who once had jobs and food, are going without, discouraged, and looking for culprits. It is likely they will create social unrest and political instability within their communities to find resolution.

Box 13.4 **General recommendations for business partners** business is a social institution as much as an economic one. Putting employees in touch with their values and the values of their business is a stepping stone for companies making a positive contribution to society.

Social auditing can also reveal internal 'social capital'. For example, one of the hidden resources and assets within businesses is its NGO contacts and relations. Employees belong to NGOs for a wide variety of reasons, whether for recreation, community development, political action, or prestige. Yet businesses are not aware of the connections that their employees have within a community. Those connections can be the difference between either a working alliance or a battle.

Know where you are

Most environmental conflicts begin wherever your company's property, including everything that goes into or comes from it, intersects with the rest of the community. The more a company knows about its physical and social surroundings, and its impact on those surroundings, the more it is able to reduce harm, promote benefit and respond effectively to critics. NGOs often know more about the issues of concern to local communities, the media and to regulators than business: it's their job. By working with NGOs, companies can access an outside perspective and improve both their self-awareness and understanding of stakeholders. This can have direct results on the bottom line. For example, the partnerships we described that used clean production as a theme increased productivity, brought new assets, and reduced waste management costs. Handled well, the partnerships also enhanced the corporations' reputation, thereby changing the 'battlefield' in favour of the company.

Know what is going on

The classic strategists afforded a high priority to intelligence. The citizens over whose territory the armies fought held extensive and exclusive information on the terrain, the enemies and what was happening. A map of the terrain was not sufficient. Neither is a map of the issues affecting a business at any one point in time sufficient: to really know *what is going on* rather than *where you are*, you need to be constantly in touch with your sources of information. Consequently, effective partnership with NGOs is not a one-off phenomenon. To be effective, it must be part of a new corporate philosophy that ties the business into the ideas and information of the partnered NGO. Only then will the business be able to understand the changing environment and society within which it operates.

Know your allies

We have argued then that business–NGO partnerships reduce the unknowns. But they do more than this, and so the Art of War metaphor must be expanded. Businesses and NGOs have begun to look for ways of fighting the enemy that faces us all: environmental degradation and social deprivation. In this mammoth battle, every individual actor will require new and unfamiliar allies. There will inevitably be misunderstandings and differences, as Co-Chair for Civil Society on the Philippine Council for Sustainable Development, Nicanor Perlas, recognises:

> The thawing of the lines between business and civil society [in most of Asia] is fairly recent. Bridges are still being built. Trust is still being developed. Common policy agendas are still being nurtured.[3]

Partnerships with new allies will not necessarily spell the end of protest. Where there is corporate irresponsibility, NGOs should be respected for their ability to call corporates to account and awaken us to social and environmental abuses. As Miguel D. de Oliveira and Rajesh Tandon argue:

> [The] exploration of opportunities for co-operative action does not imply that citizens [and NGOs] should renounce their right and duty to question and oppose corporations—and states—whenever their behavior proves detrimental to the common good. In any case labor disputes and conflicts over environmental or consumer issues will hardly disappear from the agenda of civil society (1994: 7).

A diverse network of NGOs comprises the allies of a sustainable responsible society and, therefore, the allies of a sustainable responsible business. To continue to win in today's marketplace is to understand the 'Art of Collaboration' and to *know your allies*. True allies can only be known through the test of time; now is certainly the time to test new allies and join the fight.

---

3 Personal communication with Nicanor Perlas, Philippine Council for Sustainable Development, Manilla, June 1997.

PART 5
Concepts

COMPLEMENTARY RESOURCES
The win–win rationale
for partnership with NGOs

Steve Waddell

Organizational Futures, USA

Many eyebrows were raised in 1997 when an activist environmental group, called the Conservation Law Foundation (CLF), and the multi-billion dollar US power utility, AES, made a joint bid for the $1.1 billion power-generating capacity of the New England Electric Company. After all, the two organisations were better known as adversaries than partners. In proposing to become joint owners of the region's largest power utility, the two had different goals, but they united in action. AES was focused on traditional business expansion, whereas CLF's goal was to shut down the dirtiest electricity-generating plants of the grid. By joining with CLF, AES was demonstrating its commitment to the public policy priority of cleaning up the environment. By joining with AES, CLF was gaining an opportunity to be at the board table to directly affect the policies that generate pollution. Although the partnership was outbid, it was considered a very competitive proposal.

The AES–CLF proposal was unusual. However, it contains core elements of a new type of intense working relationship that large corporations are establishing with civil society groups such as non-profit, non-governmental organisations (NGOs), or community-based interest groups. These are relationships that are not based in the gift systems of philanthropy, nor the obligations systems behind the concept of corporate social responsibility. Rather, these are relationships that address core corporate business goals and are developed by people from core functional units such as marketing, product development, strategy and planning, and product delivery.

These types of relationship are being driven, usually implicitly rather than explicitly, by the inherent ability of civil society organisations to *do* things that business corporations cannot—and vice versa. This ability is inherent in the structure and orientation that comes with being a civil society or a business organisation—the three *organisational sectors* of business, government and civil society have distinct roles in our societies. This means that they also play distinct roles in collaborations and partnerships. By joining forces, the organisations do what other partnerships aim to do: combine their resources and strengths, and offset their weaknesses. However, in *intersectoral* partnerships the roles of the different organisations are particularly complex because the organisations have such different goals, cultures, and even ways of perceiving the world. These differences can make communication problematic as words take on different meanings—for example, 'goal' in the corporate sector is associated with quantified outcomes that are critical to measuring targets, whereas for civil society groups it can have a vaguer meaning associated with longer-term objectives.

Despite these difficulties, business–civil society collaborations are increasing in number and sophistication as the significance of the rewards are better understood. However, to tap these rewards the distinct roles of business and civil society in partnerships must be better understood. This chapter aims to deepen understanding by reviewing collaborations from a corporate perspective: what they can bring to core corporate functions. It ignores corporate foundations, community relations, and public relations as supportive functions that are driven in most cases by the philanthropic tradition. Rather, this chapter focuses on relationships clearly driven by a 'win–win' or 'mutual gain' perspective. The following sections summarise eight different functions that NGOs are providing for businesses, in different industries around the world (see Table 14.1).

◢ Risk management and reduction

In various chapters the role of NGOs in creating risk for corporations is discussed. Business has been 'beaten up' in public by NGOs for such things as fleeing industrial inner cities, failing to ensure that suppliers apply human rights standards, or polluting the environment. In recent years companies operating in the oil, sportswear, timber, banana and biotechnology industries have been particularly affected. With environment (Hoffman 1997a) and in the US banking industry (Waddell 1997d) a cycle of corporate response to this type of NGO pressure can be identified: (1) initial resistance to NGOs and a response only as a public relations strategy; (2) government legislation obliging that business be responsive; (3) a more proactive framework adopted by business such as corporate social responsibility; and often a last stage (4) with identification of how to respond to the NGO-mobilised concerns in ways that recognise them as new business opportunities.

This final response recognises that the connection between NGOs and risk has a flip-side, namely that NGOs can help corporations reduce risks associated with specific projects or general operations. This is because the NGOs represent stakeholders outside of the core corporate structure, and provide a type of early warning network of potential

Corporate goal	NGO function
Risk management and reduction	☐ Providing stakeholder views as early warning of possible problems ☐ Integrating business and community goals ☐ Creating and enforcing popularly supported standards, codes, etc.
Cost reduction and productivity gains	☐ Negotiating community benefits and role ☐ Supporting transparent processes ☐ Educating publics ☐ Leveraging non-tax status ☐ Accessing altruistic energy
New product development	☐ Providing knowledge about communities and their resources ☐ Lobbying for regulatory change ☐ Providing knowledge about technical issues ☐ Providing linkages to non-commercial creativity
New market development	☐ Aggregating small and poor markets to profitable size ☐ Extending a trusting public image ☐ Creating demand through new business development ☐ Providing delivery support ☐ Educating communities about new approaches
Human resource development	☐ Teaching and training about specific communities ☐ Providing inspirational outlets for employees and boosting morale ☐ Monitoring standards
Production chain organising	☐ Organising all the chain players for total quality improvement strategies
Building barriers to entry	☐ Building a distinctive image ☐ Linking to a distinctive market
Creativity and change	☐ Providing alternative viewpoints to reveal unrecognised assumptions and develop new integrative strategies

Table 14.1 **NGO functions in business strategies: intermediaries and transformers**

problems with corporate activities. They also provide opportunities to reduce risk in more proactive ways.

Perhaps two of the best examples of corporations building relationships with civil society organisations in order to reduce general risk come from South Africa and the Philippines. Both those countries in the 1970s and 1980s had governments with low legitimacy with the general population. Partly out of concern that, when change swept out those governments, business would be swept out too, businesses joined together to create the Philippine Business for Social Progress (PBSP) and the predecessors of today's National (South Africa) Business Initiative. These organisations were instrumental in constructing dialogue with groups outside of those favoured by the governments, deepening understanding of the social situation, and creating broader social networks. This was achieved by making grants to NGOs to undertake specific activity such as community economic development or education, and through meetings with NGOs (including the Catholic Church) categorically aimed at building ties and relationships.

Sometimes general operating risk reduction takes corporations beyond marketing and into public education—something NGOs are better at doing. The major banking concern, Citigroup, saw the lack of understanding about some basic financial issues, such as the role of the Central Bank and interest rates in controlling inflation in some South American countries. Therefore, together with some NGOs, it created general programmes with materials to teach about such issues in schools.

Another way to reduce risk is to identify standards and processes to deal with problems and challenges that a business operation may pose. One of the longest NGO–business traditions in this regard is with labour unions and processes to establish a collective agreement. These standards are often very contentious, but new negotiating forums are emerging that hold some promise. One such forum addressing human rights has developed the Global Sullivan Principles, written with the convening support of the United Nations, which brought together NGOs such as Amnesty International, and businesses including General Motors and Colgate-Palmolive. Increasingly, these standards include roles for NGOs as monitors and auditors of corporate behaviour and corporate subcontractors.

NGOs can also be a good source of information that is useful in both risk management and corporate planning, which corporations would otherwise find difficult to obtain. Sometimes this develops into formal relationships, such as with the brokerage firm Salomon Smith Barney, which needs information about human rights issues to assess investment risks and obtains it in part by sponsoring research newsletters and reports prepared by the human rights organisation, Vérité.

◢ Cost reduction and productivity gains

This risk reduction activity also provides good examples of how relationships with civil society organisations can actually reduce costs for a project by building NGO relationships. For example, in San Diego, USA, the cost of housing projects in the inner city are notoriously expensive because of theft and vandalism. In response, the construction companies, bankers and an NGO representing the poor in San Diego, developed a project that built a 140-unit housing complex from a community-building perspective that ensured long-term maintenance of the investment and loan repayment through strong social structures. By integrating the community and business goals into the project, the community felt ownership of it and protected it from vandalism and theft (Waddell 1997a). The lender, Bank of America, has built a profitable strategic core competency around funding such community-building housing projects not just with the local San Diego NGO, but with similar NGOs in many communities across America.

Relationships with NGOs can also produce cost savings for corporations by their ability to mobilise volunteer energy. Volunteers can reduce project costs and make projects viable from a profitability perspective that would otherwise be impossible. What under business control would be considered exploitative, under collaboration and real partnership with NGOs becomes a civil society process to gain access to market resources. That is the approach being used to build water and sanitation systems in places as different as South Africa (Palmer 1998; Waddell 1998a) and Argentina (Fiszbein and Lowdin 1998), where NGOs have been given a central role in consortia that have undertaken the projects.

Yet still another way NGOs can help reduce costs is through their potential for enhancing transparency and reducing corruption. NGOs in general place a higher emphasis on transparency than business or government, largely because a membership-based organisation that depends on volunteer support has a much greater need to be transparent itself. For example, in the case of road building in Madagascar which intimately involved local NGO road user associations, it was estimated that reducing corruption reduced costs for company bids for road rehabilitation and construction by as much 25% (Waddell 1998b). Some businesses team up with education NGOs with the motive of reducing costs through more indirect ways. For example, Citigroup Bank supports the US NGO called Classrooms Inc. to improve teaching about information technology, in part based on the bank's need to increase usage of electronic banking systems which are much less costly than in-branch banking.

New product development

More corporations are recognising that NGOs have a particularly important role in research and development (R&D). This derives in part because of NGOs' knowledge about their communities, their ability to inspire commitment and reduce costs, their longer time-horizon, and the benefits of their tax status.

Community knowledge is critical in creating new products for particular demographic and psychographic profiles. Corporate–NGO relationships are bound to become increasingly important as competition and globalisation leads corporations to focus more on the low-income communities of developing countries. Unilever, one of the world's largest and most global manufacturers of household products, has tapped NGOs' knowledge as it takes a lead in developing new products for very low-income communities in India, Brazil and elsewhere.

Some of the earliest large-scale collaborations between NGOs and business to create new products began in the 1970s in the US banking industry (Waddell 1997a, 1997c, 1997d). Under pressure from the federal and state governments to improve services for the low-income bracket, many bankers have developed important, ongoing advisory groups with community-development, religious and other NGOs. These groups advocate for their communities and this, when the relationships are successful, produces new profitable products that integrate government programmes, include NGOs as peer groups to ensure repayment, and more closely respond to the characteristics and needs of poorer communities. In North Carolina, such an initiative was developed to address needs of migrant workers, one of the most difficult types of market for banks. And Bankers' Trust, which caters to the very wealthy, is working with NGOs such as the Accion international micro-finance network to produce a new product that provides reputable options for the bank's clients who wish to make charitable donations or social investments.

In this new product development process with NGOs, marketing departments move away from their reliance on telephone surveys and focus groups. These customer research vehicles actually provide quite shallow information, since the conversations are ad hoc and short. Moreover, they depend on people having good language skills and telephones. In contrast, conversations with NGOs on new product developments are ongoing. This means that the NGOs learn more about the business of the corporation and what it is actually capable of doing, and can participate in a much deeper dialogue about continually improving products based on community feedback. NGOs often take the initiative to suggest new products that prove good business ideas.

Sometimes NGOs find themselves with particular assets that can make them very attractive partners in emerging businesses. For example, The Nature Conservancy (TNC), a US-based environmental organisation with affiliates throughout Latin America, has focused on assembling land for eco-reserves throughout the Western hemisphere. In Belize, TNC, a local NGO, and a large British travel company, Abercrombie & Kent, aim to build a small eco-tourism site on one of the world's largest tropical rainforest reserves owned by the local NGO. The industry will provide jobs and increasing revenues as the local NGO becomes a substantial shareholder in the project; all of this creates added reason for local people to ensure the ongoing protection of the reserve.

In some cases NGOs mobilise community resources and influence to create what are essentially new products. This type of energy has often proven critical in pressuring government regulators and quasi-public utilities to become more flexible in the type of product that companies can provide. This is essentially what happened in the cases of water and sanitation projects referred to earlier, and in several locations it has been important in opening up new types of business for power utilities. In developing countries, poor communities cannot pay for such utilities based on traditional building approaches that are usually imported from developed countries. Revising these approaches and standards can produce new building processes and products to meet this market's particular needs and capacity.

The corporate–NGO collaborations often have an R&D aspect that is being integrated into common business practice. For example, there is significant intertwining between commercial pharmaceutical companies and universities, where the universities focus more on long-term and exploratory research and the pharmaceutical companies on the application. Another interesting example is the US theatre and entertainment industry. Commercial theatre is focused on profit, whereas the non-profit theatre is more mission-driven and focused on issues, innovation and excellence. A sophisticated menu of legal arrangements has been developed to support the transfer of financial resources from the commercial to non-commercial theatres, where the latter play an R&D role in developing entertainment products. Large entertainment corporations, such as Disney, have now directly entered the commercial theatre market and are developing relationships with non-commercial houses to develop products that can be films or television shows. Costs are a significant factor in these types of R&D relationship, since non-commercial theatres have much lower overheads and save on tax costs (Cherbo 1999).

New market development

NGOs' ties with poor and marginalised communities are a particularly important asset for businesses that aim to provide goods and services for them, and as Unilever has concluded, most companies should be considering the poor as a target market. Traditional delivery structures, such as bank branches, pharmacies and sales forces often are simply too expensive for companies to provide profitable services. But sometimes the biggest problem is a lack of understanding about communities and their potential. Harvard's Michael Porter has been particularly vocal about pointing out that, although individual incomes are low, within poor communities there is often more buying power per square foot than in ones where individuals are much more wealthy (Porter 1995). NGOs in these communities can help to address these issues through their own knowledge about communities and their ability to organise them.

A particularly critical role of NGOs is their ability to aggregate small markets into a scale that is meaningful for a business. This is part of the key to Grameen Bank's success in Bangladesh where it developed micro-finance lending as part of its banking strategy. Rather than use tellers and staff to monitor loans, micro-finance aggregates people into groups of five or more, with members supporting one another as they develop their businesses. This peer-lending model, growing out of local social dynamics, was first analysed in the early 1960s (Gertz 1962) and has been developed by Accion International's network to the point that it has generated a new, for-profit bank and is accessing money markets with competitive returns. Major banks are now seeing these types of activity as critical to building a base for their commercial markets, and are actively supporting micro-finance NGOs that know how to develop low-income communities in more cost-effective ways than corporations. For example, Citigroup has made this a key part of its strategy to reach its goal of 100 million customers by 2010; it reasons that it has to literally create new markets and customers, and is aggressively partnering with NGOs involved in micro-finance internationally with the insight that these NGOs are creating future bank customers.

Sometimes NGOs take a very direct role in creating demand for a company's products, because that demand can also contribute to community economic development. Such an example is unfolding in Brazil since Latin America's largest stainless steel producer, Acesita, was privatised in 1994. As commonly occurs, the privatisation was accompanied with a large number of lay-offs; however, Acesita created a foundation to, in part, address these resulting employment issues. The foundation has picked up on the fact that almost all of the stainless steel production was exported, since there were no intermediate stainless steel processors in the country. By working with the retirees association (which includes laid-off workers), a local NGO Artisans Institute has been developed to train people in manufacturing stainless steel products. These small manufacturers are creating the first significant domestic demand for the raw stainless steel product.

◢ Human resources

NGO–business relationships are proving beneficial to human resource concerns for two particular groups: those people directly hired by corporations, and those working with subcontractors. Employees are being trained by NGOs on topics and in skills that have been developed by NGOs over many years. Sometimes this is in skills in working with the poor and marginalised, and with people in specific communities. Language and culture present barriers not just for individuals, but for entire groups of people with whom the business sector often has trouble working; often the problem is that corporate employees simply do not understand how to speak with people who do not belong to their own social group. Low-income community-based NGOs are teaching bankers in the US about the informal barriers faced by the poor, such as imposing formal bank branches that are physically intimidating. And Pact, an international development NGO, provides its expertise to Cabot, an American chemical company, in developing community programmes in South-East Asia; Pact's presence also gives the programmes a higher degree of credibility and connects Cabot to Pact's own community network.

NGOs are proving adept at identifying and developing people to work in business environments. In the United States where there is a labour shortage, corporate human resource departments are partnering with NGOs and building better systems for the task of identifying and preparing people for work who have been unemployed or left outside of the mainstream workforce; NGOs have better networks, skills and knowledge appropriate for the task. Since 1991 such a partnership between the hotel group Marriott International and an NGO called Pathways to Independence has produced remarkable results, with 70% of Pathways' graduates still employed after a year and the hotel chain estimating that for every $1 it spends on the programme it is saving $4, by lowering staff turnover and absenteeism (Kanter 1999).

NGO connections with business employees also develop through volunteer pro-grammes that can have goals to build social connections, skills and employee morale. A 1999 survey of American corporations found that 81% of respondents use volunteer programmes to support core business goals, up from 31% in 1992 (Points of Light Foundation 1999). Volunteer programmes are increasingly common with lower-level employees, too. Both the billion-dollar American boot company, Timberland, and the international energy and communications company, Enron, have concluded that volun-teering provides an important morale boost for their employees. Timberland gives time off for community work, and Enron has built its 'giving programme' in part around organisations supported by its employees. The esteem of volunteers for their employer increases, and the community work increases employees' self-esteem.

The vertical disintegration of many firms through subcontracting has led to human resource problems that NGOs are helping to address. The scandals of child labour being used to produce soccer balls and below-subsistence wages for subcontracted clothing manufacturers are among the high-profile and unintended outcomes this corporate restructuring has generated. Traditional human resource strategies to avoid such prob-lems are impossible to apply to subcontractors. Agitation for improved working stan-dards by NGOs has provoked some heated exchanges and is producing some interesting results. Some NGOs are now working with corporations to assist in defining standards, monitoring them and enforcing them. This is generating a new industry of monitoring and auditing, such as with the SA 8000 initiative developed by the Council on Economic Priorities and the US President's task force on human rights and labour issues for American companies with overseas operations. Vérité is a leading NGO that specialises in providing an interface between corporations, local subcontractors and local commu-nities to address human resource issues. Vérité's international network provides an attractive vehicle for international corporations to promote standards with a consistent approach, with Vérité providing monitoring support both directly and by building capacity with local NGOs to provide the services.

◢ Production chain organising

As the geographic expanse of production chains grows with globalisation, traditional production chain linkages are often proving inadequate. Many production chains that were previously within the structure of vertically integrated firms are dissolving as 'companies have gone about . . . slicing and dicing themselves into pieces' (Wysocki 1999). New ways to build and manage production chains with NGOs are evolving under these pressures. As always, all the links have to meet the three key outcomes of quality, quantity and timeliness.

One capability of NGOs that is bringing them more centrally into some production chains is their ability to work with low-income communities. In many cases the chain includes small producers, such as farmers, who are relatively poor and without access to global markets. For example, in the Philippines, Dolefil (the Philippine subsidiary of the Dole Food Company) and a farmers' NGO have negotiated an agreement to improve the quality of rice production so that Dole can sell it to the discriminating Japanese market. In this arrangement a government research institute provides quality seeds, Dolefil guarantees a floor price for the farmers, and the NGO trains the farmers in improved production techniques, processing and packaging—profits are shared equally between the NGO and Dole's subsidiary (Ledesma 1999). In the past, government might have taken a lead in farmer training, but NGOs are found to be more effective due to their local focus, lack of large bureaucracy, and knowledge of local communities.

Sometimes NGOs take a lead in developing the entire production chain and improving its quality. This role for NGOs emphasises their ability to work with the poor and is combined with a broader community-building quality that inspires volunteer commitment and trust in a chain that can be pulled apart through competitive pressures. In India in the state of Karnataka a surprising example of this type of NGO–business collaboration is developing in a network headed by an NGO, the Center for Technology Development (CTD). It has created five different industry nodes, each with their own NGO lead organisation, in new materials (such as new metals), informatics (two nodes), food processing and agriculture; there is a small venture capital fund as well. The NGOs themselves are intersectoral, combining large businesses such as Hindustan-Lever, governments, research institutes and NGOs. An analysis of the work of the food processing and agriculture NGOs concluded that together their mission can be defined as ensuring continual quality improvement in the entire food industry production chain (Waddell 1997b). This includes working with research institutes to develop the seeds and growing technologies most appropriate for the local climate, small farmers and their NGOs to ensure appropriate application of the technologies; a farmer's co-op to improve transportation of goods, sorting and quality; a women's small business incubator organised as an NGO to establish new food businesses; Hindustan-Lever, which provides access to markets and large-scale food processing systems; and Indo-American Hybrids to assist in development of new greenhouse technologies and production. CTD and its NGOs are led by retired Indians who held very senior positions during their worklife; they volunteer their time, often many days a week, with the goal of supporting 'the upliftment' of Indians.

◢ Building barriers to entry

Relationships with NGOs can provide corporations with a distinctive network that makes entry by other companies into its market very difficult. The relationships produce a product or service that people buy because it includes the relationship with the NGO. When products are otherwise difficult to distinguish (particularly highly transactional ones such as banking or telephone services), these networks can be an important factor.

This strategy has been most commonly developed through the affinity or cause-related marketing concept. This concept was popularised through a 1993–96 partnership between an NGO called Share Our Strength, and American Express in a *Charge against Hunger* campaign. The campaign generated more than $21 million dollars for the NGO, increased public awareness about hunger and increased use of the American Express card and their participating merchants. A study revealed that nearly two-thirds of Americans, approximately 130 million consumers, would be likely to switch brands or retailers to one associated with a good cause (Cone/Roper 1999). This strategy has grown into big business with sponsorships of major sporting events such as the Olympics, and arts events, such as Edinburgh's international festival. Companies talk about 'earned visibility' because they get their name associated with public events and non-profit organisations; Enron in the US, for example, set a 1999 target of $10 million in earned recognition.

Traditionally, these relationships have been transactional—they simply access the NGO's reputation and, when mailing lists are purchased, the names of members. In these situations there is little difference from other commercial transactions and the relationships can be quite short-term. However, more long-term strategies that build much more integrated actions are beginning to be developed. Cone Communications, a leader in the field of cause-related marketing, reported in 1999 that

> companies such as Wal-Mart and McDonald's are breaking through the clutter of cause promotion in the marketplace by developing comprehensive programmes that are an integral part of their brand's identity. These companies are witnessing win–win–win business-related impacts on their employees, customers and communities (Cone/Roper 1999).

Deeper and more interesting relationships are becoming a cornerstone of some businesses' strategy. In this era of globalisation and the increasingly large scale of corporate operations, this strategy holds particular attraction for medium-sized businesses that cannot easily compete in the arenas of price and service/product range. For these businesses, the long-term and local focus of NGOs can make them particularly valuable partners to develop competitive advantages. The long-distance phone company, Working Assets, in the United States and Citizens Bank in Canada are particularly good examples of developing NGO relationships as part of their core strategy. Working Assets is tiny compared to the telephone giants, as is Citizens compared with the banks, but both have managed to carve themselves niches by unequivocally attaching themselves to NGOs such as Amnesty International. For the NGO these arrangements involve affinity-type financial arrangements, although the relationships are typically more long-term. A global competitor could strike a similar deal with Amnesty, but, because of their much broader and numerous types of relationship they have less credibility in being 'a phone company with a conscience', as Working Assets proclaims.

A yet deeper level of relationship with NGOs in a specific community can produce enormous social capital for the business and even greater barriers to market entry for competitors (Waddell 1997a, 1997c). For example, VanCity, a $6 billion Canadian financial institution, continues to build strong ties with a number of community organisations, such as ones representing the disabled; the focus is not just on the NGOs, of course, but, as was described earlier on the aggregated market that they represent, on members and families. For VanCity these relationships are growing to be quite integrated and symbiotic, as VanCity develops products more targeted to such audiences and a unique combination of structures including a foundation, community development bank, construction company, and retail banking/insurance/trust arm. When the synergies of these relationships, structures, and products are effectively developed, they represent a very powerful barrier to entry for global firms.

◢ Change and creativity support

Perhaps there is no mantra as strong today as one about the need and pressure for change and innovation. One of the greatest powers in generating innovation is uncovering assumptions that are so embedded in the way an organisation works that they are not even recognised. An outsider who can independently challenge traditions can be a particularly good agent for revealing these assumptions and supporting the develop-ment of new ways of operating. Given their different world-views, this can be a particularly useful product of NGO–business collaboration. Management guru Rosabeth Moss Kanter has been so impressed by this that she describes the product as corporate social *innovation,* in contrast to corporate social *responsibility* (Kanter 1999). Of course the trick is to manage the interactions so that they can successfully reveal the assumptions and generate new approaches; this means avoiding being superficial and 'nice', or simply descending into a pitched battle.

One assumption that development NGOs are challenging is that the poor do not constitute a viable market. Strategy expert C.K. Prahalad, working with Unilever as the company increases its emphasis on developing-country customers, identifies five assump-tions that need to be challenged: (1) the poor are not our target; (2) the poor cannot afford products; (3) only developed markets will pay for new technology; (4) the bottom of the market is not important for our long-term interests; and (5) the intellectual excitement is in the developed markets (Prahalad 1999). Challenges to these assump-tions can be seen in many of the examples already given. For example, in the United States, banking has increased its profitability by moving out of its clubby branches and into the streets, with staff meeting NGOs and their members—but this required challeng-ing basic bank assumptions about the profit potential of the low-income market.

In the NGO–business collaborations, often the traditional assumption about the role of outside 'experts' to design, build and manage systems is being challenged through more participative processes involving and developing local leadership. This can be seen in new approaches to water and sanitation systems with local committees taking leader-ship; with roads in Madagascar where the emerging lead organisations are mass-membership community-based road user associations; and in the eco-tourism models, where local people are taking leadership roles in developing sophisticated tourist facilities.

NGOs' thinking outside the traditional business box has often created opportunities for businesses that can really listen to critiques and respond effectively. This is perhaps best exemplified with environmental NGOs whose critiques have vastly reduced costs and improved production processes. Increasingly, these critics are being invited inside, such as with The Environmental Defense Fund, which is now working with BP-Amoco to help the company meet its own internal voluntary greenhouse gas reduction targets. Sometimes the presence of an NGO in a collaboration means that a company must reassess its core business. For example, in the Madagascar road-building study, the road contractors that were most successful moved from being road builders to being educators about road building and builders of a system to build and maintain roads. And in the mid-1990s Microsoft realised that it had to change its tactics with the elderly, whom it noticed use computers least but may well find them of greater benefit than most. The company decided the best approach was to work with NGOs representing the elderly such as the American Association of Retired People. But this required Microsoft to develop a capacity-building educational approach such as that used by NGOs, rather than a marketing strategy emphasising advertising and promotions. At other times, listening to NGOs can generate a whole new industry such as eco-tourism, which can be seen as a response to increasing concern about, and interest in, issues developed by environmental NGOs.

◢ Summarising the role of NGOs in business strategy

The preceding examples were grouped into eight sections, based on the function that the NGO provides for the business partner (see Table 14.1). These functions derive from a key characteristic of NGOs: they are intermediaries, building bridges between different worlds (Brown 1991, 1993; Burt 1992; Evans 1995; Westley and Vredenburg 1991). Through business collaborations, NGOs are providing a means for linking the economic and production-oriented world of business with the social and value-generating one of civil society. At one level, this translates into providing linkages to low-income people and interest groups that the comparatively wealthy, expensive and élite world of business has difficulty connecting with and understanding. At another level, this means making business aware of issues not immediately involved in production, such as the environment, poverty, inequality and social justice. The transactional corporate culture and the greater pressures of production time in a corporate world mean that it is impossible for corporations to achieve the same reflective depth, connections and understanding that the relationship civil society culture and longer time-horizons of a civil society world encourage. For the NGO communities, when this intermediary role works it means that they can access business resources in a way that is appropriate for them.

In this chapter I have described examples where, by linking with NGOs, businesses have extended their reach into a network of complementary resources. However, unlike relationships between business organisations, these are not resources that will remain accessible through traditional business growth strategies such as mergers, acquisitions, take-overs or simple competitive dominance. Using these traditional growth strategies simply ignores the fact that the value of NGOs and their function is wrapped up in both their independence and their 'NGO-ness'. Corporations, given their profit-related goals, are inherently less capable of building trust and working with and organising communities than are civil society groups. Anything that undermines these characteristics of NGOs would therefore remove the complementarity of business–NGO collaboration.

THINKING PARTNERS

Business, NGOs and
the partnership concept

David F. Murphy and Gill Coleman

New Academy of Business, UK

'Partnership' is not the first word that usually comes to mind when one thinks about business and NGOs. Over the past three decades, most relationships between the commercial sector and civil society have been founded on conflict. In different sectors and geographical settings, this pattern of business–civil society relations started to change in the early 1990s with the emergence of new forms of partnership between these long-standing adversaries.[1] Explanations for this transformation include:

O The perceived and actual decline in the regulatory role of the nation-state in the face of globalisation (see Chapter 1)

O Consequent demands for business to be more accountable for its adverse social and environmental impacts (see Chapter 2)

O The power of civil society groups to influence corporate policy because of information and communication technologies (see Chapter 3)

Others suggest that some businesses and civil society groups are beginning to find common ground around concepts such as sustainable development and corporate citizenship in order to find solutions to global–local problems which intergovernmental processes are failing to resolve (Murphy and Bendell 1997a; McIntosh *et al.* 1998).

---

1 Although most business–civil society partnerships to date have appeared in the North, many of these initiatives have significant implications for the South in that many promote international business and trading standards. Furthermore, there is some indication that Southern-based companies and NGOs are beginning to collaborate, albeit to a much lesser extent than their Northern counterparts (Murphy and Bendell 1999).

We believe that the growing prominence of the concept of partnership is also helping to bring some businesses and NGOs together. Partnership is an idea with increasing political power today, in the sense that it invokes positive connotations within society which make people act in novel ways. In this chapter we explore the meaning of the 'partnership' concept for organisations, before considering policy debates on sustainable development and discussing some examples of the partnership approach between business and civil society. Our intention is to situate innovative business–NGO initiatives within an emerging global partnership for sustainable development that brings together state, private and civil society organisations at local and international levels.

◢ A new era of partnership

Partnership is not a new idea. Historically, partnership has primarily referred to a profit-making business relationship between two or more people where the partners jointly provide the financial capital and share both control and profits. In recent years, the notion of partnership has also entered into common usage as a neutral term to describe a romantic relationship between two equal individuals (i.e. the partners). Indeed, partnership is evolving from a legalistic business concept to a more general inter-personal and inter-organisational idea. Partnership is emerging as a powerful organising principle for people and organisations throughout the world. Despite ongoing conflict within nations and many regional and global tensions, there is growing evidence that we are entering a new era of partnership.

Researchers in different disciplines have uncovered innovative forms of partnership and collaboration in a range of organisational settings. In the face of upheavals associated with economic and technological change, businesses are increasingly adopting collaborative strategies such as joint ventures and research and development consortia with academic institutions and other companies (Waddock 1988, 1991). In a related vein, companies are also entering into partnerships with suppliers (or strategic alliances with competitors) to improve product quality, reduce costs, enhance customer service, develop new technology, minimise risks and to improve competitive position (Lewis 1990; Kumar 1996).

The new era of collaboration has also seen the rise of public–private partnerships. In the aftermath of privatisation and deregulation in the 1980s, local governments in many Northern industrialised countries increasingly began to work in partnership with private-sector interests (Macintosh 1992; Hutchinson 1994). Research undertaken by the School for Policy Studies, University of Bristol, UK, suggests that public–private partnerships have become 'the most acceptable and required form of local governance' and predicts that this trend will continue (Stewart and Snape 1996: i).

The idea of partnership has also permeated NGOs and other civil society organisations. Trade unions and workers have a long history of social partnership with employers' organisations and governments via tripartite processes at the national and international levels, the latter facilitated by the International Labour Organisation (ILO). In recent years, trade unions have also begun to collaborate more closely with NGOs through North–South solidarity and linkage activities. Trade union–NGO partnership is also taking place at the international policy level through bodies such as the UN Commission on Sustainable Development (CSD). This has included co-operation in relation to the ongoing CSD review of voluntary corporate initiatives.

Since the mid-1980s, NGOs working in different sectors and geographical regions increasingly refer to each other as partners (Fowler 1991). In the age of information technology and international conferences, NGO coalitions, networks and alliances have grown considerably. The emergence of a global civil society based on partnership principles is now considered as one of the real hopes of democratising the global political economy (De Oliveira and Tandon 1994; Korten 1998).

◢ Partnership and sustainable development

Partnership has also emerged as an organising concept at international policy levels, particularly in relation to sustainable development. Three decades ago Richard Gardner and Max Millikan published a book entitled *The Global Partnership*. Although the authors acknowledged the utopian nature of 'the concept of global partnership to abolish poverty', they insisted that such a partnership was in the making and provided 'one of the notable victories for international cooperation' (1968: v). Gardner and Millikan also expressed optimism about the role of United Nations agencies in promoting international development and identified nation-states as the other major global players of the day. Remarkably, they failed to recognise any explicit role for either business or NGOs in the global partnership process. The international community in 1968 also had not seriously begun to address sustainability and corporate responsibility. The global partnership agenda then focused on the role of the UN in economic and social development, multilateral technical assistance and the need for a world development plan, and virtually ignored issues such as environmental conservation, biodiversity, ethical trade and the livelihoods of indigenous peoples.

Twenty-five years on, the official 1993 post-Rio guide to Agenda 21 offered a much more inclusive vision of partnership. *The Global Partnership for Environment and Development* emphasised themes that link the economic, the environmental and the social. Examples included: fostering growth with sustainability, sustainable living, efficient resource use, and people's participation and responsibility. The new global partnership called for at Rio grew out of recognition that international co-operation needed more than traditional forms of foreign aid. A key point was the assertion that global partnership would only be effective if based on new levels of co-operation between all key sectors of society and government (United Nations 1993).

Looking back over the past three decades, it would be easy to dismiss recent efforts to promote global partnership as another in a long line of international policy failures. Despite a seemingly endless array of conference documents, commission reports and legally binding conventions—from Stockholm to Brandt and from Brundtland to Rio and beyond—we still seem far from finding solutions to many global–local problems in the economic, social and environmental arenas. Poverty, inequality, human rights abuses and ecological destruction continue to plague the planet. However, consider the frame of the debate and the policy actors then and now. Whereas, then, partnership appeared to be the exclusive domain of the UN, other multilateral bodies and their member governments, it now officially embraces a spectrum of global citizens: business and employers' organisations, trade unions and workers, NGOs, indigenous peoples, local authorities, youth groups, women's organisations, farmers and the scientific community. One of the major achievements of the UN system both at Rio and beyond has been the integration of global partnership principles into the international policy process. Representatives of the major groups noted above are now actively engaged in the development and implementation of global frameworks for sustainable development and other international policy issues.

◢ Business–civil society partnerships

One dimension to this new era of partnership is covered in this book: collaborations between businesses and NGOs. As many of the chapters demonstrate, these partnerships cannot be understood in isolation, as they often grow out of extended periods of conflict. For example, Chapter 2 refers to the high-profile 1995 Greenpeace–Shell confrontation over the deep-sea disposal of the Brent Spar oil platform, which eventually led Shell UK to engage the Environment Council, a British NGO, to facilitate a series of European-wide dialogue forums. These events brought Shell officials face to face with a wide range of NGOs and other stakeholders to discuss alternative disposal options for the Brent Spar. By late 1996, Shell UK's chief executive Chris Fay had recognised that his company 'had no option but to pursue the goal of sustainable development' (quoted in Cowe 1996: 17).

Chapter 4 on business–NGO relationships in the forestry sector also highlights the role of environmental group campaigns in facilitating partnership. When lobbying in the late 1980s and early 1990s failed to produce effective global and national regulation of forest management practices, NGOs recognised the need to deal more directly with business. Their tools included both protest and partnership, and eventually led to the formation of the Forest Stewardship Council (FSC). Chapter 10 shows how the success of the FSC model led to the establishment in 1996 of the Marine Stewardship Council (MSC) which resulted from a conservation partnership between the World Wide Fund for Nature (WWF) and Unilever to tackle the crisis of declining fish stocks.

Although most of the examples given in this book are of environmental partnerships, similar processes of NGO protest followed by business–NGO partnership have occurred around social issues such as labour standards. Established in early 1998, the Ethical Trading Initiative (ETI) is a British-based non-profit organisation that is based on a strategic partnership between companies, NGOs, trade unions and the UK Department for International Development. The ETI has two aims: to encourage companies to implement codes of conduct that embody internationally agreed labour standards and human rights in the workplace; and to encourage the use of best practice monitoring and independent verification methods. ETI members have agreed to a 'Base Code' of labour practice that is based on core ILO conventions. Member companies are expected to adopt the Base Code or a company-specific code that incorporates the Base Code.

A similar initiative on the opposite side of the Atlantic was launched in late 1998. The Fair Labor Association is a new US-based non-profit organisation that oversees the monitoring of compliance with the Apparel Industry Partnership's Workplace Code of Conduct. Initiated by President Clinton in 1996, the Apparel Industry Partnership is comprised of apparel and footwear companies, a prominent university, human rights groups, labour and religious organisations, and consumer advocates. The Association accredits independent monitors to determine whether companies are in compliance with the Code, and issues public reports for consumers and other interested parties. Companies that wish to participate in the Association's monitoring process are expected to adopt the Workplace Code in the manufacture of their apparel and footwear products. The Association is governed by a board of directors comprising six industry members and six NGO/labour members.

As with other efforts to promote intersectoral collaboration, business–civil society partnership to promote core labour standards does not imply universal consensus. In the Fair Labor Association, some NGOs and labour groups have endorsed the scheme, whereas others have refused to participate at this time. Michael Posner of the Lawyers' Committee for Human Rights sees the Association as 'a first step in establishing accountability that will change how the industry operates' (quoted in Greenhouse 1998). Critics argue that the Association's guidelines do not require adequate monitoring and that they do not require companies to pay workers enough to meet a family's basic needs. Concerns have also been expressed about the potential of such partnerships to divert 'attention from the structural and legal changes that could eliminate sweatshops' such as reforms to trade agreements and new legislation (Howard 1998).

To date, there appears to be greater evidence of business–civil society partnerships in the North than in the South. Whereas there has been a longer history of business–civil society relations and consumer politics in the North, Miguel de Oliveira and Rajesh Tandon note that most NGOs in the South initially 'allied themselves with popular movements to oppose the state, while for all practical purposes, ignoring the market and its institutions' (1994: 7). In the face of globalisation and state deregulation, however, Southern NGOs are beginning to recognise the need to more directly influence and in some cases collaborate with business. For example, the South Korean NGO Citizens' Alliance for Consumer Protection (CACP) organises high-profile media events aimed at getting large corporations to sign agreements related to cleaner production, energy efficiency and other environmental matters. In Brazil, the Environmental Institute (OIA) has facilitated co-operation between NGOs, local authorities, community associations and various companies on the Biomass Nutrient Recycling Project. One outcome of this project was the development of the Petropolis Waste Water Treatment Plant as a commercial venture of OIA. Costa Rica's National Biodiversity Institute (INBio, an NGO) has collaborated with the American pharmaceutical company Merck on bio-prospecting in order to value and conserve biodiversity through the use of biotechnology. However, in this case serious questions have been raised about the extent to which the partnership has taken full account of the interests of all relevant stakeholders.

A different Southern partnership model emerged from Pakistan's soccer ball industry in 1997, bringing together the Sialkot Chamber of Commerce and Industry, local manufacturers, Save the Children UK, Pakistani NGOs, UNICEF and the ILO. This partnership aims to prevent and eliminate the use of child labour in the production of hand-stitched soccer balls in Pakistan. Two programmes are being developed to enable the project participants to achieve this goal. First, the Prevention and Monitoring Programme is a voluntary scheme open to all manufacturers of soccer balls. Participating manufacturers are expected to meet a number of formal registration requirements concerning use of contractors, stitching locations and proof-of-age documentation for workers. Second, the Social Protection Programme is designed to provide affected children, women and their families with educational and financial support, and to raise local awareness about child labour and the need for alternatives.

◢ Paradox and personality in the partnership process

The idea of business–civil society partnership is a relatively new phenomenon. Many of the examples noted above only became fully operational in the late 1990s. Nonetheless it is possible to identify a number of emerging trends in business–civil society partnership processes. It is also worth noting that this experience is equally relevant for UN agencies, governments and other groups that facilitate or participate in partnerships.

Partnership between business and NGOs appears to be at odds with their respective societal goals and roles. The paradox of business–civil society partnership is inevitable given that it brings together the apparently competing agendas of business and NGOs. As a social and political process, the development and implementation of such partnerships necessarily embodies paradox. The challenge facing partnering organisations is not to try to resolve paradoxes but rather how best to manage them and learn from the experience. The partners need to acknowledge each other's differences and work with them and against them simultaneously (Handy 1994; Murphy 1997).

The partners therefore need a capacity and willingness to cope with diverse perspectives and paradoxical goals throughout the process. Partnership for sustainable development implies negotiation between economic, social and environmental interests which may be problematic. Developing and implementing partnership goals usually involves a lengthy, difficult and exceedingly complex process. Given that this is largely uncharted territory for both business and civil society, much of the details of implementation usually have to be worked out as they go along. Flexibility enables partners to adapt targets and operational guidelines as circumstances change. The global dimension of many business–civil society partnerships and the multiple layers and tangents of most company supply chains and industrial processes increases the unpredictable nature of the process. At the same time, the partners may face considerable opposition from various groups within industry and civil society. Such opposition often forces the partners to revisit issues such as stakeholder legitimacy and ground rules throughout the process in order to strengthen external support for the partnership.

Power is a central feature of all social processes; however, it assumes a different form and role in partnership. Shared power emerges from a collaborative process where business and NGOs recognise each other's legitimacy and authority to define problems and propose solutions. The civil society partner needs to find positive ways for the business partner to respond to environmental, social and ethical concerns.

The idea of partnership between a multi-billion-dollar global corporation and a poor, marginalised local community group in the South appears to be at odds with the enormous power differentials and divergent interests inherent in such a relationship. On the other hand, when larger NGOs establish new collaborative relationships with business, there may be greater scope for shared power and control.

Although power differentials between participants often remain, the partners need some degree of countervailing power in order for partnership to happen. That is to say, they must be to a certain extent dependent on each other (Gray 1989; Gray and Wood 1991; Wood and Gray 1991). Despite the dominant economic power position of business, civil society embodies both the moral power of the stick (via protest) and the convening power of the carrot (via partnership) which both induce business to collaborate. In the face of protest, business needs to work with credible civil society partners to help solve commercial, social, ethical and environmental problems. In the face of globalisation, NGOs need to work with committed business partners to promote sustainable development. With much of the relationship founded on mutual trust, the partners also depend on each other's commitment to achieving shared and individual goals. Together, business and NGOs are better able to understand problems and find solutions. This also enables them to build broader support for partnership goals and activities.

On a basic level, personal contact is the critical element that makes business–civil society partnerships happen and produce results. A representative of one of the NGOs involved in the FSC forest sector partnership noted that 'success boiled down to the commitment of individuals and the support that senior management has given to those individuals'. Such partnerships also depend on mutual symbiosis—the intimate co-existence of representatives of business and civil society where both benefit. In the biological context, 'the partners are [often] melded into a single organism' in order 'to attain the highest level of intimacy' (Wilson 1992: 178).

In a related vein, research on partnerships in the USA by Fredrick Long and Matthew Arnold found that partnership champions 'not only maintain momentum, they also build morale and promote team bonding' (1995: 170). In addition to being 'convinced that what they are doing is important', partnership participants 'must feel a bond to each other that 'is almost as strong as the bond they have to their organizations' (1995: 179).

Given that partnership development depends so heavily on mutual symbiosis between motivated individuals, partnership survival may ultimately be threatened by this dependency. Partnership therefore requires much more than the personal commitment and the influence of individuals. It needs to be institutionalised via some form of referent structure such as the FSC or ETI which recognises personal commitments and their relationship to organisational roles and responsibilities without stifling the creative dynamics of intimate association between individuals.

◢ Conclusions

There are indications that the 21st century may witness closer business–civil society collaboration. A recent international study on relations between NGOs and transnational corporations (TNCs) by Price Waterhouse (now PricewaterhouseCoopers) and the University of Notre Dame reported that 61% of NGO respondents anticipated that they would have co-operative relations with TNCs in the future (Enderle and Peters 1998). Many NGOs and trade unions increasingly need to work with business in order to realise their organisational goals in a globalised economy. Their business partners need credible independent guidance in order to demonstrate their commitment to being corporate citizens and supporting sustainable development. More than ever, marginalised people and their environments depend on the efforts of non-state actors alongside those of governments and UN agencies to develop just, enterprising and sustainable alternatives.

Notwithstanding the value of closer co-operation between all three sectors of society—government, business and civil society—there will always be a need for a critical and independent civil society voice in the policy arena. Civil society protest continues to play a vital role in mobilising citizens to promote socioeconomic justice and sustainable development through policy changes at all levels of society. As noted earlier, conflict is often an important precursor to (and sometimes an ongoing feature of) meaningful forms of business–civil society partnership. Conflict resolution specialist Chris Maser nonetheless believes that adversaries have a capacity to 'perceive and understand conflict as a learning partnership' thereby enabling them to find solutions to problems in the longer term (1996: 99).

At the same time, partnership holds considerable promise as an organising principle for more equitable and sustainable world futures. Although this chapter focuses on the business–civil society partnership phenomenon, many of the lessons learned to date from this experience are also of value to UN agencies, national governments, local authorities and other groups everywhere that are seeking new partners. In a world where so many complex social, economic and environmental issues remain unresolved, there remains a need for more inclusive and participatory problem-solving models founded on partnership (Gray 1989).

In this chapter we have suggested that the changing relations between businesses and NGOs can be understood to be part of a sea change in attitudes within and between many organisations towards 'partnership thinking'. We recognise the existing debate in political science between those who believe that political ideas shape political realities, and those who see events as independent of ideas, with ideas being our way of making sense

of events rather than creating them. Our experience is that there is a mutually constituting and sustaining relationship between partnership initiatives and partnership
concepts. We believe that partnerships have the potential to bring together people and
organisations to change the way business works and potentially transform society in the
process.

CHANGE THE RULES!

Business–NGO partnerships and structuration theory

Uwe Schneidewind and Holger Petersen

University of Oldenburg, Germany

In describing partnerships between businesses and environmental groups, many classifications have already been applied (a good overview is given in Murphy and Bendell 1997a: 144). In general, these classifications follow pragmatic criteria, focusing on variables such as (1) the part of a business operation affected by the partnership; (2) the primary role played by the participating NGO; (3) the number of issues addressed (Murphy and Bendell 1997a). However, these classifications are not based on social theory. This paper uses 'structuration theory', developed by Anthony Giddens (1984), as a theoretical framework to help understand a particular kind of business–NGO partnership: namely, a partnership that aims for structure-building processes in commercial, political and societal arenas. It concentrates on the growing importance of such collaborations in an era of 'reflexive modernisation' (Beck *et al.* 1994) and shows that these collaborations are a useful means of promoting sustainable societies.

◢ Multiple playing fields: reflexive modernisation and structuration theory

Western societies are founded on notions of 'progress' and 'modernisation'. As societies, we believe we can use knowledge, science and logic to better understand and control the world we live in—and continually improve our standard of living, even quality of life. Industrial development and economic growth are often regarded as synonymous with 'progress' or 'modernisation'. It was not always so. Before the Enlightenment, superstition, mysticism and religious tradition were key to peoples' understanding of the world. Although most people would not wish a return to such values and beliefs, modernisation has its own ills. Modern institutions, such as the global market economy, the legal-rational political and bureaucratic systems or the highly developed natural sciences, have enormous social, ecological and economic implications. The confidence that Western societies have had, since the Enlightenment, in their ability to *know* the true nature of the world has therefore been shaken. In this current period of re-evaluation, it is worth noting that one of the virtues of modernisation has been the emphasis placed on analysing, testing and challenging accepted knowledge. Consequently, Western societies are characterised—by leading sociologists including Anthony Giddens, Scott Lash and Ulrich Beck—to be in a state of 'reflexive modernisation' (Beck *et al.* 1994). The current state of widespread social deprivation and environmental degradation implies that we should apply the reflective power of modernisation to the modernisation process itself: modernisation must be *itself* the object of reflection (Lash 1994: 112).

Concomitant with the erosion of traditional structures (such as religion or social classes) and conventions (such as community values), this reflection process is manifested in a more and more fragmented, individualised manner. The arenas of reflexive modernisation are no longer limited to classical political institutions. Instead, this process takes place in 'civil society', the market and in different forms of 'sub-politics' (Beck 1992: 183). People in business, in NGOs, in unions, and privately, are increasingly questioning many of the ideas taken for granted in the West. In the world of management, this questioning is evident, with business now increasingly recognised as a social and political entity as well as an economic one. On a personal level, managers are no longer prepared to leave their social and political values at home. In order to reshape society and promote greater sustainability, this form of reflection is essential, and must lead to new institutional solutions.

As this process of reflection begins within management circles, and as corporate social responsibility rises up the business agenda, it must be asked what is the true extent of a company's **'response ability'**? What can it change and what can it not change? Usually, the science of business administration regards the commercial, political and societal environment of a company as a given set of parameters (for one of the few exceptions, see Baron 1993). Accordingly, business is seen to act within a predefined framework. However, this view of business is too dependent on a concept of society as embodying a set of rules and unchanging structures. Instead, by applying 'structuration theory' to a company's operating environment, it is possible to gain a new perspective on this relationship.

British sociologist Anthony Giddens defines 'structure' as the 'rules and resources, recursively implicated in the reproduction of social systems: structure is not just "there", it is not "external" ' (Giddens 1984: 25). We, the people, have certain options open to us because of the way in which our societies are structured, yet we, the people, can change those structures through our actions, and thereby influence the actions of others in society. Through his interpretation, Giddens overcomes the opposition that has existed in social science between those who believe that systems and structures are key in determining social life, and those who believe there is no such thing as society—in the sense of systems and structures—but just individual agents pursuing their own choices. In Giddens's perspective, structure is condition *and* outcome of action, as structure is (re)produced by actors during their agency.

An analogy can be made with a game of soccer. The game could not happen without players. Yet neither could it happen without the rules of the game or resources such as a football and goalposts. Focusing on the rules or equipment alone would not help us truly understand the game, its drama and the talents of its individual stars. Nor would focusing purely on the exceptional players provide us with an understanding of the whole game. The same is true in attempting to understand society: both the structures and the individuals must be considered. Of course, the rules and resources are powerful: they not only shape the way the game is played but even the ultimate objectives of the players— scoring a 'goal'. Yet these rules and resources have been developed and changed over time by people—often players working together to make it safer, more enjoyable, and so on. Again, the same is true of society, where the process of changing rules (how structure is reproduced) has been the focus of many sociologists.

In society, 'rules' can be found in the form of **interpretative schemes** and **norms** of thought and behaviour. 'Resources' can be **allocative** (material, giving power over nature and physical artefacts) or **authoritative** (non-material, giving power over others). Giddens characterises this idea by the notion of the 'duality of structure' (see Fig. 16.1).

In the context of business administration, structuration theory has been applied mainly in our understanding of social processes within organisations and within networks of organisations (Sydow 1996). In previous studies, we showed that it is possible to go one step further: to understand markets, political arenas and public discourses— the operating environment of the company—also as **produced** 'structure' (Schneidewind 1998). Operating environments are constituted by the production and reproduction of rules and resources. Consequently, the differences between operating environments can

Figure 16.1 **The duality of structure and action**

Source: Giddens 1984

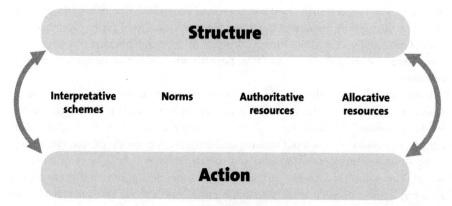

be understood by focusing on the modes of structuration: allocative and authoritative resources, interpretative schemes and norms (Schneidewind 1998: 213)

Why is Giddens's interpretation of structure of such importance to a new understanding of the relationship of companies with their environment?

☐ It makes us aware of the fact that structures can be and indeed are always influenced by actors. The business environment is both the 'medium and outcome' (Giddens 1984: 25) of acting companies: business can change the rules.

☐ Structuration theory helps us understand the means of influencing and (re)producing structures. It explicitly takes into account resources and rules as well as their interaction to describe structure-building processes. Many other social and economic theories refer to only one of these dimensions. Thus, neoclassical economic theory concentrates on the production of resources (i.e. a 'resource-based' approach), while many social theories reconstruct social reality as communication processes (i.e. a 'rules-based' approach).

We believe that, when taken together, reflexive modernisation and structuration theory help us arrive at a new understanding of collaborations and their role in the relationship between business and its operating environment. We need to be critical of our assumptions of progress, and our assumptions about the roles we assign to different social actors (reflexive modernisation), and we need to understand that business is a political entity in that it can change the social and economic structures within which it operates (structuration theory). Taken together, these concepts can act together to change the rules of the market toward a more sustainable system.

◢ The special role of collaboration

We believe that analysing business–NGO partnerships against this theoretical background will help researchers, practitioners and policy-makers recognise the importance of these initiatives. In our research, we asked: 'What role *do* and *can* companies play in the social structure-building process and what role do new forms of collaboration, such as business–NGO partnerships, play in this process?'

To answer this, we must first consider how structure is important to environmental management. The commitment of companies towards sustainable development is very often restricted by structural or institutional barriers:

☐ At the market level—if ecological product advantages are not observed or not accepted by consumers

☐ At the political level—if ecological impacts are not internalised by eco-taxes or other economic instruments

☐ At the cultural level—if social norms are hindering more sustainable lifestyles

Work on environmental issues within the subject of business administration has for a long time been bound within these frameworks in its search for ecologically sound business solutions. In the main, it has concentrated on the analysis of market structures and developed suitable mechanisms of **adaptation** to these structures for business organisations. The active **co-building** of commercial, political and societal structures by companies has been beyond its remit. It has neglected the fact that companies themselves are also involved in the creation of the structures that hinder sustainable business.

Consequently, once we recognise that business affects its own operating environment, we can explore new options for pursuing greater corporate sustainability. Collaborations between businesses and other organisations, including political organisations, non-governmental organisations (NGOs) and other businesses, on environmental issues, are one way in which operating environments are changed. These collaborative forms of sub-politics can be found at commercial, political and societal levels. They are a response to the deficits of classical political mechanisms which are increasingly unable to cope with the environmental and social side-effects of modern industrial societies.

Table 16.1 illustrates the new governance structures for solving ecological problems:

- ☐ At the **market level**, collaborating companies along the value chain, as well as industry associations, define and establish ecological standards for suppliers and customers.

- ☐ At the **political level**, voluntary agreements represent negotiated rule-making between governmental institutions and business.

- ☐ At the **level of civil society**, collaborative efforts between companies and environmental organisations are being undertaken to promote new lifestyle patterns.

Collaborations between business and NGOs have a special importance in structure-building processes for at least two key reasons. First, they can mobilise new resources. Second, by introducing managers to people with different value systems and objectives,

Table 16.1 **Institution-building through ecological business collaborations**

COLLABORATOR	KIND OF COLLABORATION
Business	Establishment of ecological standards through vertical and horizontal collaborations
Government	Voluntary agreements as negotiated rule-making on a political level
Civil society	Business–environmental group partnerships for promoting new lifestyles

they begin to question their routine actions and analyse why they have to operate in the way they do. This is important, because, as Giddens (1984: 5) argues, most of the actions of actors are executed in a routine manner and are present only in the practical conscious- ness and not in the 'discursive' consciousness of actors (where they would be seen by the individual actor to have meaning). Unintended and unacknowledged consequences of an action are a result of this routinised acting.

Collaboration with new partners brings routine actions into the discursive conscious- ness and allows for their critical assessment. In this sense, they increase the level of 'reflexivity' of action, a prerequisite for change. Norms of behaviour are affected by this growing reflexivity, which can leading to a restructuration towards greater sustainability.

◢ Three case studies

Taking these interpretations of structuration theory, it is possible to understand the institution-building effects of business–NGO alliances more clearly. Three short case studies from the German context will illustrate this. They show that business–environ- mental group partnership works on a commercial, political and societal level and that the structure-building process is in some cases more rule-oriented and in other cases more resources-oriented. Table 16.2 gives an overview of the three studies.

Changing markets: the German refrigerator market

At the beginning of the 1990s, the medium-sized refrigerator company Foron, in the former East Germany, began working with Greenpeace to promote a CFC-free refriger- ator (Härlin 1994; Hartman *et al.* 1999). The refrigerator had been developed by Foron using propane and butane. Within two years, this partnership had led to a complete

Table 16.2 **Three case studies of business–NGO collaborations and their mechanisms**

PARTNERSHIP	STRUCTURE AFFECTED	MECHANISM FOR INFLUENCING STRUCTURE
Foron–Greenpeace ('Greenfreeze' refrigerator)	Market structures	Joining of complementary resources
Group of corporations– BUND (Eco-tax support)	Policy structures	Changing interpretative schemes in the political debate
MCC–Mobility (new mobility forms)	Societal structures (lifestyle patterns)	Offering new resources and interpretation patterns

technology change in the German refrigerator market. After initial strong resistance, all large refrigerator producers in Germany adapted the new technology and made the CFC-free refrigerator the market standard. This change of **market structure** was possible because Foron and Greenpeace merged complementary resources: Foron brought its technical know-how, and Greenpeace its media presence and high moral authority, which potential customers found more convincing than any eco-label. Greenpeace, along with other environmental organisations, including the German faction of Friends of the Earth (Bund für Umwelt und Naturschutz), were involved in a number of similar business–NGO collaborations throughout the 1990s. For example, BUND worked with Cherry, the world's leading producer of computer keyboards, to develop and promote ecologically optimised computer equipment; and Greenpeace worked with Swiss engineering companies on the three-litre car.

Changing ideas: environmental tax reform

In the **political sphere**, debates about sustainable development are today characterised by high complexity and divergent interpretations and norms. An important example of such a conflict is the debate in Germany on environmental tax reform. On the one hand, environmental groups regard environmental tax reform as the cornerstone of real sustainable change in Western societies; on the other hand, business and industry associations believe environmental taxes to be one of the more significant threats to (national) competitiveness. Although many economic studies, along with the experience of countries that have already introduced such regimes, show that this can be a means of reducing unemployment and that the 'winner industries', especially in Europe, are of more commercial importance than the energy-intensive 'losers' of an environmental tax, these confrontation patterns have remained static in Germany for many years. Or, in the language of structuration theory, the routine reproduction of norms and interpretative schemes in the political and societal debate on environmental taxation has not been affected by research.

This situation encouraged certain environmentally aware corporations (many small and medium-sized companies, but also companies such as AEG Hausgeräte, one of the biggest household equipment producers in Germany) to establish a partnership with the environmental group BUND. A series of advertisements was published in major German newspapers and magazines in which participating companies and BUND jointly demanded the introduction of environmental tax reform in Germany. The advertisements were published in 1994 and in 1998, shortly before the elections for the national parliament. The aim of the campaign was to change common interpretative schemes about the opposing camps in the tax debate. This served to emphasise that the concept of environmental groups and business being in opposing and irreconcilable positions does not hold true; indeed, here was a broad base of business organisations aligning themselves with environmental groups in regarding environmental tax reform as a sound economic measure.

Changing lives: new lifestyle patterns

Progress in Western society towards sustainable development is influenced not only by market competition and political decisions. **Changes of lifestyle** and consumption patterns are also fundamental. Lifestyles can be seen as a complex mixture of norms, interpretative schemes and allocative resources for the realisation of consumers' wishes. The reproduction of these rules and resources is influenced by—among others—(social) milieus, communication strategies, and the policies of companies supplying consumer products.

One important aspect of emerging new lifestyle patterns is mobility. The enormous growth in the per capita rate of automobiles and of kilometres-driven-per-year in Western societies has a significant environmental impact. The search for more environmentally sound mobility options has to take into account the way in which cars are integrated in the lifestyle patterns of Western societies. Growing support for public transport and the rise of car-sharing schemes has had only marginal success. In 1998, the Micro Compact Car Corporation (MCC Inc., a joint venture by Daimler Benz and the SMH-Holding of Nicolas Hayek, the founder of Swatch) attempted to forge a new operating model based on collaboration with NGOs. The new, short, two-person MCC car, called 'Smart', is promoted by MCC as a means of access to a whole mobility network. As before, people are able to own a car and pursue the lifestyle usually connected with car ownership. However, with the Smart, not all mobility needs are satisfied: instead, this car allows access to many other modes of mobility, such as trains, buses and car-sharing through MCC's collaborations with the providers of such transport.

In realising this concept, business–NGO partnerships play an important role. In Switzerland, MCC co-operates with the car-sharing initiative, Mobility, which began on a volunteer basis and today is the biggest car-sharing initiative in Switzerland. By buying a Smart, every owner automatically becomes a member of Mobility free of charge. This collaboration is supported by a marketing strategy that promotes a new attitude towards individual mobility, thus trying to overcome existing 'rules' in this field.

These three examples illustrate how structuration theory can be applied to help understand new forms of business collaboration in the environmental field. It also provides some hints on how to enable companies to become responsible actors in social structure-building in the future, and to **change the rules** in favour of sustainability.

◢ Outlook

The theoretical framework presented here is just the beginning of a broad debate within business administration about the structure-building role of companies and the role of business–NGO partnerships in this context. Three aspects seem to be of importance for the future work:

☐ Empirical research in the field must be intensified. The framework presented—based on Giddens's structuration theory—helps us to describe structure-building effects only on a very general level. It is necessary to understand in more detail how the reproduction processes of rules and resources in markets, political arenas and societal discourses are influenced by companies and industry associations. This research must be interdisciplinary and requires strong collaboration with sociologists, political scientists and psychologists.

☐ Considering companies as actors in social structure-building raises many normative questions. If the actions of companies are not ruled by democratically legitimised frameworks, because business is co-producing its own frameworks, then a discussion about corporate responsibility and new legitimising procedures is increasingly needed.

☐ If the debate about reflexive modernisation is taken seriously, the role of companies (especially multinational corporations) as actors in social structure-building will gain importance, and business leaders are needed who can handle this new dimension of corporate responsibility. This makes it necessary to assess the structure-building effects of the training and discourse found in business schools. A cultural shift is therefore required in business schools—an issue that has up to now been largely neglected.

PART 6

Future Directions

NEW FRONTIERS

Emerging NGO activities to strengthen transparency and accountability in business

Jem Bendell

New Academy of Business, UK

Rob Lake

Traidcraft Exchange, UK

This book details a wide terrain of engagements between businesses and NGOs, in many parts of the world and often for very specific objectives. Whether it is a collaboration to set up a new certification council, or to mitigate the impacts of oil exploration or market a new product, relationships between businesses and NGOs can be exciting, challenging, sometimes painful and, as this book shows, increasingly powerful tools for change. However, on the horizon there is something altogether more powerful. The time has come when some NGO campaigners are recognising the common threads to their various corporate campaigns and beginning to scale up their work from specific environmental or social goals to consider the *frameworks* within which all businesses operate. Increasingly, NGOs in Europe and North America are working at more strategic levels to reframe the way in which markets and businesses operate; specifically, raising transparency and accountability as key aspects of business practice. This new frontier of business–NGO relations is about creating a stronger enabling environment within which civil society can engage with business, in order to voice concerns and expectations.

This frontier has opened up because of the seismic shifts in societies around the world, which have undermined the traditional means by which organisations achieve and maintain legitimacy with the public. These global shifts are described in detail by Peter Newell (Chapter 1) and their implications for business legitimacy covered by Cheryl Rodgers (Chapter 2). It is our contention that transparency and accountability are the essential components in the legitimating of an organisation, be it private, public or civil. This chapter charts some of the NGO work on strengthening transparency and accountability in business, a new frontier which includes areas such as criteria for investors, national and international corporate governance codes, reporting standards, stock market listing rules and company law.

◢ Frontiers in transparency

> [Corporate management] should recognise that its relationships and communications with interested parties now takes place in a society that demands greater transparency and accountability, both non-financial and financial (Commonwealth Association for Corporate Governance 1999).

The first step for a business or organisation toward generating legitimacy among a society is to be transparent. To be transparent is to provide all information that a society deems relevant to its interests, and make this widely available in an understandable format, with ample time for potential implications and responses to be discussed. For many years companies have been required by law to disclose information on their financial situation in order to protect investors and the public more generally. In many countries, therefore, companies are *financially* transparent. There are, however, other aspects to transparency, and other types of information which societies around the world now consider relevant. This new information is being asked for as a company's role in promoting or undermining sustainable social development is debated.

In response, alongside the mandatory disclosure of financial information, more and more companies are voluntarily reporting on their environmental performance. The practice has become so widespread that a whole industry has now developed among NGOs, research institutes and consultants in analysing, comparing, benchmarking, advising and standard-setting for environmental reporting.

More recently, techniques for *social* accounting and reporting have been developed. The fair trade company, Traidcraft, published its first *Social Accounts* in 1993 with the aim of reporting publicly on its relationships with all its stakeholders, from producers in developing countries that supply Traidcraft goods, to staff, secondary suppliers and shareholders.[1] Meanwhile, interest in social accounting and reporting among major companies has grown dramatically in parallel with the general upsurge of interest in corporate social responsibility. Some companies now experimenting in this area include BP, Shell, NatWest Bank, Co-operative Bank, Co-operative Wholesale Services, BT and The Body Shop.

The key driving factor behind increased transparency on environmental and social performance is the concept of risk—identifying it, understanding it and controlling it. Environmental and social malpractice poses three types of risk: reputational, operational and legal—legal, as companies can suffer fines and sometimes closures for environmental or social malpractice, and even incur future liabilities; operational, as

---

1   Information on Traidcraft's latest Social Accounts can be found at www.traidcraft.co.uk.

direct action by disaffected communities can stop production; and reputational, as poor performance transmitted through the media and by NGO 'risk agents' can negatively affect a corporate's reputation and therefore its sales, staff commitment, stakeholder ties and stock valuation. Consequently, professional bodies around the world are taking steps to improve the transparency of a company's exposure to such risks. In the UK the Institute of Chartered Accountants in England and Wales has published guidance for directors of listed companies that require them to certify that they have adequate control systems in place for all the significant risks to which their business is exposed. Compliance with this guidance is a requirement for listing on the London Stock Exchange (ICAEW 1999). According to the British newspaper, *The Guardian* (Buckingham and Cowe 1999),

> the focus will be on risks which could have an adverse implication for the business. That includes issues such as child labour and pollution because they can damage a company's reputation and therefore shareholder value.

Social reporting is still relatively underdeveloped compared with environmental reporting, in terms of both the number of companies involved and the maturity and stability of the methodology. However, significant efforts are now under way to address this. In the UK, the Institute for Social and Ethical Accountability has been established to develop professional standards for social and ethical accounting, auditing and reporting. Membership of the Institute includes both companies and NGOs, and mechanisms are being developed to draw NGO expertise into the organisation's detailed work with companies in individual sectors. At an international level the Global Reporting Initiative (GRI), under the auspices of the US-based NGO Coalition for Environmentally Responsible Economies, has been developing a standardised framework for sustainability reporting embracing environmental and social dimensions, and some companies are already using this as their template for sustainability reporting.[2]

Development NGOs are beginning to provide valuable specialist input into these initiatives. While some aspects of environmental reporting lend themselves to the use of quantified indicators (emission per unit of product, for example), many social issues require a more qualitative approach. It is not appropriate, for example, for a Western company with operations in the developing world to adopt a limited range of quantified social indicators to be applied to all its operations. The important thing will be to find indicators of the processes of stakeholder consultation and dialogue through which the company needs to go in order to allow local stakeholders to contribute to the development of locally relevant indicators. Thus, instead of asking from corporate headquarters 'how many clinics have we built?', companies will need to ask questions such as 'have the processes we have followed for talking to local communities allowed all those affected by our operations, including marginalised groups, women and indigenous people, to voice their views and expectations of us?' These challenges are familiar to development NGOs and others involved in international development work. Wheels do not need to be re-invented. The lessons learned from participatory approaches to devel-

---

2   Information on the Global Reporting Initiative can be found at www.globalreporting.org.

opment need to be transferred to the operations of multinational companies (and indeed domestic companies in developing countries).

Yet companies face the risk of developing social reporting systems that will not provide information considered relevant by the community of organisations working on development issues. Such reporting would fail to fulfil its function of delivering transparency. Through dialogue with development NGOs, companies could identify the important issues to report on and in turn reshape their actual policies and practices to deliver improvements in these areas. As NGOs are key risk agents turning corporate malpractice into reputational damage, so engaging them in this process will help a company to prioritise its efforts on social issues so as to optimise their risk-management benefit.

The need for greater corporate transparency is now spreading across the globe, catalysed by international organisations such as the World Bank. Researchers from the World Bank have recommended a number of measures to buttress environmental law enforcement where government agencies have limited resources. These include efforts to open up companies to scrutiny of their environmental performance by civil society, by introducing structured programmes to release firm-specific information about environmental performance, and empowering local communities and stakeholders to act on this information through environmental education programmes (Dasgupta *et al.* 1998). It seems that there is no turning back from the frontiers of transparency.

◢ Frontiers in accountability

As developments in social reporting have illustrated, efforts toward greater transparency inevitably lead to considerations of the responsiveness of the organisation to civil society, and therefore its accountability. Ann M. Florini of the Carnegie Endowment for International Peace makes this clear:

> transparency is always closely connected to accountability. The purpose of calls
> for transparency is to permit citizens, markets, or governments to hold others
> accountable for their policies and performance (Florini 1999: 1).

Debates about corporate accountability constitute another new frontier. With increased corporate power and ability to reshape markets and their rules, as described by Uwe Schneidewind and Holger Petersen in this volume (Chapter 16), so society is calling for more accountability from its corporations. But to what extent can a company owned by shareholders be accountable to employees, communities and wider society, and what mechanism can ensure this? The answer is not simple, and brings the debate about accountability on to the issue of corporate governance—who should own the corporation, who should run it, and how.

The debate about corporate governance is not only being opened up by civil society but also by the financial community. In the Asian financial crisis of 1997–98, many Western investors lost considerable sums, which made them realise that they had not had sufficient information about how their investments were being managed, and that the governance of the companies entrusted with those investments left much to be desired. This sparked a proliferation of activity on corporate governance at the national and international levels by governments, international institutions, institutional investors and their organisations. Consequently, management is walking a tightrope between greater levels of shareholder scrutiny and greater levels of stakeholder scrutiny. How can a company balance the interests of shareholders and stakeholders? We can identify three types of approach from management in dealing with this scrutiny, and therefore the corporate governance issue more generally: these are **insular**, **responsive** and **democratic** approaches.

In light of this increased scrutiny, some businesses are maintaining an **insular** approach to corporate governance, keeping shareholders or stakeholders at arm's length. The argument for keeping *shareholders* at arm's length is that, although financial institutions might know a lot about money management but little about the specific business, individual shareholders know even less. The argument for keeping *stakeholders* at arm's length is that those who are important to the operation of the business are remunerated (employees, suppliers) while the interests of more distant stakeholders (communities, suppliers' suppliers) should be protected through the legislature. From this perspective, to do anything more for stakeholders than obey the law is considered to be a waste of shareholders' money. This is the insular management approach to corporate governance.

Some argue that the interests of all the stakeholders affecting or affected by a company should be taken into account in corporate governance, because that is *the just thing to do* as stakeholders invest 'social' capital in a company, and because it is *the prudent thing to do* as good stakeholder relations generally means a healthy company (Wheeler and Sillanpää 1997; McIntosh *et al.* 1998). The obvious question then is: how can this be done? There are two broad corporate governance approaches that seek to provide accountability to shareholders and stakeholders: **responsive** and **democratic** approaches.

The second approach to corporate governance is the **responsive** management approach. This is either because management recognises the legitimacy of shareholder and stakeholder scrutiny and wants to manage the company in a responsive fashion or because it wishes to be *seen* to be responsive. Management can be proactively responsive toward the interests of shareholders or stakeholders, consulting with them on the information they require and the suggestions they have. For stakeholders, this can extend to the appointment of an environmental or social activist as a non-executive director. However, some management is only responsive in a reactive fashion, appearing defensive toward increased scrutiny and trying to supply the minimum information and minimum dialogue necessary in order to satisfy critics. In either case most managers are more shareholder-responsive than stakeholder-responsive, unless they have been convinced by the theory of a symbiotic relationship between good stakeholder relations and share value.

Third, there is the **democratic** management approach to corporate governance. This is where management recognises that true accountability can only be ensured if there are mechanisms enabling shareholders or stakeholders to control, via a democratic process, the actions of managers. One means is through the election of representatives to the board of directors—this is called representative democracy. The other is through formal but direct involvement in internal decision-making processes, which is called participatory democracy. Either can focus on the shareholders, employees, or on a host of stakeholders, the latter giving rise to a pluralistic form of corporate democracy.

In Germany, corporate representative democracy is practised under the *Mitbestimmung* (co-determination) system where the employees and the shareholders each elect half of the directors (Mintzberg 1989). Other companies consider democracy to imply joint ownership and they operate as co-operatives where the employees or consumers own the shares and elect the board. This allows social and environmental issues relevant to the company's employees and communities to be put on an equal footing with financial considerations. However, this does not include wider stakeholders in the democratic process, such as suppliers and dwellers in the local and global environment. Yet a pluralistic form of representative democracy, where most stakeholders would be able to have a vote in the election of the board, is difficult to imagine: problems with defining a stakeholder and the logistics of an election would most likely rule it out. Therefore participatory forms of democracy appear more workable for achieving accountability with a wider range of stakeholders.

There are examples of employee participatory democracy in action, such as collective bargaining agreements with unions, workers councils, or co-operative staff meetings. Pluralistic participatory democracy with wider stakeholders is pursued through partnerships with NGOs, when there is a commitment from the corporation on which they cannot easily renege. However, although participatory, business–NGO partnerships are only as democratic as the strength of the partner NGO's mandate from the constituents it purports to represent. Consequently, companies need to assess the accountability of potential NGO partners and also consider various systems for enhancing accountability—for example, working with coalitions of NGOs, and establishing new democratic institutions to mediate between the corporation and NGOs, such as the Forest Stewardship Council (see Chapters 4 and 12). If management does not consider these issues when in partnership with an NGO, then it has embraced only a responsive form of corporate governance, not a participatory democratic form.

The three approaches are illustrated in Figure 17.1. In some cases, shareholders and stakeholders are the same, such as in an employee co-operative or consumer co-operative. Although we have no empirical evidence to supply on the matter, our perception is that companies are moving along the tightrope, away from an insular approach toward a responsive approach: democratic approaches to corporate governance are still few and far between.

As business is recognised as a key player in sustainable development, so NGOs are becoming engaged in the debate about corporate accountability and corporate governance. There are three developments worth discussing. First, there is the UK company law review (DTI 1999).[3] A wide-ranging consultation paper published in March 1999

---

3   Copies of the document *Modern Company Law for a Competitive Economy: The Strategic Framework* are available from the DTI by telephoning +44 (0)171 215 0409. A summary of key issues for stakeholders in the company law review can be found on the Traidcraft website, www.traidcraft.co.uk, in the report of the seminar on this subject held on 13 April 1999.

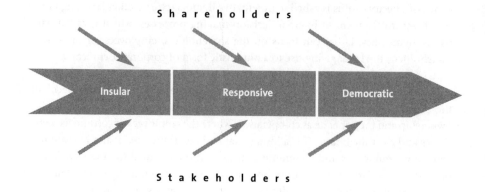

Figure 17.1 **Changing management approaches to corporate governance**

discussed key issues in the transparency and accountability debate. It asked questions on previously taboo subjects, such as whether company directors should be legally account-able only to shareholders, and have legal duties only to the 'the company' (as at present); or whether they should be required by law to take into account the interests of other stakeholders in the company and, if so, how widely the boundaries of the stakeholder group should be drawn? The company law consultation paper recognised two possible government responses:

☐ **Non-interventionist:** assuming that in order to be competitive in today's world companies will value stakeholder relations that contribute to their success—such as relations with staff, customers and suppliers—and that the law does not need to be changed to make this happen

☐ **Interventionist:** assuming that companies will not necessarily take appropriate account of these stakeholders and that the law should be changed to ensure that they do

Neither approach considers those stakeholders who do not contribute in an immediate sense to the success of the company, or who are not perceived as doing so. Indigenous and other poor or marginalised people in developing countries where foreign com-panies are investing, or the workers of developing-country suppliers to a retailer, may not affect a company's immediate economic performance but are themselves affected by the company. Consequently, NGOs such as Traidcraft Exchange have lobbied for changes to company law so that the framework for doing business will be more supportive of those businesses who extend their responsibility to a wider set of stakeholders.

The UK consultation paper goes further than the 'Principles of Corporate Governance' of the Organisation for Economic Co-operation and Development (OECD 1999). These are intended to be used as an international benchmark both by OECD governments and by the international financial institutions in the way they deal with non-OECD countries. The Principles are viewed by G7 ministers as a cornerstone of the new international 'financial architecture' intended to prevent a recurrence of the 1997–98 financial crisis in Asia. Given this background, the OECD Principles are tilted heavily towards the interests of shareholders. Stakeholders are taken into account essentially to the extent that they make an identifiable contribution to the company's success, rather than because they are important in their own right and are affected by the company. Recommendations in the Principles on transparency and disclosure of information to stakeholders focus on 'material information', which is defined as being material to the company's financial success rather than material to the stakeholders' interests. This is unacceptable to most NGOs working on corporate governance and their battle to convince hearts, minds and bank accounts has only just begun.

A stronger endorsement of an approach that is responsive to stakeholders as well as shareholders is contained in the Commonwealth Secretariat's (1999) *Principles of Best Business Practice for the Commonwealth*. They argue that:

> The board should exercise its responsibilities to employees, customers, suppliers and other interested parties in the wider community, and ensure that this is amply demonstrated by the enterprise in its conduct and dealings in all respects . . . The board must take into account the legitimate interests of other organisations, groups and individuals who may have a direct or indirect interest in the achievement of the commercial and other objectives of the enterprise. The board should promote goodwill with these parties and be prepared to be accountable for the organisation's actions.

This stance reflects that of many leadership companies today. However, in keeping with the position of the majority of companies, it is really emphasising the need for *responsibility* rather than accountability. 'Being prepared to be accountable' means, in this case, to be prepared to explain your actions—systems for stakeholders to exercise some control over the actions of corporations are not considered. It is our contention that, if there is a mutual relationship between a well society and a healthy company, then a successful company should demonstrate compliance with the concerns and aspirations of civil society: and the best way of doing this is to open itself up to democratic processes. Therefore we agree with management theorist Henry Mintzberg that:

> in a society of organizations democracy can have meaning only if it applies to the organizational activities that most impinge upon citizens in their daily lives—as workers, consumers and neighbors. Organizations that prove unresponsive to other forces will have to be opened up to external control, one way or another. Indeed, as the legitimacy of a large closed system of organizations becomes increasingly questioned by workers inside as well as pressure groups outside, generating greater levels of [internal] politicization, the issue will become no less one of economic efficiency than of social democracy (Mintzberg 1989: 313).

Whether representative, participatory, employee, consumer or pluralistic forms of democracy are more appropriate for a specific case, there are a variety of mechanisms that corporations can adopt to become truly accountable before the fact, not after it. For companies adopting such approaches, NGOs will become ever more important, as will a closer assessment of NGOs' own accountability to the constituents they purport to represent.

◢ Financing frontiers

In recent years more NGO staff have come to accept the economic reality of management in a stock market-quoted corporation. This has led to a focus on the win–win situations, which deliver environmental or social improvements while helping to build share value. Energy efficiency programmes or activities that boost staff commitment are examples of apparent win–wins. However, there is another side to this realisation: the scope for a manager to undertake social and environmental initiatives is fundamentally restricted unless the financial community starts giving different signals to companies from its traditional mantra—'thou must maximise profit, increase market share and control emerging categories'. NGOs have woken up to the fact that institutional investors are the real force. In the UK, pension funds, insurance companies, unit trusts and the like now own over 60% of shares in UK companies. The 60 or so fund managers responsible for these investments control funds worth more than the combined national incomes of the Netherlands, Austria and Sweden. Consequently, a coalition of activists and organisations in civil society is slowly coming together to try to make this immensely powerful financial community change its mantra and become more supportive of the advances being made by pragmatic NGOs and leadership companies on sustainable social development issues.

But why should the investment community take notice? After all, it must look after the beneficiaries whose funds it is managing, not the ethical impulses of managers in companies in which it invests. Thankfully, it might not need to be an either/or situation. There are two key 'bottom-line reasons' why the financial community should start considering its relations with NGOs more strategically. These relate to the external and internal risks and resources posed by the investors', and the invested companies', relations with civil society. We deal with each in turn.

First, there are external risks and resources: namely, risks and resources associated with companies in an investor's portfolio, because of the nature of their relations with NGOs. There is a growing body of research that indicates that good environmental and social performance coincides with healthy stock performance (WRI 1998). In the US, the Domini Social Index developed by the investment research firm Kinder Lydenberg Domini, tracking companies with high social and environmental standards, has consistently outperformed the Standard & Poor's 500 Index—this is shown in Figure 17.2.

Research by the World Bank has found a direct correlation in emerging markets between press reports of companies' environmental performance and movements in share prices—up in response to positive news and down in response to news of pollution incidents or fines or other regulatory action by government (Dasgupta *et al.* 1998).

Why does there seem to be a relationship between better performance on environmental or social issues and buoyant share value? It could be argued that it is those

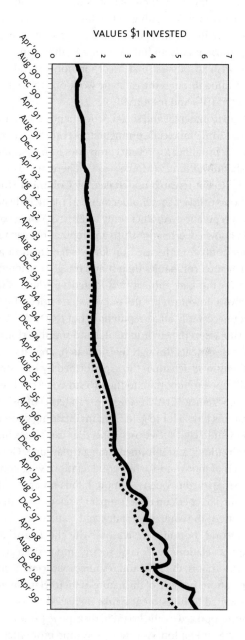

Figure 17.2 **Performance of the Domini Social Index**

VALUES $1 INVESTED

Domini Social Index

Standard & Poor's 500

companies who have the most environmental and social impacts who require the best policies, and therefore these statistics are meaningless. Alternatively, it could be that companies who are operating well in financial terms can afford to think ahead and adopt social and environmental policies and programmes. In this way good environmental and social performance is an indicator of a healthy company. Yet there is another explanation we wish to pursue: that a corporation's social and environmental performance affects it value through the catalytic work of NGOs which transforms that performance into a set of risks and resources.

Poor environmental and social performance poses risks in terms of fines, closures and liabilities. Some financial commentators consider these to be significant risks and have argued that by failing to prevent companies from flouting environmental legislation they are mishandling funds (Monks 1998). There are also risks to corporate reputation to consider. Recent research undertaken by Columbia University in the USA suggests that around one-third of shareholder value in many industry segments is accounted for by company reputation. Another study by Ernst & Young estimated that the intangible assets of skills, knowledge, relationships and reputation averages two-thirds of the total market value for companies focused on knowledge creation and/or market position (Coates 1998). For such companies their brand image is a significant asset and, if it is negatively affected by the bad publicity associated with an NGO campaign, the company may experience a downturn in sales or even share price. The key here is that malpractice itself does not necessarily affect reputation, but NGOs do. And, if we consider that it is often NGOs who assess the environmental and social performance of corporations, or contribute to assessments through their research, and that their assessments are often more trusted within society than those performed by industry or government, so NGOs automatically appear important to the investment community.

The importance of NGOs is not only in terms of risk. Simon Zadek (1999) argues that corporations have a lot to gain from maintaining good relations with civil society. From involvement in civil society networks they can access information and ideas that lead to new innovations, and informed strategic planning. Good relations with staff can ensure high levels of motivation, while good relations with communities can enhance sales and recruitment. In consequence a more hands-on approach is required from the financial community, to check up on a company's relations with civil society, as part of an overall assessment of the company's status and value.

The second 'bottom-line reason' why the financial community should start considering its relations with civil society more strategically concerns *internal* risks and resources—that is, the risks and resources associated with the investment organisations' own operations because of the nature of their relations with NGOs. In the late 1990s direct actions aimed at investment banks increased. These ranged from shareholder resolutions not supported by the board to disruptive protests such as the 18 June 1999 'Stop the City' march in London. As activists become more literate about the economics behind the activities they are trying to stop, so direct action against investment houses without ethical policies is set to increase. Meanwhile, as more investment houses become *au fait* with social and environmental issues and thereby develop best practices in this area or even discuss changes in legislation, so industry laggards could find it difficult to adapt to subsequent changes imposed from professional bodies and regulators. Similarly, such companies could be left behind as leadership financial institutions diversify their products by offering ethically screened investments.

This brings us to the resources offered by NGOs, which relate to product development, maintenance and marketing. There is currently a major growth in ethical investment, driven by the consciousness-raising activities of NGO staff and supporters.[4] The development of the wider investment community's response to this growing market, through its provision of ethically screened funds or funds that seek ethical businesses, is helped by information provided by NGOs, and the marketing of these new financial products over time will depend on ongoing assessments by NGOs of companies in a particular investment portfolio. An example of NGO work in this area is Traidcraft Exchange. Working with a group of investors and the government's Department for International Development, Traidcraft Exchange is aiming to develop a systematic approach to evaluating companies' policies and management systems in relation to the developing world, and to research the business case for a specifically 'pro-poor' dimension to corporate social responsibility.

Governments are now beginning to support greater transparency in investment choices, which suggests that NGOs may increasingly become a potential resource or risk to investors. One example is the British government's proposal to require occupational pension fund trustees to disclose what consideration they have given in their investment policy to social, environmental and ethical matters (Timms 1999). This will open up the management of £850 billion in pension funds to the scrutiny of NGOs working on social and environmental issues. NGOs could provide a useful resource for fund managers in helping them decide what to include in their investment policy and then monitoring compliance with the policy. Alternatively, a weak or inappropriate policy might lead to negative relations with NGOs and subsequent difficulties with pension holders.

Many within the investment community have already started working on these issues. For example, clients of the Pensions Investment Research Consultants Ltd (PIRC), which offers advice to institutional investors on corporate social responsibility and governance issues, represent some £250 billion of investment. PIRC's latest shareholder voting guidelines recommend that companies should disclose their environmental, social, employment and ethical policies, and that they should provide documentation on these issues to shareholders on request (PIRC 1999). PIRC's surveys of corporate environmental and social reporting are creating pressure on companies for greater disclosure by benchmarking performance and highlighting best as well as less-impressive practice.

Despite this, dialogue between NGOs and the investment community is limited. Collaboration has been largely confined to individual high-profile cases such as Shell's operations in Nigeria. In this case, a shareholder resolution co-ordinated by PIRC and the Ecumenical Council for Corporate Responsibility presented to the company's 1997 AGM was instrumental in bringing about a significant change of attitude by the company both to its activities in Nigeria and to its approach to the environment, human rights and relations with external stakeholders overall (PIRC 1998). Yet there has not been

---

4 The total volume of 'retail' ethical investment in personal pensions, PEPs, etc. is some £2 billion.

systematic collaboration between investors and development NGOs to develop strategic approaches to the international development dimension of corporate citizenship, or the social aspects of sustainable development. There is a need for collaboration to develop policies, criteria and benchmarks of corporate behaviour of the kind that are increasingly being used in the environmental arena. Although there exists a wealth of expertise within development NGOs on development issues and a wealth of expertise in business on how to do business, there is limited knowledge on how to link the two. On the one hand, international social development issues are new to business and seem far removed from the financial city centres of the world. On the other hand, development NGOs have only recently begun looking at investment and corporate codes.

◢ Conclusions

The frontier between businesses and NGOs is widening and as it does there is a capacity-building issue for both sectors to address. This book is a contribution to business's engagement with that process, but NGOs will also need support to effectively perform their role as agents of 'civil regulation', as described in the following chapter. Environmental NGOs have been working steadily on reporting and transparency issues, but they are new to corporate governance and accountability issues and fairly new to finance. Meanwhile, development NGOs are latecomers to the frontiers of work on corporate transparency and accountability (although dealing with these issues in relation to government), having paid little attention to market-based mechanisms before now. Previously they focused on public policy and regulation as mechanisms for achieving their objectives—overseas aid, debt relief, trade and investment policy. Their approach to business has often been to concentrate on working for international regulation of corporate behaviour, and on ensuring that international policy allows governments to regulate and place constraints on business at the national level. Therefore, what we have charted in this chapter are tentative frontiers, but we believe the ongoing power shifts in society mean that they will widen, and deepen.

The building blocks of the framework within which business operates are starting to vibrate from the new corporate social responsibility and sustainable development agendas. Socially responsible investors are bullish, corporate governance codes and stock market listing rules are responding (cautiously) to the concept of environmental and social risk, voluntary environmental and social disclosure is burgeoning, and even company law may develop in ways conducive to civil society input. NGOs and leadership companies can work with the grain of these trends and make them more profound. As society's expectations of business grow, the business case for greater transparency and accountability can only strengthen.

CIVIL REGULATION
A new form of democratic governance for the global economy?

Jem Bendell

New Academy of Business, UK

> Through our scientific genius we have made of the world a neighborhood; now through our moral and spiritual genius we must make of it a brotherhood (Martin Luther King, Jr).

At the start of this new century there is much with which we can be satisfied. Democracy has replaced authoritarian government in most nations on Earth, and world wars now seem unlikely, especially as most of Europe is working together. The human race has conquered once devastating illnesses such as smallpox and polio, increased life expectancy in less-industrialised countries by over a third and witnessed their infant mortality rates fall by more than half in 30 years (UNDP 1993). Meanwhile, new technologies are allowing people to communicate across great distances instantaneously, minimising national and cultural barriers, keeping people in touch, and creating new opportunities for people with vision, energy—and luck.

Yet, while this new digital economy drives forward on a pneumatic Nasdaq, and venture capitalists make millions within a month, approximately 1 billion of the world's people struggle to survive on less than a dollar a day. Their traditional means of providing for themselves through fishing or farming are continually undermined as time and time again their resources are expropriated by others to feed the global market. Even in the world's industrialised countries, high levels of unemployment, falling real wages and the increasing use of short-term contracts are creating a climate of stress and insecurity for the majority. The more extreme symptoms of this malaise can be found in growing violent crime rates around the world and increased levels of armed conflict within states (UNDP 1994).

Meanwhile, increasing numbers of people face environmental catastrophe. In the last few years freak weather episodes have become more common and devastating, such as the 1998 hurricane 'Mitch' in Central America, which killed approximately 20,000 people, and the 1999 floods in Venezuela which killed still greater, if unknown, numbers. For the people left to rebuild their lives, climate change is not a theory. Nevertheless, our societies continue to increase the rates of deforestation, air and water pollution and extinctions of flora and fauna. Biologists estimate that half of all life on earth is at threat from extinction, because of the actions of humankind. Disrupting the web of life may have untold effects on our own security. Already, environmental pollution is affecting our health and it is probable that you are currently reading this book with 500 more chemicals circulating in your body than was the case for someone living in the 1920s, increasing your risk of allergy, infection, infertility and cancer (Colborn *et al.* 1997).

The environmental degradation and social dislocation we are facing is a direct result of the policy paradigm that now dominates political discourse in most of the world's nations. There are two pillars upholding this policy paradigm. The first pillar is the idea that increasing the production, consumption and amount of money changing hands in an economy is intrinsically good for society. The second pillar is the notion that international trade helps in this expansion and is consequently an important goal for society to pursue. Study after study proves these pillars are made of sand and that we need to reassess what really benefits people—yet business, the media and politicians 'carry on regardless':

> The continued quest for economic growth as the organising principle of public policy is accelerating the breakdown of the ecosystem's regenerative capacities and the social fabric that sustains human community; at the same time, it is intensifying the competition for resources between rich and poor—a competition that the poor invariably lose (Korten 1995: 11).

That quest for growth has been accelerated by the globalisation of the world economy and the unveiling of a form of hypercapitalism where trillions of dollars are switched around the world in a day, where companies that have never turned a profit are worth billions, and where the future of corporations is decided by a handful of investment managers who are primarily interested in short-term share price. The collective opinion of these investment managers is the compass from which the courses of corporations are set, and in turn the course of governments seeking the favour of investors. Hypercapitalism is spiralling out of control, becoming disconnected from the people living in its midst. This disconnection is heightening the negative social and environmental consequences of the growth paradigm:

> Lacking a reliable human-based signalling system for identifying investments that have damaging, even transgeneric effects, today's capitalism—indifferent, remote and numbers driven—continues to direct resources into projects that endanger our planetary resources (Gates 1998: xxv).

The growing frustration of the disconnected and disempowered has been expressed at rallies against the organisational icons of the global market, including protests at the May 1998 meeting of the G8 in Birmingham, the January 2000 meeting of the World Economic Forum (WEF) in Davos, and the November 1999 meeting of the World Trade Organisation (WTO) in Seattle where 50,000 demonstrators took to the streets. Secretary-General and CEO of the Citizens' Alliance for Participation (CIVICUS), Kumi Naidoo, considers the social unrest in Seattle a direct result of people's disconnection with the institutions of hypercapitalism:

> The actions of the WTO impact on the lives of billions all around the world, yet civil society is not a full partner in the process. The frustration demonstrated by so many individuals and citizen groups in Seattle was a reaction to this marginalization (Naidoo 1999: 1).

NGOs working on a wide variety of issues from turtle conservation to child labour are uniting in opposition to the unfettered and unaccountable hypercapitalism that globalisation is producing (Lynch 1998). In this book a variety of instances of protest against corporations have been mentioned, from demonstrations at home-improvement stores about deforestation (Chapter 4) to occupations of oil installations as a protest against dumping at sea (Chapter 2). This same understanding of how global economic processes affect our social and environmental realities has also led some NGOs to work with corporations to effect change. The reasons why businesses have responded positively to NGOs and the management lessons of the resulting partnerships have been discussed in the previous chapters. What I want to do in these concluding pages is to outline a concept that explains something of the significance of what is happening and that invites you to work in support of this change.

In this chapter I describe the growing importance of consumer politics and how NGOs are using it to drive changes in corporate practice. I move on to describe the different tactics used by NGOs, presenting them as part of the same process of 'regulating' business. I argue that this form of regulation is helping to make up the deficit of democratic governance which we face as a result of economic globalisation. I argue that current emphases on voluntarism and corporate social responsibility are misguided, as they sidestep the need to create new mechanisms for the democratic control of markets and the accountability of its institutions. I emphasise the reasons why business should embrace a radicalised concept of corporate citizenship and address core corporate governance issues. In the final sections I discuss some of the limitations of civil regulation in delivering sustainable development and democratic governance, by considering the partial reach of consumer politics and questions about the accountability of NGOs to their constituents. I conclude by calling on intergovernmental agencies to become more involved in multi-stakeholder processes for the regulation of business, and for corporations to support them in this endeavour.

◢ NGOs' mobilisation of consumer politics

It is widely understood that worker unrest with factory owners and other capitalists in most Northern countries at the start of the 20th century led to the establishment and legal protection of trade unions and a democratic political force for workers. This was an incorporation of worker demands that served to head off the revolutions against capitalism that had occurred in other countries. Critics of capitalism argued for the development of a 'producer politics' where workers unite in order to control capitalists' access to labour. The social democracies that emerged from this period embodied the notion that capitalism worked best if there was a counterbalancing force to capitalists through strong government and trade unions: capitalists needed the workers while workers, it was argued, needed the capitalists.

This social democratic system led to, or coincided with, a huge expansion of many economies during the 20th century. As we start the 21st century, this balance has been lost. Neoliberal governments have largely rejected the social democratic model, rolling back the state both internally, and externally by promoting international free trade. Trade union power and influence has also declined. The result is that global business does not have an effective counterbalancing force of globally organised producers. Increasingly, the offer of the lowest pay and working conditions wins the capitalist investment.

Meanwhile, in most Northern countries, work has changed. People are changing jobs more quickly than before. Family members no longer do what their parents did. Personal identity is not determined so much by one's work but increasingly by how one spends one's money and spare time. Thus the most recent political issues of our time are leading to different outcomes. 'There has been a dramatic increase over the last five years in international collective action through consumption', states a recent report by the NGO New Economics Foundation (Zadek *et al.* 1998: 8). In industrialised countries during the 1990s, concern about environmental and social issues not only led to workers uniting to demand better corporate performance, but to consumers uniting to do so as well. Whereas the establishment of trade unions and political parties incorporated the workers' movement, the establishment of NGOs has incorporated a 'consumer movement'.

Whereas producer politics gained its power through controlling access to labour, consumer politics gains its power through controlling access to customers. The examples in this book show that NGOs are mobilising consumer politics to change the behaviour of corporations in a number of ways. Corporate boycotts and direct action protests are the confrontational outcomes of consumer politics, in contrast to the strikes and lock-outs of producer politics. Business–NGO partnerships are the co-operative tools of consumer politics, in contrast to the business–union deals of producer politics. The following typology of NGO activities to influence corporations employs two variables: the 'style' of the NGO activities in relation to the market and the 'place' of the NGO activities in relation to the corporate activity they seek to change. This is illustrated by Figure 18.1.

The first variable is the 'style' of the activity being used by the NGO to change the behaviour of a corporation. The style of an NGO activity is the result of a number of factors, such as the ideology of the NGO, the skills it possesses, the success or failure of previous campaigns, and the responsiveness of the businesses in question. On the one hand there are confrontational approaches to corporations—the 'stick' approach—and on the other hand, there are collaborative approaches—the 'carrot' approach. The second variable is the 'place' of the NGO activity in relation to the market economy: in other words, whether the NGO activity is dependent on raising revenue in the market economy, or not.

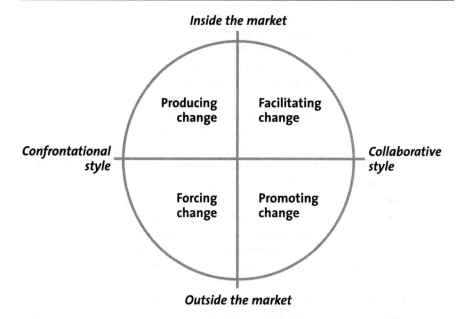

Figure 18.1 **NGO activities to change corporate behaviour**

In this book a number of examples have been presented where NGOs use voluntary donations of time, resources and money to try to force changes in corporate behaviour. This type of approach is described as *forcing change*. Campaigns for the boycotting of companies or products have been powerful catalysts for change in a variety of industries. Boycotts of consumer products from companies such as Levi Strauss and Pepsi, because of these companies' operations in Burma, were successful in persuading them to withdraw from the country: not before Pepsi had lost a $1 million contract with Harvard University because of the 'Free Burma Campaign' boycott (see Chapter 3). Boycotts of timber retailers across Europe throughout the 1990s because of their trade in wood originating from destroyed forests were key to the widespread adoption of responsible wood purchasing policies (see Chapter 4). General attempts to increase public outrage via the media are also important NGO tactics in this category, and were key in forcing Shell to change its policy on Brent Spar and its operations in Nigeria (see Chapter 2). Demonstrations at corporate offices, retail outlets, or annual general meetings are another tactic used against companies. Direct actions against biotechnology corporations in Asia and Europe, including the destruction of field trials of GM crops added to pressure which resulted in policy U-turns from Monsanto, Novartis and others (see Chapter 6). The publishing of critical research is also a key NGO activity for *forcing change*, and has underpinned a variety of the NGO campaigns covered in this book. Three more traditional activities are strikes, court action and lobbying for legislation—all of which remain significant confrontational tactics.

Another group of activities that operate outside the market, in the sense that they also rely on voluntary donations of time, resources and money, are aimed at *promoting change* in corporate behaviour. These collaborative activities include negotiating agreements with corporate management, advising companies on best practice, endorsing or promoting best practice (thereby supporting ethical consumerism and investment), conducting and publishing helpful research, or jointly developing new products or techniques. The World Wide Fund for Nature's work with timber retailers in the WWF 1995 Plus Group involved a number of these techniques, with the WWF negotiating standards and targets for responsible wood sourcing with member companies and providing advice on implementation issues (see Chapter 12). The Environmental Defense Fund has developed a number of projects from solid waste management to carbon emissions, while emphasising its financial independence from the corporations with whom it works (see Chapter 14). The Ethical Trading Initiative (ETI), which brings together companies, unions and development groups to increase learning on how to improve labour conditions in the suppliers of UK companies, is another example. Member NGOs provide research and advice on implementation issues as well as endorsing the labour standards being promoted by member companies.

While these activities do not rely on generating an income from the market in order to be successful in changing corporate practice, there are a variety of NGO activities that operate inside the market. In recent years a number of NGOs have started to provide services that are *facilitating change* in corporate practice, while generating revenue for the NGO. Consultancy services that aim to help corporations with change processes are one example. Another group of services relate to systems of company and/or product endorsement. Some NGOs run certification systems such as the US-based Rainforest Alliance's Eco-OK programme for agricultural products. Set up in 1992, the Alliance has certified, along with its partner organisations in Latin America, tens of thousands of hectares of banana plantations, including most of those run by Chiquita Brands International. There are now NGOs that specialise in providing corporations with monitoring services, such as Vérité, which focuses on labour rights issues. Accreditation bodies such as the Forest Stewardship Council (FSC) and Marine Stewardship Council (MSC) set standards for a particular industry through a multi-stakeholder process and then accredit organisations to go and audit companies using these standards; successfully certified companies can market their products accordingly (see Chapters 4 and 10). Although these stewardship councils are supported by grants, membership fees and accreditation revenues, their ultimate success in facilitating change in corporate practice depends on the acceptance of their certifications in the business community and the success of their logos in the marketplace.

Another group of NGO activities are those aimed at *producing change* in the market, by providing alternative production systems based on a different value system to mainstream business practice. NGO-owned alternative trading companies such as Max Havelaar, Fairtrade Foundation, Traidcraft Exchange and Oxfam Trading Company are examples. These NGO activities operate inside the market, in the sense that their success depends on sales in the marketplace. They are also confrontational to those corporations that are seen to be socially or environmentally questionable, because they advertise themselves as ethically preferable to such companies and compete with them for a market share. One example is Cafédirect, a UK-based marketing company that promotes a brand of fairly traded coffee. In 1999, Cafédirect already had a 4% share of the UK roasted coffee market and 2% of the freeze-dried market.

The typology therefore describes four types of NGO activity that mobilise consumer politics to change corporate practice: *forcing, promoting, facilitating* and *producing* change. Different NGOs are inclined to different types of activity depending on a number of factors, such as whether or not they discriminate between companies depending on their environmental and social performance and seek to work with the leaders (see Chapter 11). Many NGOs undertake different types of activity for a given objective, depending on the responsiveness of the corporation, but there appears to be a trend toward more collaborative activities. For example, Chapter 4 showed a progression of tactics, from protests to partnerships, as corporations began to respond to the deforestation issue. To begin with, NGOs were primarily protesting and boycotting to try to change corporate policy, and, once this was achieved within certain companies, some NGOs began exploring collaborative opportunities, which ultimately led to the formation of the FSC. Although the entry point for relations is often a *forcing change* approach, the trend for *facilitating change* approaches is strong, particularly with the establishment of multi-stakeholder accreditation councils. These councils may be the most formal system for civil society control of corporate behaviour, but the reason for their existence cannot be understood in isolation from the other activities with which NGOs have been attempting to tip the market in favour of sustainable development.

◢ Conceptualising civil regulation

The NGO attempts at mobilising consumer politics described above are becoming more effective as a result of developments in information technology, and more significant because of the affect of globalisation on the ability of governments to regulate and businesses to maintain legitimacy. Barbara Rose Johnston (1997: 332) believes that these NGO activities constitute 'a political force whose power and impact cannot be over-stated'. This political force is a real phenomenon for corporate managers, who report that dealing with stakeholders is one of their primary challenges for the start of this century (*Financial Times* 1999). However, to fully comprehend these forces we must question long-standing assumptions about the place of politics, the nature of governance and the source of regulation.

The chapters in this book deal with political processes just as much as they do with management, yet the nation-state and government rarely feature. To understand the significance of these processes we need, for one moment, to set aside the concept of state sovereignty and government as the place of political life. As Shapiro (1991: 474) points out, 'the present global condition of sovereignty is a relatively recent and contentious set of practices rather than a naturally evolving wisdom', and it should not limit our political horizon. Business and the market economy are forms of social organisation and as such are also sites for political thought and action, in addition to the traditional political sphere of government. Drawing on the sociological theory of structuration, the power of businesses and NGOs to 'change the rules' of markets was described clearly in Chapter 16. These non-state actors are involved in the politics of their own governance:

> Whereas before the large corporation may have looked like an economic entity with political power, now it appears to be a political entity that happens to operate in the economic sphere (Mintzberg 1989: 366).

Political scientist James Rosenau (1997: 145) argues that 'any actors who resort to command mechanisms to make demands, frame goals, issue directives, and pursue policies' are partaking in governance:

> [Whereas] governments exercise rule, governance uses power . . . [with] each party trying to induce, or to force the other party to do certain things it otherwise would not have done (Rosenau and Czempiel 1992: 250).

This conception of governance is shared by thought leaders in civil society. The Secretary-General and CEO of the Citizens' Alliance for Participation (CIVICUS), Kumi Naidoo, argues that 'governing can no longer be left only to government' and that we should focus 'less on the institutions of government and more on solving problems and making and implementing decisions that are in the public's interest' (Naidoo 2000).

Liberated from anachronistic conceptions of state-centred politics and governance, it is now possible to comprehend the revolutionary changes that are occurring. Reflecting on the new forms of business–NGO relations, BP's Chris Marsden suggests that 'there is . . . a new form of global governance evolving' that is made up of:

> codes and accountability systems, which are becoming a kind of 'soft law'. It is being developed and enforced by increasingly sophisticated civil society activism, leadership by both socially responsible and responsive companies and thereby, increased public expectation.[1]

The evidence in this book adds weight to this perspective, by demonstrating that, as either business provocateurs or partners, NGOs are playing catalytic roles in changing corporate policy and practice. It is the thesis here that NGO campaigns are constituting a new and emerging form of regulation for international corporations, called *civil regulation*. NGOs are setting the standards for corporate behaviour, through dialogue with management, and corporates are increasingly choosing to adopt these standards. For corporations that adopt the standards, a number of benefits are available, relating to social and intellectual capital, as described in this book's introduction, as well as support for specific corporate operations, as outlined in Chapter 14. For those companies choosing not to adopt these standards, the confrontational tools of consumer politics can be expected from civil society (boycotts, direct action, ethical disinvestment, etc.), with deleterious effects on company sales, costs and social or intellectual capital. Whereas government fines for pollution violations now rarely affect company value, consumer politics brings greater financial risks. Although governments may have the purported monopoly on

1   Personal communication with Chris Marsden, 21 May 1999.

force—and therefore the 'final say'—in reality, the ability of NGOs to regulate business behaviour through financial carrots and sticks is rapidly becoming more powerful.

I recognise that, traditionally, government has been regarded as the sole source of regulation. However, if we consider the classical concept of regulation, we can liberate it from the traditional view that also limited our perception of—and involvement in— politics and governance. From a reworking of Kantian writings (Kant 1964), a *regulatory framework* can be defined as a norm-creating and norm-enforcing system, which must exhibit the following five components:

☐ An agent, or agents, who can make choices between alternative norms of behaviour

☐ Alternative norms of behaviour between which to choose

☐ A subject, be it something or someone, on which a chosen norm is imposed

☐ A resolution regarding which of the alternative norms should apply to the subject

☐ A mechanism for ensuring that the chosen norm is adhered to by the subject(s)

In terms of a national government and the legislature, the *resolution* regarding which *norm* to choose is called 'legislation' and the preferred *norm* is called a 'law'. However, it is incorrect to assume a government to be the only *agent* considering different *norms* of behaviour and making *resolutions* about which should apply to different *subjects*, and then using a *mechanism* to ensure compliance. A discussion of the current situation using the classical conception of a regulatory framework reveals the fallacy of such an assumption.

☐ A chosen *norm*, or law, without a *mechanism* for enforcing it on a *subject* or subjects is mere wishful thinking on the part of an *agent*, and the system is therefore not a real *regulatory framework*. Yet this is the situation today with many states and intergovernmental organisations, who lack the will and resources to implement their *resolutions*, or legislation.

☐ An *agent* who does not have a number of alternative *norms* to choose from in coming to a *resolution* is not a real *agent*, and the system is not a *regulatory framework*. Yet this is the situation for most governments today who are locked into a process of deregulation and tax cuts in order to attract investment in a global market.

☐ A *subject* of a *resolution* who is also the *agent* making that choice between *norms* is neither a *subject* nor an *agent*, and the system is not a *regulatory framework*. Consequently the concept of industry self-regulation is a contradiction.

In civil regulation the *agent* is civil society, where—given concerns with sustainable development—different *norms* of behaviour for corporations are debated. NGOs then make *resolutions* about the standards that should be upheld by the *subjects* of the regulation, the corporations. The mechanism for compliance is provided by consumer politics. Therefore, from a reworking of the classical roots of modern thought about government and the rule of law, we find that, whereas legal regulation is in decline and self-regulation is illogical, civil regulation is a valid depiction of modern business–NGO relations.

◢ Challenging 'self-regulation'

From a consideration of what is and what is not real 'regulation', I have suggested that industry self-regulation is an oxymoron. What could be occurring, however, is the regulation of some companies by other companies. This is occurring as particular companies are organising to change the rules of access to markets with the help of intermediary institutions, such as trade associations and professional bodies (see Chapter 16). Using examples such as the informal rule-making by accountants and lawyers Günther Teubner (1997) demonstrated how key actors in the private sector develop laws and law-like systems of rules. Claire Cutler *et al.* (1999) consider that these forms of 'private authority', being created through co-operation among businesses, hold potential for substituting government authority. Similarly, Mathias Finger and Ludivine Tamiotti believe that the growing significance of standards set by organisations such as the International Organization for Standardization (ISO) represents a 'privatisation of environmental regulation' (1999: 11).

Throughout the 1990s 'self-regulation' was championed as a way of promoting business contributions to sustainable development by allowing flexibility in addressing environmental issues and by creating incentives for environmental innovations (WBCSD 1997). 'Voluntarism' became a popular concept in government circles as social and environmental regulations were seen to be inflexible and anti-competitive, and collaborative relations between business and government more desirable. However, 'voluntarism' has been attacked on a number of fronts.

By comparing the results of voluntarist policies with stiffer regulation, analysts have questioned whether voluntarism motivates environmental innovation and socially above-compliance performance by corporations (Maltby 1995). Others have drawn on economic theory to argue that voluntarism is insufficient, as 'markets tend to become uncompetitive' and in a global economy corporations tend to monopolise market power so that 'the policy implication . . . [is] to create a countervailing power so that . . . the market can be made to work more effectively again'.[2] Barque simply states that the 'free market is not an effective instrument for raising up a civilisation founded on and governed by ethical values' (1993: 164). Korten believes that leaving the future of society to be shaped by business is unethical as 'corporations should obey the laws decided by the citizenry, not write those laws' (1995: 308). In a similar vein, the UN Research Institute for Social Development (UNRISD) contends that 'international business cannot be expected to author their own regulation: this is the job of good governance' (UNRISD 1995: 19). Moreover, we could say that this is the job of good *democratic* governance.

2   Personal communication with Chris Marsden, 21 May 1999.

What are the principles of democratic governance? I could present a variety of perspectives with a review of the literature on political thought through the ages, but my purpose here can be better served by stating a view that is developed from a post-state analysis of the writings of Dahl (1961) and which I hope can be widely supported. That is, in a democratically governed society a community of people should have meaningful participation in decisions and processes that affect them and they should not be systematically adversely affected by another group of people, without being able to rectify the situation. This conception of democratic governance is based on a belief in the human right to self-determine one's life-world. A number of other human rights stem from this, once we recognise the material foundations of self-determination, and self-actualisation: namely, the right to basic necessities of life, which includes a safe environment. David Korten suggests that 'there are few rights more fundamental than the right of people to create caring, sustainable communities and to control their own resources, economies and means of livelihood' (1995: 307).

From this approach to human rights and democratic governance, organisations or persons that affect you and your community, especially when they affect the material foundations to your self-determination, must be able to be influenced by you and your community. In other words, they must be accountable. However, as argued in Chapter 1, economic globalisation has undermined national state systems for the democratic governance of the economy: corporations are no longer acceptably accountable to the citizens of a nation through the machinery of national government. Organisation theorist Henry Mintzberg therefore asks us, 'how can we call our society democratic when many of its most powerful institutions are closed to governance from the outside and are run as oligarchies from within?' (1989: 328). Although voluntary steps taken by corporations to deal with some of the social and environmental challenges that arise from, or just surround, their operations should be welcomed, from a democratic perspective they are not sufficient. What are required are new forms of democratic governance so that people can determine their own futures in a sustainable environment and safe society. In providing a means by which people can hold corporations accountable for their actions and change their policies and operations, civil regulation offers a novel channel for the democratic governance of the global economy by civil society.

◢ Radical corporate citizenship

This preceding analysis challenges current thinking on corporate social responsibility (WBCSD 1999) and corporate citizenship (McIntosh *et al.* 1998). The pragmatic rationale of these approaches is illustrated by management guru Charles Handy's (1998) assertion that 'we have to rely on [corporations'] internal values to keep them honest and decent. We have to hope that those values are focused on what is best for all of us.' Here we see that the onus is placed on the corporation to take action on social and environmental issues. The agency is with the company, not the people; the power to do the right thing is assigned to the company, not the people. In direct opposition to this, I agree with

Mintzberg that 'society cannot sit by and be dictated to by systems that were created to serve it' (Mintzberg 1989: 103). This issue does not arise for advocates of corporate social responsibility (CSR) and corporate citizenship, because they assume a win–win world and do not recognise intractable conflict between corporate interests and those of civil society. At most, conflict is seen as a process issue, an outcome of paradoxes which should be managed carefully (Chapter 16).

However, fundamental conflicts do exist. In Chapter 6 on the biotechnology industry the possibility was raised that in some circumstances there will be no win–win solution, unless fundamental environmental and social principles are compromised. It was argued above that it is a human right for a group of people not to have their future health, environmental and economic security threatened by institutions working for the profit of another group. Therefore it is essential for institutions with this power to be accountable to society; in other words, it is essential for corporations with this power to be less powerful. The needed outcome is a win–lose scenario. The win–win paradigm therefore papers over fundamental political concerns about human rights and democracy so that CSR and corporate citizenship do not deal adequately with the rights of individuals over commercial institutions in society. While CSR and corporate citizenship remain wedded to the view that we live in a win–win world, their usefulness in helping to build sustainable governance of the world economy will be limited.

The concept of the civil regulation of corporations is not based on a win–win world-view. In the case of biotechnology, the outcome of civil regulatory processes may be to make most commercial applications of the technology unviable—a distinct win–lose (see Chapter 6). From the fundamental principles of democracy and self-determination, civil regulation is demanding corporate accountability. In direct refutation of the argument that we must rely on corporations' internal values, Korten asserts that 'it is the people's right to demand that . . . corporations remain accountable to the public will and interest' and reminds us that 'the powers of the private corporation are grants extended' by society so that the corporation may 'serve the collective human interest' (1995: 330). People come before profit and so our goal should be to create a system that works well for people, with corporations being merely one mechanism for meeting human needs. If there are useful roles for corporations, then they have much to offer, 'but the right to decide must reside with people' (Korten 1995: 324).

A radicalised version of corporate citizenship that recognises the role of civil regulation and embraces the need for greater corporate accountability may provide a progressive policy discourse for corporations. For this we need to consider what it means to be a real 'citizen'. Management thinker Peter Drucker observes that 'as a political term citizenship means active commitment. It means responsibility. It means making a difference in one's community, one's society, one's world, one's country' (1993: 155). I agree that active responsibility is one aspect of citizenship, but no less important is active accountability. A citizen is a member of a political community, subsuming itself to the authority of that community, believing that all members will submit equally and so that all will benefit. This is because if all individuals or groups in a society pursued their unrestrained self-interest then the majority would suffer; and so, by giving up certain rights to a higher authority, the individual citizen helps to guarantee the rights of all citizens to life, liberty, property and the pursuit of happiness. This has direct implications for *corporate* citizenship.

Of which communities are corporations members, and to which authority should they submit? The financial community is currently the *de facto* authority controlling corporations, but radical corporate citizenship demands that new channels of authority are consolidated with other, non-financial, communities. This is not a simple exercise as corporations operate at many levels, cross-cutting a number of geographical and cultural communities; the fact that a defined democratic world community does not yet exist also causes complication. Three types of non-financial community are particularly relevant here: stakeholders, staff and international agencies. Building democratic systems of accountability with these groups and integrating their signals into corporate policy is a major challenge for corporations, giving renewed importance to questions of corporate governance. Insular, responsive and democratic approaches to corporate governance were discussed in Chapter 17. Radical corporate citizenship suggests a democratic approach to corporate governance, where systems would be put in place for stakeholders to participate in strategic planning and even for them to elect non-executive directors to the board. This democratic approach would imply that staff should also have an input in policy decisions, including the election of some board members. A direct method for creating corporate accountability with staff, their families and communities is to close the gap between those who own the institution and those who work for it. Having diagnosed hypercapitalism and 'absent owners' as the driving factor behind the growth in unaccountable market institutions, Jeff Gates argues that we need more 'up-close ownership' if we are 'to link a nation's people to their workplace, their community, their economy, their environment—and to each other' (Gates 1998: xxv). Employee share ownership plans should therefore be an integral element of a radical corporate citizenship strategy.

Transnational corporations are also members of an emerging global community. For managers who support radical corporate citizenship there is a logical business case for supporting the development of institutions for democratic global governance. While profitability may rise in the short term as a result of lax regulation, this is not a stable climate for business in the longer term, as resources are squandered, communities alienated and potential markets left undeveloped. Individual companies cannot respond to this emerging social and environmental crisis alone. To do so, for example, by unilaterally pulling out of a gas development project in Peru, might affect investor confidence in the competitiveness of the company. However, if companies collaborate to improve environmental and social standards, they may succeed in creating a more favourable business climate in the long term. To achieve this, business requires an external force that can push reluctant companies forward. In this sense business requires a global civil society and a strong intergovernmental community. Radical corporate citizenship suggests that companies should begin by submitting to the authority of fledgling intergovernmental processes and by not lobbying against their regulatory functions. Moreover, there is good reason for companies to lobby for heightened regulation at the intergovernmental level in order to raise the common standard of practice and ensure greater benefit for all.

◢ Limitations of civil regulation

The regulatory vacuum created by economic globalisation is being filled, to some extent, by NGOs. Yet the archaic—perhaps anarchic—nature of civil regulation means that it will not be sufficient on its own to deliver a system of democratic governance for sustainable development. There are a series of limitations that need to be addressed if we are to create a robust system of democratic governance for the global economy.

The first limitation arises because of the limited geographical reach of consumer politics in non-Western countries. For example, in the case of forestry, Western businesses' support for the FSC has not stopped Asian companies with poor management practices from increasing their logging activities in tropical forests. This is because the growing demand for timber in the emerging economies is not yet matched by a growing consumer politics. Even as Northern-based companies in other sectors develop higher social and environmental standards for their operations in the South, their Asian or Latin American competitors are likely to continue to cut corners when supplying Southern markets. This means that civil regulation, as expressed through certification and labelling schemes, may merely serve to shift international trading patterns and have little effect on environmental protection or sustainable development in the South (see Chapter 4).

The second limitation relates to the limited social reach of consumer politics. Certain groups of consumers (and their advocates) do not have the same power as other consumers. Consumer power is directly related to spending power: in consumer politics it is 'one dollar, one vote', not 'one person, one vote'. This poses major problems for people with little, or no, consumer power: citizens of Southern countries have far less of this political power than their counterparts in the North. However, in producer politics power is not gained by an individual's worth as a worker but is gained through collective action and collective bargaining. Consumer solidarity with those in the midst of social or environmental troubles is therefore key:

> the idea of 'lending' consumer power in the market has emerged, whereby leverage through the purchasing power of wealthy consumers has been used to support the workplace demands of people in other countries who have inadequate leverage through their own collective action (Zadek *et al.* 1998: 27).

A further limitation relates to the potential of civil society to mobilise consumer politics when the ability to organise, take direct action and speak freely is not always protected. Without the ability to wield the 'stick', Southern NGOs and communities will not be able to realise the benefits of civil regulation. The ability to do this relies on government protecting civil liberties, which is not the situation in all countries:

> One reason why Latin American environmental campaigners are more vulnerable than their fellow activists in Europe or North America is that Latin America's democratic and judicial institutions are still weak and protesters often have limited recourse to the law (Collinson 1996: 1).

Again, the answer might lie in North–South linkages. From the examples provided, it appears that to become active in civil regulation, Southern NGOs need to be linked with supportive NGOs in countries with developed consumer politics. The Shell Nigeria example also reminds us that Southern campaigning on its own is not always effective in changing corporate practices. Protests by local Delta communities against Shell began in the late 1980s, but it only became an issue in the North much later when Northern NGOs, companies and the media joined the cause (see Chapter 2). Radical corporate citizenship also suggests that businesses should take a leadership role in ensuring that basic human rights and freedoms are respected in the countries and regions where they operate.

A fourth limitation relates to the democratic credentials of civil regulation. P.J. Simmons (1998) has acknowledged the important role that NGOs play in demanding more accountability of governments and international organisations, but also points out their own problematic lack of accountability, and suggests that the growing influence of NGOs is a mixed blessing. The same issue arises with the civil regulation of corporations. Those who claim to be acting for the interests of a particular group have a great deal of power in determining the future of that group; therefore the accountability of NGOs to the constituents they purport to represent is key to democratic governance. However, many Southern NGOs continue to complain that Northern NGOs impose agendas on them (Murphy and Bendell 1999) and in Chapter 5 we saw how certain indigenous peoples' concerns can be marginalised by environmental NGOs that push their own agendas. In turn, Ann Hudock (1999) found that many Southern NGOs are not particularly accountable to grass-roots interests and concerns because they need to be more aware of the grant-givers' priorities and appear attractive to them. Despite these thorny issues, some campaigners continue to see NGO accountability as a 'non-issue' (Greenpeace's Thilo Bode, quoted in WEF 2000). Businesses will need to be clear about their interest in accountability and democratic governance and support those NGOs that subscribe to such principles. Ultimately, a triple democratisation of state, private and civil organisations should be the goal of radical corporate citizens.

◢ Conclusion

> A highly problematic process of stakeholder engagement seems to be emerging as an informal model of global governance. This, in time and with the right kind of influence and encouragement from national governments and emerging agents of global governance, could harden up into an effective regulatory system.[3]

Both the potential and limitations of civil regulation open a way for the leadership role of intergovernmental agencies, to 'harden' it into an effective system of democratic global governance for sustainable development. In launching the Global Compact with business and civil society, the United Nations is beginning to take up that leadership role.[4]

3 Personal communication with Chris Marsden, 21 May 1999.
4 www.unglobalcompact.org

In parallel with this process, NGOs have called on the UN to endorse a 'Citizens' Compact' which would set out a course for the UN to develop a legal framework, including monitoring, to govern corporate behaviour around the world (CEO 2000).

This book has provided ample evidence why businesses should support such a process. For those who are aware of the urgency of our social and environmental predicament, cognisant of the limitations of the growth paradigm, conscious of the emergent power of civil society, and convinced of the relevance of democratic principles to corporations, a battle awaits to convert others to the cause of radical corporate citizenship. In taking up that battle, you become part of a growing civil society and help realise the vision of the International NGO Forum's Declaration at the Earth Summit in 1992. Reflect on its truth, and consider its calling:

> We the people of the world will mobilise the forces of transnational civil society behind a widely shared agenda that bonds our many social movements in pursuit of just, sustainable and participatory human societies. In so doing we are forging our own instruments and processes for redefining the nature and meaning of human progress and for transforming those institutions that no longer respond to our needs. We welcome to our cause all people who share our commitment to peaceful and democratic change in the interest of our living planet and the human societies it sustains (International NGO Forum 1992).

BIBLIOGRAPHY

Adams, W.M. (1993) 'Sustainable Development and the Greening of Development Theory', in F. Schuurman (ed.) *Beyond the Impasse* (London: Zed Books).

Alvesson, M., and P.O. Berg (1992) *Corporate Culture and Organizational Symbolism* (Berlin: de Gruyter).

Aspinwall, R., and J. Smith (eds.) (1996) *Environmentalist and Business Partnerships: A Sustainable Model? A Critical Assessment of the Impact of the WWF UK 1995 Group* (Cambridge, UK: White Horse Press).

Babin, R. (1995) 'Les enjeux de la regulation écologique: des contraintes du marché à l'action des citoyens' (Working paper; Département de Sociologie, Moncton, Canada).

Barboza, D. (1999) 'Biotech companies take on critics of gene-altered food', *New York Times*, 12 November 1999: 14.

Baron, D.P. (1993) *Business and its Environment* (Englewood Cliffs, NJ: Prentice–Hall).

Barque, C. (1993) *The End of Economics?* (London: Zed Books).

Beck, U. (1992) *Risk Society: Towards a New Modernity* (London: Sage).

Beck, U., A. Giddens and S. Lash (1994) *Reflexive Modernisation: Politics, Tradition and Aesthetics in the Modern Social Order* (Stanford, CA: Stanford University Press).

Bell, E., and D. Fraser (1999) 'Evangelist gets £10m pay-off', *The Observer*, 6 June 1999.

Bendell, J. (1998) 'Citizens Cane? Relations between Business and Civil Society', paper presented at the *International Society for Third-Sector Research (ISTR) 3rd International Conference*, Geneva, 8–11 July 1998 (available on-line at www.mailbase.ac.uk/lists/business-ngo-relations/files/citizenscane).

Bendell, J., and F. Sullivan (1996) 'Sleeping with the Enemy? Business–Environmentalist Partnerships for Sustainable Development: The Case of the WWF 1995 Group', in R. Aspinwall and J. Smith (eds.), *Environmentalist and Business Partnerships: A Sustainable Model? A Critical Assessment of the Impact of the WWF UK 1995 Group* (Cambridge, UK: White Horse Press).

Bendell, J., and D. Warner (1996) 'If you can't beat 'em, join 'em: The Costs and Benefits of Collaborating with the Environmental Movement', in *Proceedings of the Business Strategy and the Environment Conference 1996* (Leeds, UK: ERP).

Benton, T. (1997) 'Beyond Left and Right? Ecological Politics, Capitalism and Modernity', in M. Jacobs (ed.), *Greening the Millennium? The New Politics of the Environment* (Oxford, UK: Blackwell).

Bioengineering Action Network (1999) Press Release, 4 September 1999.

Bonoma, T.V. (1985) 'Case Research in Marketing: Opportunities, Problems, and a Process', *Journal of Marketing Research* 22 (May 1985): 199-208.

Bray, J. (1995) *Burma: The Politics of Constructive Engagement* (Discussion Paper 58; London: Royal Institute of International Affairs).

Broad, R., and J. Cavanagh (1999) 'The Corporate Accountability Movement: Lessons and Opportunities', *Fletcher Forum* 23 (Fall 1999).

Brown, A.D. (1995) *Organizational Culture* (London: Pitman).

Brown, L.D. (1991) 'Bridging Organisations and Sustainable Development', *Human Relations* 44.8: 807-31.

Brown, L.D. (1993) 'Development Bridging Organisations and Strategic Management for Social Change', *Advances in Strategic Management* 9: 381-405.

Brummer, A. (1999) 'The People's Plutocrat', *The Guardian*, 12 June 1999.

Buckingham, L., and R. Cowe (1999) 'Rude Awakening to the Dawn of a Risk Revolution. News Analysis: Corporate hazard management is being overhauled', *The Guardian*, 20 April 1999.

Burt, R. (1992) *Structural Holes: The Social Structure of Competition* (Cambridge, MA: Harvard University Press).

Business in the Environment (1997) *The Index of Corporate Environmental Engagement* (London: BiE).

Carroll, A.B. (1993) *Business and Society: Ethics and Stakeholder Management* (Cincinnati, OH: South-Western).

Carson, R. (1962) *Silent Spring* (Boston, MA: Houghton Mifflin).

CEO (Corporate Europe Observatory) (2000) *Groups Launch 'Citizens Compact' on the UN and Corporations* (Press Release; Corporate Europe Observatory and the Transnational Resource and Action Center; Davos, Switzerland, 28 January 2000).

Chatterjee, P., and M. Finger (1994) *The Earth Brokers: Power, Politics and World Development* (London: Routledge).

Cherbo, J.M. (1999) 'Creative Synergy: Commercial and Non-profit Live Theater in America', paper presented at the *Independent Sector Spring Research Forum*, Washington, DC, 1999.

Christian Aid (1999) *Selling Suicide: Farming False Promises and Genetic Engineering in Developing Countries* (London: Christian Aid).

Clair, J.A., J. Milliman and I.I. Mitroff (1995) 'Clash or Cooperation? Understanding Environmental Organizations and their Relationship to Business', *Research in Corporate Social Performance and Policy*, Supplement 1: 163-93.

Coates, B. (1998) 'Managing Consumer Pressure', speech presented at the first conference of the Ethical Trading Initiative, London, December 1998.

Cobbe, J.H. (1979) *Governments and Mining Companies in Developing Countries* (Boulder, CO: Westview).

Cohen, J. (1995) 'Interpreting the Notion of Civil Society', in M. Walzer (ed.), *Toward Global Civil Society* (New York: Berghahn Books).

Colborn, T., D. Dumanoski and J. Peterson Myers (1997) *Our Stolen Future* (New York: Plume).

Colchester, M. (1993) 'Forest Peoples and Sustainability', in M. Colchester and L. Lohman (eds.), *The Struggle for Land and the Fate of the Forests* (London: Zed Books).

Collinson, H. (ed.) (1996) *Green Guerrillas: Environmental Conflicts and Initiatives in Latin America and the Caribbean* (London: Latin American Bureau).

Commonwealth Association for Corporate Governance (1999) *Principles of Best Business Practice for the Commonwealth: Towards Global Competitiveness and Economic Accountability* (London: Commonwealth Association).

Conca, K. (1993) 'Environmental Change and the Deep Structure of World Politics', in R. Lipschutz and K. Conca (eds.), *The State and Social Power in Global Environmental Politics* (New York: Columbia University Press).

Cone/Roper (1999) '1999 Cone/Roper Cause Trends Report: The Evolution of Cause Branding' (Cone Communications, www.conenet.com/website/crm/report.htm).

Control Risks Group (1997) *No Hiding Place: Business and the Politics of Pressure* (London: Control Risks Group).

Corporate Watch (1999) *Animal Food and Genetic Engineering* (Oxford, UK: Corporate Watch).

Corry, S. (1993) 'Harvest Moonshine Taking You for a Ride: A Critique of the Rainforest Harvest, its Theory and Practice' (Discussion paper; London: Survival International): 1-15.

Cowe, R. (1996) 'Shell comes clean to its green critics', *The Guardian*, 26 November 1996: 17.

Crane, A. (1995) 'Rhetoric and Reality in the Greening of Organisational Culture', *Greener Management International* 12 (October 1995): 49-62.

Crane, A. (1998) 'Exploring Green Alliances', *Journal of Marketing Management* 14.6: 559-79.

Crowfoot, J., and J.M. Wondolleck (1990) *Environmental Disputes: Community Involvement in Conflict Resolution* (Washington, DC: Island Press).

Cummins, R. (1998) ' "Cremate Monsanto": Global opposition intensifies', *Food Bytes* 15 (7 December 1998), www.purefood.org.

Cutler, A.C., V. Haufler and T. Porter (eds.) (1999) *Private Authority and International Affairs* (New York: SUNY).

Dahl, R.A. (1961) *Who Governs? Democracy and Power in an American City* (New Haven, CT: Yale University Press).

Danker, S. (1999) in *Earth Times*, 12 August 1999.

Dasgupta, S., B. Laplante and N. Mamingi (1998) *Capital Market Responses to Environmental Performance in Developing Countries* (Washington, DC: World Bank; available at www.worldbank.org/nipr/work_paper/index.htm).

De Jonquières, G. (1998) 'Network Guerrillas', *Financial Times*, 30 April 1998.

De Oliveira, M.D., and R. Tandon (eds.) (1994) *Citizens Strengthening Global Civil Society* (Washington, DC: CIVICUS World Alliance for Citizen Participation).

Dodds, F. (ed.) (1997) *The Way Forward: Beyond Agenda 21* (London: Earthscan).

Dore, E. (1996) 'Capitalism and Ecological Crisis: Legacy of the 1980s', in H. Collinson (ed.), *Green Guerrillas: Environmental Conflicts and Initiatives in Latin America and the Caribbean* (London: Latin American Bureau).

Drohan, M. (1998) 'How the net killed the MAI: Grassroots groups used their own globalization to derail deal', *The Globe and Mail*, 29 April 1998; cited on the Corporate Watch website, www.corpwatch.org/trac/corner/worldnews.

Drucker, P. (1993) *Post Capitalist Society* (Oxford, UK: Butterworth–Heinemann).

DTI (UK Department for Trade and Industry) (1999) *Modern Company Law for a Competitive Economy: The Strategic Framework* (London: DTI).

Dubash, N.K., and M. Oppenheimer (1992) 'Modifying the Mandate of Existing Institutions: NGOs', in I. Mintzer (ed.), *Confronting Climate Change: Risks, Implications and Responses* (Cambridge, UK: Cambridge University Press).

Economist (1997) 'Meltdown', *The Economist*, 1 March 1997: 94.

EDF (Environmental Defense Fund) (1999) *Catalyzing Environmental Results: Lessons in Advocacy Organization–Business Partnerships* (ed. E. Fastiggi; New York: EDF).

Elkington, J. (1997a) Foreword, in D. Murphy and J. Bendell, *In the Company of Partners: Business, Environmental Groups and Sustainable Development Post-Rio* (Bristol, UK: The Policy Press).

Elkington, J. (1997b) *Cannibals with Forks: The Triple Bottom Line of 21st Century Business* (Oxford, UK: Capstone Publishing).

Elkington, J. (1998a) 'Quakers', *The Guardian*, 14 March 1998.

Elkington, J. (1998b) Speech at the *Sustainable Business Conference*, British Library, London, 22 October 1998.

Emerson, R. (1962) 'Power–Dependence Relations', *American Sociological Review* 27: 31-40.

ENDS (Environmental Data Services) (1999) 'The Environment Daily' e-mail, 22 March 1999.

Enderle, G., and G. Peters (1998) *A Strange Affair? The Emerging Relationship between NGOs and Transnational Companies* (London: Price Waterhouse in partnership with the University of Notre Dame).

Epstein, J. (1999) 'Brazilians boil over ban on altered beans', *Christian Science Monitor*, 25 August 1999, available at my.csmonitor.com.

Epstein, M.J., and M.-J. Roy (1997) 'Environmental Management to Improve Corporate Profitability', *Journal of Cost Management*, November/December 1997: 26-34.

Evans, P. (1995) 'Possibilities for Synergy: Evaluating the Comparative Evidence', preliminary draft paper prepared for the meeting of the *Economic Development Working Group: Social and Public Affairs Project*, Cambridge, MA, 1995.

Evans, R. (1997) 'Accounting for Ethics: Traidcraft plc, UK', in S. Zadek, P. Pruzan and R. Evans, *Building Corporate Accountability: Emerging Practice in Social and Ethical Accounting, Auditing and Reporting* (London: Earthscan).

Fabig, H., and R. Boele (1999) 'The Changing Nature of NGO Activity in a Globalising World: Pushing the Corporate Responsibility Agenda', *IDS Bulletin* 30.3: 58-67.

Fay, C. (1998a) Speech to the Institute of Chartered Accountants, *21st Century Annual Report Conference*, London, 11 September 1998.

Fay, C. (1998b) 'The Wider Responsibilities of Business', speech to *New Statesman 'Toward a Radical Century' Conference*, London, 17 September 1998.

Financial Times (1999) 'World's Most Respected Companies', *Financial Times*, 7 December 1999: Survey Section.

Fineman, S., and K. Clarke (1996) 'Green Stakeholders: Industry Interpretations and Response', *Journal of Management Studies* 33.6: 715-30.

Finger, M. (1993) 'Foxes in Charge of the Chickens', in W. Sachs (ed.), *Global Ecology: A New Arena of Political Conflict* (London: Zed Books).

Finger, M., and L. Tamiotti (1999) 'Institutional Innovation', *IDS Bulletin* 30.3 (July 1999): 8-15.

Fischer, K., and J. Schot (eds.) (1993) *Environmental Strategies for Industry* (Washington, DC: Island Press).

Fisher, R. (1983) 'Negotiating Power: Getting and Using Influence', *American Behavioral Scientist* 27.2: 149-66.

Fisher, R., and W. Ury (1992) *Getting to Yes: Negotiating Agreements without Giving In* (Boston, MA: Houghton Mifflin).

Fiszbein, A., and P. Lowdin (1998) *Working Together for a Change: Government, Business and Civic Partnerships for Poverty Reduction in LAC* (Washington, DC: World Bank).

Florini, A.M. (1998) 'The End of Secrecy', *Foreign Policy*, Summer 1998, available at http://216.51.17.154/articles/art7.htm.

Florini, A.M. (1999) 'Does the invisible hand need a transparent glove? The Politics of Transparency', paper prepared for the *Annual World Bank Conference on Development Economics*, Washington, DC, 28–30 April 1999, available at www.worldbank.org/research/abcde/washington_11/papers.html.

FoE (Friends of the Earth)-UK (1991) 'Friends of the Earth brings DIY stores into line', Press Release, 11 December 1991, London.

FoE (Friends of the Earth)-UK (1992) 'Timber Agreement under Fire', *Earth Matters* 17 (Winter 1992): 5.

Fowler, A. (1991) 'Building Partnerships between Northern and Southern Development NGOs: Issues for the 1990s', *Development in Practice* 1.1: 5-18.

Freeman, R.E. (1984) *Strategic Management: A Stakeholder Approach* (Boston, MA: Pitman).

Friedman, M. (1962) *Capitalism and Freedom* (Chicago: University of Chicago Press).

Fukuyama, F. (1995) *Trust: The Social Virtues and the Creation of Prosperity* (New York: Free Press).

Gardner, R., and M.F. Millikan (eds.) (1968) *The Global Partnership: International Agencies and Economic Development* (New York: Praeger).

Gates, J. (1998) *The Ownership Solution* (Harmondsworth, UK: Penguin).

Gertz, C. (1962) 'The Rotating Credit Association: A "Middle Run" in Development', *Economic Development and Cultural Change* 10: 249-63.

Giddens, A. (1984) *The Constitution of Society: Outline of the Theory of Structuration* (Berkeley, CA/Los Angeles: University of California Press).

Giddens, A. (1994) *Beyond Left and Right: The Future of Radical Politics* (Cambridge, UK: Polity Press).

Gills, B. (1997) 'Globalisation and the Politics of Resistance', *New Political Economy* 2.1: 11-17.

Glaser, B.G., and A.L. Strauss (1967) *The Discovery of Grounded Theory* (New York: Aldine).

Glover, D. (1999) 'Defending Communities: Local Exchange Trading Schemes from an Environmental Perspective', *IDS Bulletin* 30.3: 75-82.

Goldstick, M. (1987) *Wollaston: People Resisting Genocide* (Montreal: Black Rose Books).

Gramsci, A. (1992) *Prison Notebooks: Volume I* (ed. J.A. Buttigieg; trans. J.A. Buttigieg and A. Callari; New York: Columbia University Press).

Gray, B. (1989) *Collaborating: Finding Common Ground for Multiparty Problems* (San Francisco: Jossey-Bass).

Gray, B., and D. Wood (1991) 'Collaborative Alliances: Moving from Practice to Theory', *Journal of Applied Behavioral Science* 27.1: 3-22.

Greenhouse, S. (1998) 'Two more unions reject agreement for curtailing sweatshops', *New York Times*, 6 November 1998, sourced from www.sweatshopwatch.org/swatch/headlines/1998/aip_nov98.html.

Greenpeace (1998) *The Turning of the 'Spar'* (London: Greenpeace).

Griffith, D.A., and J.K. Ryans, Jr (1997) 'Organizing Global Communications to Minimize Private Spill-Over Damage to Brand Equity', *Journal of World Business* 32.3 (Fall 1997): 130-42.

Grolin, J. (1998) 'Corporate Legitimacy in a Risk Society: The Case of Brent Spar', *Business Strategy and the Environment* 7: 213-22.

Grove-White, R. (1997) 'Environment, Risk and Democracy', in M. Jacobs (ed.), *Greening the Millennium? The New Politics of the Environment* (Oxford, UK: Blackwell).

Hall, A. (1996) 'Did Chico Mendes die in vain? Brazilian Rubber Tappers in the 1990s', in H. Collinson (ed.), *Green Guerrillas: Environmental Conflicts and Initiatives in Latin America and the Caribbean* (London: Latin American Bureau).

Hamel, G., Y.L. Doz and C.K. Prahalad (1989) 'Collaborate with your Competitors—and Win', *Harvard Business Review*, January/February 1989: 133-39.

Handy, C. (1994) *The Age of Paradox* (Boston, MA: Harvard Business School Press).

Handy, C. (1998) 'The Real Challenge of Business', *Visions of Ethical Business, Financial Times* Supplement No. 1.

Härlin, B. (1994) 'Die "Greenfreeze"-Erfahrung', in S. Hellenbrandt and F. Rubik (eds.), *Produkt und Umwelt* (Marburg, Germany: Metropolis): 221-32.

Harmon, A. (1998) 'Hactivists of all persuasions take their struggle to the Web', *New York Times*, 31 October 1998.

Harris, P.G. (1996) Letter to WWF (London: Timber Trade Federation, 19 April).

Hartman, C.L., and E.R. Stafford (1996) 'The Dynamics of Environmental Alliance Relationships: Some Preliminary Propositions', in E.A. Blair and W.A. Kamakura (eds.), *American Marketing Association's Winter Educators' Conference Proceedings* (Chicago: American Marketing Association): 414-21.

Hartman, C.L., and E.R. Stafford (1997) 'Green Alliances: Building New Business with Environmental Groups', *Long Range Planning* 30.2: 184-96.

Hartman, C.L., and E.R. Stafford (1998) 'Crafting "Enviropreneurial" Value Chain Strategies through Green Alliances', *Business Horizons*, March/April 1998: 62-72.

Hartman, C.L., E.R. Stafford and M.J. Polonsky (1999) 'Green Alliances: Environmental Groups as Strategic Bridges to Other Stakeholders', in M. Charter and M.J. Polonsky (eds.), *Greener Marketing: A Global Perspective on Greening Marketing Practice* (Sheffield, UK: Greenleaf Publishing).

Haufler, V. (1997) 'Private Sector International Regimes: An Assessment', paper presented at *Non-State Actors and Authority in the Global System* conference, Warwick University, UK, 31 October–1 November 1997.

Hecht, S., and A. Cockburn (1990) *The Fate of the Forest: Developers, Destroyers and Defenders of the Amazon* (London: Penguin).

Herkströter, C.A.J. (1996) 'Dealing with Contradictory Expectations: The Dilemmas Facing Multinationals' (speech by the President of Royal Dutch Petroleum Company, The Hague, 11 October 1996).

Hilary, J. (1999) *Genetically Modified Seeds: Corporate Control over Farmers in the Third World* (London: World Development Movement).

Hill, J., D. Fedrigo and I. Marshall (1997) *Banking on the Future* (London: The Green Alliance).

Hirst, P., and G. Thompson (1996) *Globalisation in Question* (Cambridge, UK: Polity Press).

Hoffman, A. (1996a) 'Trends in Corporate Environmentalism: The Chemical and Petroleum Industries: 1960–1993', *Society and Natural Resources* 9: 47-64.

Hoffman, A. (1996b) 'A Strategic Response to Investor Activism', *Sloan Management Review* 37.2 (Winter 1996): 51-64.

Hoffman, A. (1997a) *From Heresy to Dogma: An Institutional History of Corporate Environmentalism* (San Francisco: New Lexington Press).

Hoffman, A. (1997b) 'Public letter on Chile's Native Forests' (Santiago, Chile: Defensires del Bosque Chileno, 22 May 1997).

Hofstede, G. (1980) 'Angola Coffee or the Confrontation of an Organization with Changing Values in its Environment', *Organization Studies* 1.1: 21-40.

Howard, A. (1998) 'Partners in Sweat', editorial in *The Nation*, 29 December 1998, sourced from www.sweatshopwatch.org/swatch/headlines/1998/aip_nov98.html.

Hudock, A.C. (1999) *NGOs and Civil Society: Democracy by Proxy?* (Cambridge, UK: Polity Press).

Humphreys, D. (1997a) 'Environmental Accountability and Transnational Corporations', paper presented to the *International Academic Conference on 'Environmental Justice: Global Ethics for the 21st Century'*, University of Melbourne, Australia, 1–3 October 1997.

Humphreys, D. (1997b) *Forest Politics: The Evolution of International Cooperation* (London: Earthscan).

Hutchinson, J. (1994) 'The Practice of Partnership in Local Economic Development', *Local Government Studies* 20.3: 335-44.

Hydro-Quebec (1994) *Programme de participation publique provinciale au plan de développement 1996* (Report BPP-058; Montreal: Hydro-Quebec, February 1994).

ICAEW (Institute of Chartered Accountants in England and Wales) (1999) *Internal Control: Guidance for Directors of List Companies Incorporated in the United Kingdom. Consultation Draft April 1999* (London: ICAEW, available at www.icaew.co.uk/internalcontrol).

Independent (1998) 'Electronic Warfare', *The Independent*, 10 December 1998: Education Section.

Inez-Ainger, K. (1999) 'In India, peasants are burning crops, mocking their leaders and dying: Here's why', *The Guardian*, 27 January 1999: 4-5.

International Lake Constance Conference (ed.) (1999) *Measurement Plan Agriculture/Protection of Water Resources in the Lake Constance Watershed: Intermediate Report 1999* (Zurich: International Lake Constance Conference); English translation of: Internationale Bodenseekonferenz (Hrsg.), 'Massnahmenplan Landwirtschaft/Gewässerschutz für den Bodenseeraum' (Zürich: Infras Zwischenbericht, 1999)

International NGO Forum (1992) *The People's Earth Declaration: A Proactive Agenda for the Future* (Rio de Janeiro: International NGO Forum of the UN Conference on Environment and Development, 12 June 1992).

Ito, M., and M. Loftus (1997) 'Cutting and Dealing: Asian loggers target the world's remaining rain forests', *US News and World Report*, 10 March 1997.

ITTO (International Tropical Timber Organisation) (1997) 'A Success Story in Eucalyptus Plantations', *Tropical Forest Update* 7.2 (Yokohama: ITTO).

Jacobs, M. (1997) 'The Quality of Life: Social Goods and the Politics of Consumption', in M. Jacobs (ed.), *Greening the Millennium? The New Politics of the Environment* (Oxford, UK: Blackwell).

Jacoby, H. (1998) 'The Lake Constance Foundation: Contact Partner for Nature and Cultural Issues in the International Lake Constance Area', in *Sustainable Lake Constance* (Konstanz, Germany:

Lake Constance Magazine Company); English translation of: H. Jacoby, 'Die Bodensee-Stiftung: Ansprechpartner für Natur und Kultur in der internationalen Seeregion', in *Zukunftsfähiger Bodensee* (Konstanz: Bodensee-Magazin Verlag, 1998).

James, C. (1997) *Global Status of Transgenic Crops in 1997* (ISAAA Briefings, 5; Ithaca, NY: International Service for the Acquisition of Agri-Biotech Applications).

James, C. (1998) *Global Review of Commercialised Transgenic Crops* (ISAAA Briefings, 8; Ithaca, NY: International Service for the Acquisition of Agri-Biotech Applications).

Jenkins, R. (1998) 'Bt in the Hot Seat', *Seedling* 15.3: 13-21.

Johnson, G., and K. Scholes (1999) *Exploring Corporate Strategy* (London: Prentice–Hall Europe, 5th edn).

Johnston, B.R. (ed.) (1997) *Life and Death Matters: Human Rights and the Environment at the End of the Millennium* (Walnut Creek, CA: AltaMira Press).

Kant, I. (1964) *Groundwork of the Metaphysic of Morals* (trans. H.J. Paton; New York: Harper & Row).

Kanter, R.M. (1999) 'From Spare Change to Real Change: The Social Sector as Beta Site for Business Innovation', *Harvard Business Review*, May/June 1999: 122-32.

Kelman, S. (1992) 'Adversary and Cooperationist Institutions for Conflict Resolution in Policy-making', *Journal of Policy Analysis and Management* 11.2: 178-206.

Knight, A. (1992) *B&Q's Timber Policy towards 1995: A Review of Progress* (Eastleigh, UK: B&Q plc).

Kobrin, S.J. (1987) 'Testing the Bargaining Hypothesis in the Manufacturing Sector in Developing Countries', *International Organization* 41: 609-38.

Korten, D. (1987) 'Third Generation NGO Strategies: A Key to People-Centred Development', *World Development* 15, Supplement: 145-59.

Korten, D. (1990) *Getting to the 21st Century* (Hartford, CT: Kumarian Press).

Korten, D. (1995) *When Corporations Rule the World* (London: Earthscan).

Korten, D. (1998) *Globalizing Civil Society: Reclaiming our Right to Power* (New York: Seven Stories Press).

Kumar, N. (1996) 'The Power of Trust in Manufacturer–Retailer Relationships', *Harvard Business Review* 74.6: 92-106.

Kuper, S., and J. Mackintosh (1998) 'Big companies "miss point" of interest', *Financial Times*, 26 January 1998.

Lachowicz, M. (1998) *The Non-Listening Banks and those that Like to Say Yes: The Effects of Banking on the Environment* (London: London Environment Centre).

Lash, S. (1994) 'Reflexivity and its Doubles: Structure, Aesthetics, Community', in U. Beck, A. Giddens and S. Lash, *Reflexive Modernisation: Politics, Tradition and Aesthetics in the Modern Social Order* (Stanford, CA: Stanford University Press): 110-73.

Ledesma, C. (1999) 'Attaining Food Security: A Cause for Multi-Sectoral Collaboration', paper presented at the *Independent Sector Spring Research Forum*, Washington, DC, 1999.

Lee, K., D. Humphreys and M. Pugh (1997) 'Privatisation in the United Nations System: Patterns of Influence in Three Intergovernmental Organisations', *Global Society* 11.3 (September 1997): 339-59.

Lewis, J.D. (1990) *Partnerships for Profit: Structuring and Managing Strategic Alliances* (New York: Free Press).

Lober, D.J. (1997) 'Explaining the Formation of Business–Environmentalist Collaborations: Collaborative Windows and the Paper Task Force', *Policy Sciences* 30 (February 1997): 1-24.

Long, F.J., and M.B. Arnold (1995) *The Power of Environmental Partnerships* (New York: Dryden Press).

Lukes, S. (1974) *Power: A Radical View* (London: Macmillan).

Lund, B., and M.L. Duryea (1994) *Conflict and Culture: Report of the Multiculturalism and Dispute Resolution Project* (Victoria, Canada: Institute for Dispute Resolution, University of Victoria).

Lynch, C. (1998) 'Social Movements and the Problem of Globalisation', *Alternatives* 23: 149-73.

Lynch, R. (1997) *Corporate Strategy* (London: Pitman).

Macintosh, M. (1992) 'Partnership: Issues of Policy and Negotiation', *Local Economy* 7.3: 210-24.

Maltby, J. (1995) 'Setting its Own Standards and Meeting those Standards: Voluntarism versus Regulation in Environmental Reporting', paper presented at the 1995 *Business Strategy and the Environment Conference*, University of Leeds, UK, 20–21 September 1995.

Martin, J. (1992) *Cultures in Organizations: Three Perspectives* (New York: Oxford University Press).

Martinez-Alier, J. (1997) 'The Merchandising of Biodiversity', in R. Guha and J. Martinez-Alier (eds.), *Varieties of Environmentalism: Essays from North and South* (London: Earthscan): 107-27.

Maser, C. (1996) *Resolving Environmental Conflict: Towards Sustainable Community Development* (Delray Beach, FL: St Lucie Press).

McCormick, J. (1991) *British Politics and the Environment* (London: Earthscan).

McIntosh, M., D. Leipziger, K. Jones and G. Coleman (1998) *Corporate Citizenship: Successful Strategies for Responsible Companies* (London: Pitman/Financial Times).

Milne, G.R., E.S. Iyer and S. Gooding-Williams (1996) 'Environmental Organization Alliance Relationships within and across Non-profit, Business, and Government Sectors', *Journal of Public Policy and Marketing* 15.2: 203-15.

Mintzberg, H. (1989) *Mintzberg on Management: Inside our Strange World of Organizations* (New York: Free Press).

Mitchell, J. (1997) *Companies in a World of Conflict* (London: RIIA/Earthscan).

Mittelman, J. (1998) 'Globalisation and Environmental Resistance Politics', *Third World Quarterly* 19.5: 847-72.

Monks, R.A.G. (1998) *The Emperor's Nightingale* (London: Capstone Publishing).

Moorhead, G., and R. Griffin (1992) *Organizational Behavior: Managing People and Organizations* (Boston, MA: Houghton Mifflin).

MSC (Marine Stewardship Council) (1996) *Marine Stewardship Council Initiative Newsletter*, 1996.

MSC (Marine Stewardship Council) (1998) *Marine Stewardship Council Initiative Newsletter*, 1998.

MSC (Marine Stewardship Council) (1999) *Our Empty Seas: A Global Problem, A Global Solution* (London: MSC).

Murphy, D.F. (1996a) *DIY–WWF Alliance: Doing it Together for the World's Forests* (working paper; Bristol, UK: University of Bristol School for Policy Studies/New Consumer).

Murphy, D.F. (1996b) 'In the Company of Partners. Business, NGOs and Sustainable Development: Towards a Global Perspective', in R. Aspinwall and J. Smith (eds.), *Environmentalist and Business Partnerships: A Sustainable Model? A Critical Assessment of the Impact of the WWF UK 1995 Group* (Cambridge, UK: White Horse Press).

Murphy, D.F. (1997) 'The Partnership Paradox: Business–NGO Relations on Sustainable Development in the International Policy Arena' (unpublished doctoral thesis, School for Policy Studies, University of Bristol, UK).

Murphy, D.F., and J. Bendell (1997a) *In the Company of Partners: Business, Environmental Groups and Sustainable Development Post-Rio* (Bristol, UK: The Policy Press).

Murphy, D.F., and J. Bendell (1997b) 'The Politics of Corporate Environmentalism: Civil, Legal or Self-Compliance for Sustainable Development?', paper presented at United Nations Research Institute for Social Development (UNRISD) conference, *Business Responsibility for Environmental Protection in Developing Countries*, Heredia, Costa Rica, 22–25 September 1997.

Murphy, D.F., and J. Bendell (1999) *Partners in Time? Business, NGOs and Sustainable Development* (UNRISD Discussion Paper, 109; Geneva: UN Research Institute for Social Development).

Murphy, D.F., and C. Carey (1998) *International Review of Forest and Trade Networks* (Study commissioned by WWF-International; London: New Academy of Business).

Myers, N. (1992) *The Primary Source: Tropical Forests and our Future* (London: W.W. Norton).

Naidoo, K. (1999) 'Editorial', *E-CIVICUS* 48 (Washington, DC: CIVICUS, 7 December 1999).

Naidoo, K. (2000) 'Editorial', *E-CIVICUS* 54 (Washington, DC: CIVICUS, 1 February 2000).

NCC (National Consumer Council) (1996) *Green Claims: A Consumer Investigation into Marketing Claims about the Environment* (London: NCC).

Neal, M., and C. Davies (1998) *The Corporation under Siege* (London: Social Affairs Unit).

Newell, P. (1999) Globalisation and the Environment: Exploring the Connections', *IDS Bulletin* 30.3: 1-8.

Newell, P. (forthcoming) 'Environmental NGOs, TNCs and the Question of Governance', in V. Assetto and D . Stevis (eds.), *International Political Economy and the Environment* (Lynne Rienner Press).

Newell, P., and M. Paterson (1998) 'Climate for Business: Global Warming, the State and Capital', *Review of International Political Economy* 5.4: 679-704.

Newton, T.J., and G. Harte (1997) 'Green Business: Technicist Kitsch?', *Journal of Management Studies* 34.1: 75-98.

NGO Task Force on Business and Industry (1997) *Minding our Business: The Role of Corporate Accountability in Sustainable Development* (Independent assessment submitted to the UN Commission on Sustainable Development, prepared by J. Barber, Integrative Strategies Forum; Washington, DC: NGO Task Force on Business and Industry).

Nomura, T. (1999) 'Japanese press for labels on their tampered tofu', *Christian Science Monitor*, 25 August 1999, available at my.csmonitor.com.

Nuffield Foundation (1999) *Report of the Nuffield Council on Bioethics, 27 May 1999* (London: Nuffield Foundation).

O'Connor, A. (1998) 'The Role of Corporate Disclosure in Reducing Financial Risk', paper given at the *Sustainable Business Conference*, British Library, London, 22 October 1998.

O'Riordan, B. (1996) 'The MSC and the Market: Who is seducing who?', *Samudra* 18 (Madras: The International Collective in Support of Fishworkers, July 1996): 10-11.

OECD (Organisation for Economic Co-operation and Development) (1998a) 'The Multilateral Agreement on Investment: Frequently Asked Questions and Answers', www.oecd.org.

OECD (Organisation for Economic Co-operation and Development) (1998b) 'Multilateral Framework for Investment', www.oecd.org/daf/cmis/mai/maindex.htm, updated 23 October 1998.

OECD (Organisation for Economic Co-operation and Development) (1999) 'Principles of Corporate Governance', www.oecd.org.

Oliver, C. (1990) 'Determinants of Interorganizational Relationships: Integration and Future Directions', *Academy of Management Review* 15 (April 1990): 241-65.

Osborn, D. (1997) 'Making Environmental Policy', in M. Jacobs (ed.), *Greening the Millennium? The New Politics of the Environment* (Oxford, UK: Blackwell).

Pallast, G., and B. Laurance (1999) 'Bank of Scotland counts cost of US misadventure', *The Observer*, 6 June 1999.

Palmer, I. (1998) *A Case Study of an Independent Approach to Rural Water Supply and Sanitation* (Johannesburg: Mvula Trust).

Parliament of the Commonwealth of Australia (1997) *Report of the Senate Select Committee on Uranium Mining and Milling* (Canberra: Australian Government Publishing Service).

Pasquero, J. (1991) 'Supraorganizational Collaboration: The Canadian Environmental Experiment', *Journal of Applied Behavioral Science* 27.1: 38-64.

Patten, D.M. (1991) 'Exposure, Legitimacy and Social Disclosure', *Journal of Accounting and Public Policy* 10: 297-308.

Pearce, F. (1991) *Green Warriors* (London: Bodley Head).

Pestoff, V.A. (1990) 'Nonprofit Organizations and Consumer Policy: The Swedish Model', in H.K. Anheier and W. Seibel (eds.), *The Third Sector Comparative Studies of Nonprofit Organizations* (Berlin/New York: de Gruyter): 77-92.

Peters, G. (1999) *Waltzing with the Raptors: A Practical Roadmap to Protecting your Company's Reputation* (Chichester, UK: John Wiley).

PIRC (Pensions Investment Research Consultants Ltd) (1998) *Environmental and Corporate Responsibility at Shell: The Shareholder Role in Promoting Change* (London: PIRC, available at www.pirc.co.uk).

PIRC (Pensions Investment Research Consultants Ltd) (1999) *PIRC Intelligence* (London: PIRC).

Points of Light Foundation (1999) *Corporate Volunteer Programs: A Strategic Resource. The Link Grows Stronger* (Washington, DC: Points of Light Foundation).

Polanyi, K. (1946) *The Great Transformation* (Boston, MA: Beacon Press).

Porter, M.E. (1995) 'The Competitive Advantage of the Inner City', *Harvard Business Review*, May/June 1995: 55-71.

Porter, M.E., and C. van der Linde (1995) 'Green and Competitive: Ending the Stalemate', *Harvard Business Review* September/October 1995: 120-34.

Prahalad, C.K. (1999) presentation at session entitled 'Creating Sustainable Development: Strategies for the Bottom of the Pyramid', *Academy of Management 1999 Annual Meeting*, Chicago, 1999.

RAFI (1999a) 'Traitor Technology: The Terminator's Wider Implications', *RAFI Communique*, January/February 1999.

RAFI (1999b) 'The Gene Giants: Masters of the Universe?', *RAFI Communique*, March/April 1999.

Rappaport, A., and Flaherty, M.F. (1992) *Corporate Responses to Environmental Challenges* (New York: Quorum).

Repetto, R., and M. Gillis (1988) *Public Policies and the Misuse of Forest Resources* (Cambridge, UK: Cambridge University Press).

Revkin, A. (1990) *The Burning Season: The Murder of Chico Mendes and the Fight for the Amazon Rain Forest* (London: Collins).

Roberts, J. (1995) 'UK cash props up terror mine', *The Independent on Sunday*, 26 November 1995: 13.

Rodgers, C. (1998) 'Producer Responsibility and the Role of Industry in Managing End-of-Life Products' (unpublished DPhil thesis).

Rodman, K. (1998) 'Think Globally, Punish Locally: Non-State Actors, MNCs and Human Rights Sanctions', *Ethics and International Affairs* 12: 19-43.

Roome, N. (1998) *Sustainability Strategies for Industry* (Washington, DC: Island Press)

Rosenau, J. (1997) *Along the Domestic–Foreign Frontier: Exploring Governance in a Turbulent World* (Cambridge, UK: Cambridge University Press).

Rosenau, J., and E. Czempiel (eds.) (1992) *Governance without Government: Order and Change in World Politics* (Cambridge, UK: Cambridge University Press).

Rowell, A. (1996) *Green Backlash: Global Subversion of the Environment Movement* (London: Routledge).

Rowen, D. (1998) 'Meet the new world government', *The Guardian*, 13 February 1998.

Ruggie, J.G., and G. Kell (1999) 'Global Markets and Social Legitimacy: The Case of the Global Compact', paper presented at *Governing the Public Domain beyond the Era of the Washington Consensus*, York University, Canada, 4–6 November 1999.

Salamon, L.M., H.K Anheier, R. List, S. Toepler, S.W. Sokolowski and Associates (1999) *Global Civil Society: Dimensions of the Nonprofit Sector* (Baltimore, MD: The John Hopkins University Centre for Civil Society Studies).

Saurin, J. (1993) 'Global Environmental Degradation, Modernity and Environmental Knowledge', *Environmental Politics* 2.4: 46-64.

Savage, G., T. Nix, C. Whitehead and J. Blair (1991) 'Strategies for Assessing and Managing Organizational Stakeholders', *The Executive* 5.2: 61-75.

Schein, E.H. (1992) *Organizational Culture and Leadership* (San Francisco: Jossey-Bass, 2nd edn).

Schelling, T. (1960) *The Strategy of Conflict* (Cambridge, MA: Harvard University Press).

Schmidheiny, S. (1992) *Changing Course: A Global Business Perspective on Development and the Environment* (Cambridge, MA: MIT Press).

Schneidewind, U. (1998) *Die Unternehmung als strukturpolitischer Akteur* (Marburg, Germany: Metropolis).

Shapiro, M.J. (1991) 'Sovereignty and Exchange in the Orders of Modernity', *Alternatives* 16: 447-77.

Shapiro, R.B. (1999a) Open Letter to Rockefeller Foundation President, Gordon Conway, 4 October 1999.

Shapiro, R.B. (1999b) Address to Greenpeace Business Conference London, 6 October 1999.

Shiva, V., and R. Holla-Bhar (1993) 'Intellectual Piracy and the Neem Tree', *The Ecologist* 23.6: 223-27.

Simmons, P.J., (1998) 'Learning to Live with NGOs', *Foreign Policy*, Fall 1998, available at http://216.51.17.154/Fall98/articles/PIRT8.htm.

Sklair, L. (1994) 'Global Sociology and Global Environmental Change', in T. Benton and M. Redclift (eds.), *Social Theory and the Global Environment* (London: Routledge).

Smircich, L. (1983) 'Concepts of Culture and Organizational Analysis', *Administrative Science Quarterly* 28 (September 1983): 339-58.

Smith, D.N., and L.T. Wells, Jr (1975) *Negotiating Third World Mineral Agreements: Promises as Prologue* (Cambridge, MA: Ballinger).

Smith, N.C. (1990) *Morality and the Market: Consumer Pressure for Corporate Accountability* (London/New York: Routledge).

Smith, N.C. (1991) 'The Case Study: A Vital yet Misunderstood Research Method for Management', in N.C. Smith and P. Dainty (eds.), *The Management Research Handbook* (London: Routledge).

Snow, C.C., R.E. Miles and H.S. Coleman (1992) 'Managing 21st Century Network Organisations', *Organisational Dynamics*, Winter 1992: 5-19.

Spinney, L. (1998) *Biotechnology in Crops: Issues for the Developing World* (Oxford, UK: Oxfam GB).

Stafford, E.R., and C.L. Hartman (1996) 'Green Alliances: Strategic Relations between Business and Environmental Groups', *Business Horizons*, March/April 1996: 50-59.

Starik, M., G. Throop, J. Doody and M.E. Joyce (1996) 'Growing an Environmental Strategy', *Business Strategy and the Environment* 5: 12-21.

Stea, D., S. Elguea and C.P. Bustillo (1997) 'Environment, Development and Indigenous Revolution in Chiapas', in B.R. Johnston (ed.), *Life and Death Matters: Human Rights and the Environment at the end of the Millennium* (Walnut Creek, CA: AltaMira Press).

Stewart, M., and D. Snape (1996) *Keeping up the Momentum: Partnership Working in Bristol and the West* (unpublished study for The Bristol Chamber of Commerce and Initiative; Bristol, UK: School for Policy Studies, University of Bristol).

STOP (1996) 'STOP 1970–1995', *STOP Press*, Special Edition.

Stopford, J., and S. Strange (1991) *Rival States, Rival Firms* (Cambridge, UK: Cambridge University Press).

Strange, S. (1996) *The Retreat of the State* (Cambridge, UK: Cambridge University Press).

Strauss, A., and J. Corbin (1990) *Basics of Qualitative Research: Grounded Theory Procedures and Techniques* (Newbury Park, CA: Sage).

Suchman, M.C. (1995) 'Managing Legitimacy: Strategic and Institutional Approaches', *Academy of Management Review* 20.3: 571-610.

Susskind, L., and P. Field (1997) *Dealing with an Angry Public: The Mutual Gains Approach* (New York: Free Press).

SustainAbility (1996) 'Strange Attractor: The Business–ENGO Partnership Strategic Review of BP's Relationships with Environmental NGOs. Summary of Findings, *Trends*, July 1996.

Sydow, J. (1996) 'Inter-Organizational Relations', in M. Warner (ed.), *International Encyclopedia of Business and Management* (London: Routledge).

Tandon, R. (1989) 'The State and Voluntary Agencies in India', in R. Holloway (ed.), *Doing Development: Governments, NGOs and the Rural Poor in Asia* (London: Earthscan in association with CUSO).

TAPOL (1995) 'Freeport killings confirmed', *TAPOL Bulletin* 129 (June 1995): 1-3.

Temple, G. (1997) 'Globalization as the Triumph of Capitalism: Private Property, Economic Justice and the New World Order', in T. Schrecker (ed.), *Surviving Globalism: The Social and Environmental Challenges* (London: Macmillan).

Tennyson, R. (1998) *Managing Partnerships* (London: Prince of Wales Business Leaders Forum).

Teubner, G. (ed.) (1997) *Global Law without a State* (Dartmouth, MA: Aldershot).

Tickell, O. (1999a) 'First the Forests, Now the Fish', *Green Futures*, May/June 1999: 38-42.

Tickell, O. (1999b) 'Model Trade', *The Guardian*, 17 March 1999.

Timms, S. (1999) Speech by Stephen Timms, Minister of State for Pensions, to the PIRC (Pensions Investment Research Consultants Ltd) *Corporate Social Responsibility Conference*, 21 April 1999; available at www.pirc.co.uk.

Turcotte, M.-F. (1995) 'Conflict and Collaboration: The Interfaces between Environmental Organizations and Business Firms', *Research in Corporate Social Performance and Policy*, Supplement 1: 195-229.

Turcotte, M.-F. (1997a) *Prise de décision par consensus: Leçons d'un cas en environnement* (Paris: l'Harmattan).

Turcotte, M.-F. (1997b) 'Case Analysis of a Multistakeholder Collaborative Process in the Environmental Domain: Consensus, Learnings, and Innovations as Outcomes of the "3R" Roundtable', *Business and Society* 36.4: 430-34.

TWN (Third World Network) (1996) *Biosafety: Scientific Findings and Elements of a Protocol. The Report of the Independent Group of Scientific and Legal Experts on Biosafety* (Panang, Malaysia: TWN).

Understanding Global Issues (1997) 'Multinational Business: Beyond Government Control', *Understanding Global Issues* 97/11 (Special Issue).

UNDP (United Nations Development Programme) (1993) *Human Development Report* (New York: Oxford University Press).

UNDP (United Nations Development Programme) (1994) *Human Development Report* (New York: Oxford University Press).

UNEP (United Nations Environment Programme) (1994) *A Statement by Banks on the Environment and Sustainable Development* (Geneva: UNEP).

Unilever (1996) *Environment Report: Our Worldwide Approach* (London/Rotterdam: Unilever Environment Group).

Unilever (1997) 'Sustainability: Unilever's Approach', paper based on a speech given by Dr Iain Anderson, Unilever Strategy and Technology Director, to the *American Oil Chemists' Society Environmental Challenges Conference*, Brussels, 5 March 1997.

Unilever (1998) *Annual Review* (London/Rotterdam: Unilever).

United Nations (1993) *The Global Partnership for Environment and Development* (New York: United Nations Publications).

United Nations (1997) WWF/The World Bank: Press Release 97 (New York: United Nations, 25 June 1997).

UNRISD (United Nations Research Institute for Social Development) (1995) *States of Disarray: The Social Effects of Globalization* (Geneva: UNRISD).

Varadarajan, P.R., and D. Rajaratnam (1986) 'Symbiotic Marketing Revisited', *Journal of Marketing* 50.1 (January 1986): 7-17.

Viana, V., J. Ervin, R. Donovan, C. Elliot and H. Gholz (1996) *Certification of Forest Products* (Washington, DC: Island Press).

Vidal, J. (1997) 'Industry terrified at the outbreak of ethics', *The Guardian* Ecosoundings, 23 April 1997.

Vidal, J. (1999) 'Power to the People', *The Guardian*, 7 June 1999.

Waddell, S. (1997a) 'Building a New Form of Enterprise: A Study of Partnerships between Banks and Community-Based Organisations', in A.A. George (ed.), *Expanding Housing Opportunities for all Americans: Partnerships Provide the Best Avenue* (Washington, DC: National Community Reinvestment Coalition).

Waddell, S. (1997b) *Intersectoral Collaboration in Agriculture and Food Processing with the Center for Technology Development, Bangalore, India* (Boston, MA: Institute for Development Research).

Waddell, S. (1997c) 'Outcomes of Social Capital Strategies of Banks and Community-Based Organisations in the US: The Four Pros of Property, Profit, Processes and Products', *IDR Reports* 13.1.

Waddell, S. (1997d) *The Rise of a New Form of Enterprise: Social Capital Enterprise* (Ann Arbor, MI: UMI Dissertation Information Service).

Waddell, S. (1998a) *Mvula Trust: Building the Mission with a Pty (Forprofit) Affiliate: A Report on Issues and Strategies to Develop a Pty-Affiliate of the Trust* (Johannesburg: Mvula Trust).

Waddell, S. (1998b) *Road-Building in Madagascar: Civil Society in the Lead* (Boston, MA: Institution for Development Research).

Waddock, S. (1988) 'Building Successful Social Partnerships', *Sloan Management Review,* Summer 1988: 17-23.

Waddock, S. (1991) 'A Typology of Social Partnership Organizations', *Administration and Society* 22.4: 480-515.

Wadsworth, J. (1996) *Study on Markets and Market Segments for Certified Timber and Timber Products* (ITTC[XX]/7; Manilla: ITTO, 11 April 1996).

Wallach, L.M. (1998) 'A Dangerous New Manifesto for Global Capitalism', *Le monde diplomatique,* February 1998; English text available at www.monde-diplomatique.fr/en/1998/02/07mai.html.

Walzer, M. (1995) *Toward Global Civil Society* (New York: Berghahn Books).

Wapner, P. (1996) *Environmental Activism and World Civic Politics* (New York: SUNY).

Washington Post (1999b) 'What on Earth? The New Crops', *Washington Post,* 9 October 1999: A15.

WBCSD (World Business Council for Sustainable Development) (1996) *Towards a Sustainable Paper Cycle* (summary report of a study on the pulp and paper industry by IIED commissioned by the WBCSD; Geneva: WBCSD).

WBCSD (World Business Council for Sustainable Development) (1997) *Signals for Change* (Geneva: WBCSD).

WBCSD (World Business Council for Sustainable Development) (1999) *Corporate Social Responsibility: Meeting Changing Expectations* (Geneva: WBCSD).

WCED (World Commission on Environment and Development) (1987) *Our Common Future* (Oxford, UK: Oxford University Press).

WDM (World Development Movement) (1999) *GMOs and the WTO: Overruling the Right to Say No* (London: WDM).

WEF (World Economic Forum) (2000) *NGOs and Business: A Relationship in the Making* (Session Summaries; Davos, Switzerland: WEF, 29 January 2000).

Weiss, R. (1999) 'British revolt grows over "genetic" foods', *Washington Post,* 29 April 1999: E02.

Welford, R. (1995) *Environmental Strategy and Sustainable Development* (London: Routledge).

Westley, F., and H. Vredenburg (1991) 'Strategic Bridging: The Collaboration between Environmentalists and Business in the Marketing of Green Products', *Journal of Applied Behavioral Science* 22.1: 65-90.

WFAFW (World Federation of Agriculture, Food, Hotel and Allied Workers) (1999) *Theme 9: Genetically Modified Organisms* (GMOs) (WFAFW/FEMTAA Presentation Paper; Brussels: WFAFW, September 1999; http://attac.org/fra/toil/doc/femtaaen.htm).

Wheeler, D., and M. Sillanpää (1997) *The Stakeholder Corporation: A Blueprint for Maximising Stakeholder Value* (London: Pitman).

Willets, P. (1998) 'Political Globalization and the Impact of NGOs upon Transnational Companies', in J. Mitchell (ed.), *Companies in a World of Conflict* (London: Royal Institute for International Affairs and Earthscan).

Wilson, E.O. (1992) *The Diversity of Life* (Cambridge, MA: The Belknap Press of Harvard University Press).

Winter, M., and U. Steger (1998) *Managing Outside Pressure: Strategies for Preventing Corporate Disasters* (Chichester, UK: John Wiley).

Wood, D.J., and B. Gray (1991) 'Toward a Comprehensive Theory of Collaboration', *Journal of Applied Behavioral Science* 27.2: 139-62.

World Bank (1999) *Business as Partners for Development* (New York: World Bank, available at www.worldbank.org/html/extdr/extme/1962.htm).

WRI (World Resources Institute) (1998) *Green Shareholder Value: Hype or Hit?* (Washington, DC: WRI, available at www.wri.org/meb/sei/perspec.html).

WWF (World Wide Fund for Nature) (1991) *Truth or Trickery?* (Godalming, UK: WWF-UK).

WWF (World Wide Fund for Nature) (1997) *Annual Report* (Godalming, UK: WWF-UK).

WWF (World Wide Fund for Nature) (1998) *WWF News: The Newsletter of WWF-UK* (Godalming, UK: WWF-UK, Autumn 1998).

Wysocki, B. (1999) 'Corporate America confronts the meaning of a "core" business', *Wall Street Journal,* 9 November 1999: A1.

Zadek, S. (1999) 'Can Corporations Be Civil?', paper presented at the conference, *NGOs in a Global Future,* Birmingham, UK, January 1999.

Zadek, S., S. Lingayah and S. Murphy (1998) *Purchasing Power: Civil Action for Sustainable Consumption* (London: New Economics Foundation).

Zollinger, P., and J. Elkington (1999) 'Corporate Governance in a CNN World', www.SustainAbility. co.uk, November 1999.

ABBREVIATIONS

AGM	annual general meeting
AIDS	acquired immuno-deficiency syndrome
ASEAN	Association of South-East Asian Nations
BAA	British Airports Authority
BATNA	Best Alternative to a Negotiated Agreement
BCSD	Business Charter for Sustainable Development
BELA	Bangladesh Environmental Lawyers' Association
BIO	Biotechnology Industry Organisation (USA)
BOD	biological oxygen demand
BoS	Bank of Scotland
BP	British Petroleum Group
BSE	bovine spongiform encephalopathy
BT	British Telecom
Bt	*bacillus thuringiensis*
BUND	Bund für Umwelt und Naturschutz (German faction of Friends of the Earth)
BVQI	Bureau Veritas Quality International
CACP	Citizens' Alliance for Consumer Protection (South Korea)
CBD	Convention on Biological Diversity
CCME	Canadian Council of Environmental Ministers
CEO	chief executive officer
CEO	Corporate Europe Observatory (Switzerland)
CEP	Council on Economic Priorities
CERES	Coalition for Environmentally Responsible Economies
CFCs	chlorofluorocarbons
CIVICUS	Citizens' Alliance for Participation (USA)
CLF	Conservation Law Foundation (USA)
COD	chemical oxygen demand
CSA	Canadian Standards Association
CSR	corporate social responsibility
CT	clean technology
CTD	Center for Technology Development (India)
CUM	Communauté Urbaine de Montréal
CUT	Brazilian confederation of trade unions
DIY	do-it-yourself
DNA	deoxyribonucleic acid
DTI	Department of Trade and Industry (UK)
EBRD	European Bank for Reconstruction and Development
EC	European Commission
EDF	Environmental Defense Fund (USA)
EMAS	EC Eco-Management and Audit Scheme

EMS	environmental management system
EMS	eosinophiliamyalgia syndrome
ENDS	Environmental Data Services (UK)
ENGO	environmental NGO
ERIN	Environmental Resources Information Network (USA)
ETI	Ethical Trading Initiative (UK)
EU	European Union
FAO	Food and Agriculture Organisation of the United Nations
FBC	Free Burma Campaign
FDI	foreign direct investment
FoE	Friends of the Earth
FSC	Forest Stewardship Council
FTC	Free Tibet Campaign
FTI	Federation of Thai Industries
FUNAI	National Indian Foundation (Brazil)
FUNDE	Fundación Nacional para el Desarrollo (El Salvador)
GM	genetically modified
GMO	genetically modified organism
GNP	gross national product
GRI	Global Reporting Initiative
GUP	Gono Unnayan Prochesta (Bangladesh)
IBAMA	Instituto Brasileiro do Meio Ambiente e dos Recursos Naturais Renováveis (Brazil)
ICAEW	Institute of Chartered Accountants in England and Wales
ICC	International Chamber of Commerce
ICSF	International Collective in Support of Fishworkers
IEM/FTI	Industrial Environmental Management Office at the Federation of Thai Industries
IIED	International Institute for Environment and Development
ILO	International Labour Organisation
INBio	National Biodiversity Institute (Costa Rica)
INGO	indigenous rights NGO
INTRAC	International NGO Training and Research Centre
ISAAA	International Service for the Acquisition of Agri-Biotech Applications
ISEA	Institute of Social and Ethical Accountability
ISO	International Organization for Standardization
ITTA	International Tropical Timber Agreement
ITTO	International Tropical Timber Organisation
LCA	life-cycle assessment
LDC	less developed country
LO	Landsorganisasjonen (Norway)
MAI	Multilateral Agreement on Investment
MCP	multi-stakeholder collaborative process
MOGE	Myanmar Oil and Gas Enterprise
MSC	Marine Stewardship Council
MUC	Montreal Urban Community
NAFTA	North American Free Trade Agreement
NCC	National Consumer Council (UK)
NDRC	Natural Resources Defense Council (USA)
NEF	New Economics Foundation (UK)
NGO	non-governmental organisation
NLD	National League for Democracy (Burma)
NO_x	oxides of nitrogen
NPRI	National Pollutant Release Inventory, Canada
OECD	Organisation for Economic Co-operation and Development
OIA	Environmental Institute, Brazil

PAN	Pesticide Action Network of Asia
PBSP	Philippine Business for Social Progress
PEP	personal equity plan
PIRC	Pensions Investment Research Consultants Ltd
PTT	Petroleum Authority of Thailand
RAFI	Rural Advancement Foundation International (USA)
RAG	Rainforest Action Group
RAN	Rainforest Action Network
RIGDIM	Régie intermunicipale de gestion des déchets sur l'île de Montréal
RSA	Republic of South Africa
RTZ	Rio Tinto Zinc
SEHD	Society for Environment and Human Development (Bangladesh)
SINTICEL	Trade union of Aracruz employees, Brazil
SKEPHI	NGO Network for Forest Conservation in Indonesia
SLORC	State Law and Order Restoration Council (Burma)
SO_2	sulphur dioxide
SPDC	State Peace and Development Council (Burma)
STCUM	Société de Transport de la Communauté Urbaine de Montréal
TAPOL	Indonesia human rights organisation (UK)
TIN	Tibet Information Network (UK)
TNC	transnational corporation
TNC	The Nature Conservancy (USA)
TRIP	trade-related intellectual property rights
TSP	Tea Sourcing Partnership
TWN	Third World Network (Malaysia)
UNCED	United Nations Conference on Environment and Development
UNCSD	United Nations Commission on Sustainable Development
UNCTAD	United Nations Conference on Trade and Development
UNCTC	United Nations Centre for Transnational Corporations
UNDP	United Nations Development Programme
UNEP	United Nations Environment Programme
UNICEF	United Nations Children's Fund
UNRISD	United Nations Research Institute for Social Development
UPOV	International Convention for the Protection of New Varieties of Plants
US–AEP	United States–Asia Environmental Partnership
VOC	volatile organic compound
WBCSD	World Business Council for Sustainable Development
WCED	World Commission on Environment and Development
WDM	World Development Movement (UK)
WEF	World Economic Forum
WFAFW	World Federation of Agriculture, Food, Hotel and Allied Workers
WMC	Western Mining Corporation
WRI	World Resources Institute
WTN	World Tibet News
WTO	Word Trade Organisation
WWF	World Wide Fund for Nature
WWI	World Watch Institute

BIOGRAPHIES

Saleem H. Ali is completing his doctorate in environmental planning from the Massachusetts Institute of Technology as a Voorhees Scholar. His research focuses on environmental conflicts involving mining companies and aboriginal groups, particularly around issues of water usage. Before beginning his doctorate, he worked as an environmental specialist at General Electric. He has a Bachelor of Science degree in Chemistry and Environmental Studies from Tufts University and a Masters in Environmental Studies from Yale University.

Jem Bendell is a researcher, writer and consultant on strategic environmental management and corporate social responsibility. He has worked on projects for the World Wide Fund for Nature (WWF), International Labour Organisation (ILO) and United Nations Research Institute for Social Development (UNRISD). His earlier work on the relationships between business and environmental groups was published in a book co-authored with David F. Murphy, *In the Company of Partners: Business, Environmental Groups and Sustainable Development Post-Rio* (The Policy Press, 1997).

John Bray is Principal Research Consultant of Control Risks Group, the London-based business risk consultancy. He is the principal author of *No Hiding Place: Business and the Politics of Pressure* (Control Risks Group, 1997). His current research interests include the politics of corruption, and the contemporary politics of South and South-East Asia.

Gill Coleman is the Director of the New Academy of Business and was the co-founder of the MSc in Responsibility and Business Practice, a joint initiative with the University of Bath. In addition to leading the New Academy's education programmes, Gill is also responsible for programme development in business and gender. She is currently working on an action-learning project on gender and organisational change with Simmons College, Boston. Gill is a Visiting Fellow at Lancaster University and the University of Bath. She is co-author of *Corporate Citizenship: Successful Strategies for Responsible Companies* (FT/Pitman, 1998).

Andrew Crane received his PhD from the University of Nottingham, UK, and is currently a lecturer at Cardiff Business School. His principal research interests are in the areas of business ethics and organisational greening, particularly in their relationships with marketing, strategy and organisational behaviour. He has published articles on these subjects in *The Journal of Marketing Management*, *The Journal of Business Ethics* and *Greener Management International*.

John Elkington is Chairman and founder of strategy consultants SustainAbility, Chairman of The Environment Foundation, author of *Cannibals with Forks: The Triple Bottom Line of 21st Century Business* (Capstone Publishing, 1997), and a member of the Council of the Institute of Social and Ethical Accountability (ISEA) and of the Steering Group of the Global Reporting Initiative (GRI).

Shelly Fennell is a Director of SustainAbility Ltd. In addition to her work with BP on the partnership study described in this volume, she has consulted for a number of other energy company clients on environmental and sustainability strategy. Her most recent publication is the UNEP/SustainAbility report, *The Oil Sector Report: A Review of Environmental Disclosure in the Oil Industry.*

Penny Fowler, currently Policy Advisor on Trade at Oxfam UK, was formerly a researcher at INTRAC, where she participated in a two-year project on 'NGOs, the Private Sector and their Constituencies'. Prior to joining INTRAC, she was a policy officer with the Catholic Institute for International Relations and an Overseas Development Institute Fellow in Fiji.

Simon Heap is Senior Researcher at INTRAC conducting a two-year project on 'NGOs, the Private Sector and their Constituencies'. He was previously the Kirk-Green Junior Research Fellow in Tropical African Studies at St Antony's, Oxford, UK, after gaining his doctorate from the University of Ibadan, Nigeria.

Mike Lachowicz is a consultant, researcher and trainer in environmental management. Mike currently works as a consultant with Safety and Environmental Risk Management Rating Agency Ltd, measuring risks against capital. He joined the London Environment Centre at London Guildhall University as an Associate in 1995 assisting with the development and delivery of their short course, research and management programmes. His main research interests are environmental management performance in the financial sector along with environmental reporting, sustainable development and social accountability. He is the author and editor of several publications; most recently *The Environment, Employment and Sustainable Development* as joint editor (Routledge, 1998) and the chapter, 'Financial Sector and the Environment', in *Corporate Environmental Performance 2000* (*Management Today*, 1999).

Rob Lake is Director of Policy at Traidcraft. The charity arm of Traidcraft works at a policy level on fair and ethical trade that benefits the developing world; corporate accountability and social responsibility and corporate governance; social reporting and accounting; and socially responsible investment. The organisation also carries out practical small business development initiatives in developing countries. Current projects within Traidcraft's policy work relate to the company law review; the development of standards for voluntary corporate social reporting; corporate codes of conduct for ethical trading; the future of fair trade initiatives; and the role of pension fund trustees in promoting socially responsible business.

David F. Murphy is Programme Director with the New Academy of Business, with responsibility for education and research initiatives on partnerships and human rights. Recent research and consultancy experience includes a study on corporate responses to HIV/AIDS for the International Labour Organisation and a review of forest sector business–NGO partnerships for WWF-International. David has a PhD in International Policy from the University of Bristol and extensive development NGO experience in West Africa and Canada. He is the co-author of *In the Company of Partners: Business, Environmental Groups and Sustainable Development Post-Rio* (The Policy Press, 1997).

Dr **Peter Newell** is a Research Fellow at the Institute of Development Studies, Sussex University. His key research interests lie in corporate social and environmental responsibility and international environmental politics. He has books forthcoming on the global politics of climate change (*Climate for Change*, Cambridge University Press) and EU environmental policy, and is currently researching the politics of crop biotechnology regulation in developing countries.

Holger Petersen is writing his PhD thesis on business–NGO alliances.

Christopher Plante is Program Officer for the NGO–Business Environmental Partnership at The Asia Foundation. For the last three years, he has advised and followed over 50 partnership projects in Asia.

Dr **Cheryl Rodgers** is a principal lecturer in corporate strategy and strategic environmental management at the University of Portsmouth Business School. Her research interests focus on issues of corporate social responsibility, notably environmental protection. Her doctoral thesis (Sussex, 1998) examines the effects of producer responsibility on the electronics industry. Prior to pursuing an academic career, Cheryl was a management consultant, and she continues her consultancy work alongside her teaching and research.

Uwe Schneidewind is Professor of Business Administration at the University of Oldenburg, Germany. His latest book, *Die Unternehmung als strukturpolitischer Akteur* (*The Company as a Social Structure Building Actor*) employs the conceptual approach of structuration theory in analysing the active influencing of market and political environments by companies. Within this context, it focuses on the meaning of different forms of collaboration.

Marie-France Turcotte, PhD, is professor of management at Concordia University. She also has a Masters degree in communication studies and a BSc in biology. This multidisciplinary background prepared her to approach complex problems such as environmental issues. In 1997, she published with l'Harmattan Éditions a book on consensual decision-making based on a case study of a multi-stakeholder roundtable process. Her current research projects concern multi-stakeholder initiatives, and environmental and ethical mutual funds.

Steve Waddell has 20 years of experience with collaborations involving business, government and civil society organisations. This experience has involved diverse issues in numerous countries. Currently a senior researcher and consultant with Organizational Futures, Steve lives in Boston. He has a Doctorate and MBA from Boston College, where he teaches on an executive management programme that he founded.

Anne Weir, Manager of Community and Non-governmental Affairs, Unilever plc, joined Unilever in 1988 after spending her early career as an economist and information specialist in the public sector. Anne has led continuous improvement programmes and communications and marketing initiatives around improving environmental performance and has produced Unilever's first two corporate environment reports. Currently, her work includes advising on the development of Unilever's approach to sustainable development and promoting and facilitating dialogue with non-governmental organisations.

INDEX